Holistic Innovation
The New Driver For Excellent Enterprises

Phillip P. Andrews
Lynn W. Scarborough
Doug M. Berman
Kurt J. Wall

DEDICATION

This book is dedicated to our colleagues and friends that have served as coaches and mentors to us through the years. They have provided us with much insights, wisdom and great information on the subjects of innovation and creative disruption. They have contributed in more ways than we could express in words. We thank them all!

CONTENTS

Acknowledgments   i

Prologue   Pg #1

1 Why Innovation Is Important   Pg #6

2 The Emergence Of The Conceptual Age And Its Importance To Innovation   Pg #16

3 Analytical vs. Holistic Thinking   Pg #26

4 Disruptive and Radical Innovation   Pg #34

5 Delving Deeper Into Creative Disruption / Creative Innovation   Pg #46

6 Triggers and Obstacles For Creative Innovation and Disruption   Pg #52

7 The Essence Of Holistic Innovation   Pg #60

8 The Innovation Ecosystem   Pg #72

9 The Right Strategy, Business Model, and Business Practices For Innovation Pg #83

10 The Right Organization Structure, Culture and Style Of Management For Innovation Pg #93

11 Mind Of The Innovator   Pg #104

12 The Innovation Thought Matrix   Pg #118

13 The Role Of Spirituality In Innovation   Pg #127

14 Steve Jobs And The Process Of Innovation   Pg #138

15 The Sparks Of Innovation   Pg #153

Epilogue   Pg #165

Author Bios   Pg #171

ACKNOWLEDGMENTS

Gene Makie, Ford Motor Company
John Van Blois, IBM
Bob Cavanaugh, GE
Bob Bonsack, Deloitte
Hiten Varia, EDS
Mike Fischer, EDS
Mike DeGroot, CBIZ
John Mikus, NL Industries
Christopher Gifford, The Brown Lab
Nicole Turner, Harvard Companies

.

PROLOGUE

First priority is to clarify the difference between **Invention** and **Innovation**. Everyone knows that they are different[1], but in this book we will treat them as being one and the same because they both require the same processes, patterns of thinking, frameworks, tools and techniques.

The concept of **Holistic Innovation** has been around for several years, but it is still being refined and redefined as the word "holistic" is very broad and can have several meanings and interpretations based on the person making the case for it. In several **Holistic Innovation seminars** and workshops the presenters have offered their own versions and models to audiences. Here are some of them:

- **Left Brain + Right Brain = A Whole Mind**
- **Cognitive Thinking + Conceptual Thinking**
- **Analytical Thinking + Synthetic or Systems Thinking**
- **Convergent Thinking + Divergent Thinking**
- **Industrial Era Thinking + Digital Era Thinking**
- **Humanism + Transhumanism**
- **People + Processes + Culture**
- **People + Organizations + Artifacts**
- **Ideas + User Experience + Brand Strategy + Visual Branding + Tools & Structures + Graphic Design + Social Media + Web and Mobile Apps**
- **Creative Thinking + Inspiring Dream + Self-Confidence**
- **Feasibility + Desirability+ Viability**
- **Strategy Innovation + Product Innovation + Marketing Innovation + Process Innovation Technology Innovation + Organizational Innovation**

All these models are correct ... and yet none of them are complete because **Holistic Innovation is all that and more!** In this book we will briefly address some of them (such as Culture, People and

---

[1] **Invention** is the creation of a product or introduction of a process for the first time, while **Innovation** is the improvement (and significant contribution) to something that has already been invented. Thomas Edison is considered to be as an inventor and Steve Jobs is considered to be both an inventor and an innovator. As one can see the difference is meaningless.

Brain Power, along with mental models, processes, and frameworks) because of their strategic importance and value pertaining to innovation, but our main focus is on subjects that normally are not addressed in most seminars either due to lack of understanding, or lack of sufficient knowledge to present them in a compelling and convincing manner. Moreover, we know that culture and attitudes not only impact innovative thinking, but also the very model that one follows to pursue holistic solutions.

The difficulty with all holistic solutions is that it becomes difficult for one to draw the limits of the topic because by its very definition "holistic" implies all approaches, all tools, all techniques, all processes ... well, all of everything. It is the same thing as trying to describe the cosmos. Thus, the smart thing to do is to describe only the things that are new and valuable, where one can gain new insights, new awarenesses, and a better overall perspective on the subject matter.

The main point in this book is that innovation in the past was dealt as something that was a routine process in the R&D Departments of large enterprises, and the output of haphazard "*AHA! Moments*" of entrepreneurs and inventors. Innovation was always a strategic weapon, but it usually lacked the urgency and company-wide promotion and encouragement. Today innovation has become the #1 strategic weapon and the only one that matters long term in sustainable development for businesses, communities and entire societies.

The days of having Suggestion Programs and in-house R&D departments are over. The days of looking only at minor improvements and tweaks are also over. And the proof is in the pudding. With almost 80% of enterprises gone since the early '70s it is imperative to understand that the old ways of approaching innovations are over. Most companies have now abolished Suggestion Programs because their own employees have ignored them. The new approach is to deal with innovation with reverence, amazement, wonder and a sense of urgency, as if the company's very future depends on it --- and it does.

There are numerous graves and deathbeds of enterprises that did not focus on innovation and lost it all. **US Steel, Digital Equipment Corp., Wang Laboratories, Compaq, Polaroid Corporation, Borders Group** and hundreds of other major corporations are sad reminders of what happens when innovation is lost or falls behind the speed of the industry and leading competitors. Speed matters. Staying in lockstep mode with the leaders matters. Taking calculated risks matters. Utilizing state-of-the-art technologies matters. Leapfrogging the leaders ... is even better. Upsetting the entire industry and value chain is the best way to impress customers and consumers around the world and create unimaginable wealth for all involved. There is no more BAU (Business As Usual) mode of operation. BAU implies stagnation ... and stagnation is the kiss of death.

We still call innovation a strategic weapon, but now it means something more than it did before. Innovation today is equivalent to the air that we breathe. One stops innovation and the whole "body" of the enterprise starts feeling weak, dizzy, and ready to collapse. Yes, innovation is that important!

The challenge is a) how does one maintain a good rhythm of breathing (to ensure that the body (of the enterprise) never starves for air (= innovation)), and b) how to increase the oxygen content of the air. The oxygen represents the ingredients that enrich innovation. The holistic approach looks at all the key ingredients --- from the location of the innovators to the very tools that they use, to the amount of leisure time allotted to them for rejuvenating their thoughts and "recharging their batteries", to the way the "rewire" their own brains.

In the past, working in an R&D Department meant being an employee working "normal hours" and going home around 5:00p, like most other people. The attitude was *"Tomorrow is another day!"* (as Scarlet O'Hara famously declared in the movie "**Gone With The Wind**". It was unheard then for an employee to say to the boss, *"I need to stay home for a few days to meditate on how to come up with a new design …"*. R&D employees were not granted special privileges and perks in order to improve their ideas. They were treated as all other employees (it was the fair thing to do). But all that is changing now because everyone finally understands that creative juices do not follow the pattern of working normal hours or being cooped up in the same place all the time.

Smart companies today invite all employees to participate in the innovation effort, and better yet they invite the entire world to be part of it. The new Business Models go well beyond these traditional questions:

- o **Internal** (What you have and offer) (This is all cost related)
- o **What are you offering?** (Product and Service Portfolios)
- o **What do you need?** (Key Resources ➔ Core People and Skills, Core Competencies/Capabilities, Core Technologies, Core Assets, etc.)
- o **How do you do it?** (Key Activities ➔ Operations and Outsourcing)
- o **Who will help you and how?** (Partners and Suppliers ➔ Value and Supply Chains)
- o **External** (What the customers need and want) (This is all revenue and profit related)
- o **Who do you help?** (Target Customers, Target Markets, Target Geographies)
- o **How do you reach them?** (Market, Sales and Distribution Channels)
- o **How do you interact with customers?** (Customer Relationships)
- o **Value Proposition** (Connecting the Internal and External)
- o What is the **value that customers need and want**?
- o What is the **differentiation**?

As you can see the Business Model does <u>not</u> directly address innovation. It is implied in the Offering and Value Proposition. The Offering describes what it is, and the Value Proposition describes what makes it special. Value and differentiation are (or should be) driven by innovation, not by having more "bells and whistles" than the competitors. Unfortunately, when most companies strategize, their Value Propositions are not driven by innovation(s), but by marketing fluff that will impress and (in some cases fools) targeted customers/consumers. Real Value Propositions showcase the innovation itself.

Innovation also affects the rest of the Business Model because it adds more "beef" to the aspects and questions of competing effectively and supporting a sustaining **Growth Strategy**.

Reminder: *"Faster, Bette[2]r, Cheaper"* are not anymore enough to create the perception of great value in the minds of buyers. Value today is a lot more than those simple dimensions that were deified by the old capitalistic model because they paid more attention to people's basic needs. Here are the **basic values** that satisfy the basic needs:

---

[2] This word leaves the door wide open to any translation and any flavor one wants to imbed in it. However, the traditional term only refers to additional "bells and whistles".

- Providing safety, security and comfort
- Saving money, time and grief
- Satisfying one's ego (incl. esteem and status)
- Supporting self-gratification through style and luxury

Value today is derived by a combination of all of the above, plus playing up and satiating these benefits (= **Higher Values**):

- **Emotional** (beyond aesthetics --- addressing feelings and even spiritual aspects)
- **Altruistic** (doing good)
- **Social** (incl. relationships and improving society --- even addressing touchpoints)
- **Intellectual** (being at the cutting edge of knowledge and technology)

In other words, people today are looking for **Aggregate Value** rather than one dimensional value. They take it for granted that the product or service provider has integrated all the basic values into her/his offering. Customers and consumers are looking for the total experience, which goes well beyond great customer service and return policies. Most of the Total Experience is built in and integrated into the offering itself. It is Total Experience by design. There is such a science today (called **Total Experience Design**) that focuses on designing every part that goes into the product, for great customer experience … and innovation plays a major role in all of that.

People do not want to see or deal with customary and traditional stuff. The Digital Age has convinced people that there is always something better than they had yesterday. More importantly, information and knowledge now offer more value than anything other type value offered before. **Smart Anything is it (including Smart Cities, Smart Buildings, Smart Appliances, Smart Value and Supply Chains, Smart Social and Government Agencies, etc.)! Welcome to The Smart Age!**

This may sound very strange, but very few companies (even among the biggest corporations) have such strategies, because they take Innovation and Growth as givens because they assume that their R&D and Engineering departments are on top of all that and are doing all they can to keep them in business. It's time that companies reconsider their approach, as innovation has now become the name of the game. Smart companies have specific strategies and business models that encourage management teams to address their in-house mentalities, methods, cultures … and even their styles of leadership that affect innovation and growth.

Before we plunge to the main course, it is appropriate to define innovation the right way. And although we know that invention and innovation are different, for all practical purposes in this book we treat them as being one and the same because they both require the same thought patterns, same processes and same behaviors. In simple terms, **invention** can be defined as the creation of a product or introduction of a process for the first time, while **innovation** is about significantly improving on or making a crucial/vital contribution to an existing product, process, service, lifestyle, or means of experiencing life. To struggle with defining Uber's new business model as an invention or as an innovation is a meaningless exercise.

Defining Innovation

The traditional definition is:

1: the introduction of something new
2: a new idea, method, or device: novelty

The verb **Innovate** is defined as:
Transitive verb:
      1: to introduce as or as if new
      2: to effect change in
Intransitive verb:
      1: To make changes
      2: Do something in a new way

It is a pretty simple definition and yet very incomplete. Here are some additional concepts that could enhance the definition and view/perspective regarding innovation:

Innovation is about:

- Ideation, imagination, ingenuity, originality, resourcefulness
- Creativity, inventiveness, invention
- Novelty, uniqueness, exclusivity
- Modernism, modernization, progress
- (Positive) Radicalism, progressivism, reformism
- The introduction of new ideas, concepts, methods, tools, techniques, way of thinking, etc.

Moreover, in the business world innovation plays a major role in:

- Problem Solving (in innovative ways)
- Meeting Unmet Customer and Market Needs (inventing things in the **"White Space"**)

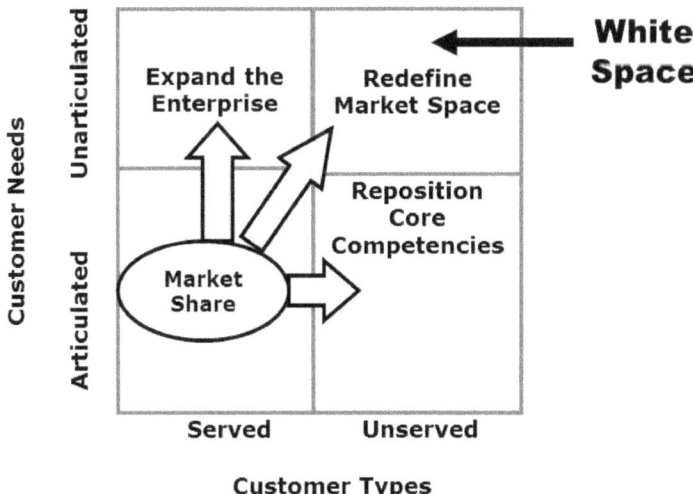

- Pioneering R&D (incl. Product Development)
- Business Model Modification/Revision (in disruptive ways)
- Intellectual property (incl. patents, copyrights, trademarks)

The best opportunities lie in the white space because that's where imagination, vision, dreams, intuition … even revelations commingle together to give birth to the most amazing creations of our civilization. Computers, the internet and smart phones are typical examples of products that were born in the white space. This book offers several suggestions of how to approach creative thinking in the white space.

Although the above graph depicts "white space" as a square, in reality it a wide open space without borders or limits. It is not about thinking outside-the-box, as much as it is not seeing any boxes at all. This is an important point because most engineers are lost in numbers, formulas, cold logic, hard data, analytical tools, and numerous other devices and means that offer limited answers and options. White space, as we shall see in the following chapters, leaves all that behind in favor of thinking what is the end product is all about, and then working backwards from there.

In other words, one must immerse her/himself in her/his work because it's then that intuition and visualization become clearer. The problems that most engineers have are that a) they love problem solving and following specific processes/steps, and b) they have hard time visualizing because they are not polymaths, which limits their vision and ability to synthesize the numerous options that are available out there. All of that will become clearer in the chapters ahead.

1 WHY INNOVATION IS IMPORTANT

Phillip Andrews

Introduction

Everyone knows that innovation is important and there is no need to argue the point. However, what most people miss is the point that innovation now has a different scope and a different objective from previous times and eras. The main difference is that up to this time in our history innovation for the most part took the same path as evolution. Civilizations, societies and companies allowed (and still allow) innovation to be a natural outgrowth of existing and prevalent norms, trends, models, tendencies, longings, affinities, wishes and requirements. Humanity simply follows its urges, needs and wants and innovation is aimed at satisfying exactly what the world desires and craves for.

Thus, the Age (or Era) Of Enlightenment was not a major surprise as the world was ready for a major awakening after several centuries of Dark Ages. The same is true with the Industrial Revolution, which was a natural outgrowth of both the Enlightenment Era (in parallel with the sharp decline of the Agrarian Era). The result was not simply mass migrations to the big cities. The result was inventing a new civilization based on machines, factories, industrialization ... and innovation. What happened in the 19th Century was nothing short of another mass awakening; realizing that we (humans) are more than just another species on this planet. We are the architects and builders of a fantastic future!

The last two hundred years humanity has seen an infinite amount of innovations that have catapulted our civilization to much higher levels of existence in terms of conveniences, luxuries, frills, new ways of life and lifestyles. And although most of that is positive and beneficial to all people, there is a negative side that most people avoid thinking or addressing. The two major negatives regarding industrialism and capitalism are: a) they were based on **exploitation** of resources and people (and even the exploitation of entire nations), and b) they were based on many faulty assumptions, of which **infinite (abundant) resources** was one of the main ones.

This is not a criticism of industrialism or capitalism; just a realization of what is the impact of it all on all of us and our civilization. Back then humanity did not have all the required knowledge and understanding to make good and globally beneficial decisions. It's only the last few decades that humanity was awakened to new perspectives and holistic views. **The new perspectives and views are begging for new solutions and approaches in moving forward with our civilization.**

New Realizations Affecting All Of Humanity

After two hundred plus years of Industrial Revolution, the world has finally realized that the revolution has created some major problems and issues for everyone on the planet, such as:

- **Depleting several key resources, such as oil and lithium.** And although the planet has more of it, the awareness is that it will be a lot more difficult (and by implication a lot more expensive) to extract such resources out of the ground and make them available to the masses. This is begging for:
  - New technologies to discover and extract raw materials
  - New technologies for creating new substitute materials that will replace the old materials (no different than oil replacing wood, coal and even whale oil as burning fuel)
  - New technologies for converting the new materials into finished products
- **Polluting the planet.** Pollution comes in many forms, including waste material, land, air and water pollution, noise pollution, and even light pollution.
- **Poisoning of the planet.** The chemicals, pesticides and other harmful substances have found their way into our food and water supplies and ecosystems creating a variety of physical, mental and emotional health problems that create other severe consequences and implications for the general populations. Only now people are getting to the point of understanding the magnitude of the damage being done to us individually and collectively. However, there is no conspiracy going on here. It is mass ignorance and inanity that has afflicted most politicians around the world. The problems are so huge that they don't which way to turn because for each good solution they propose there are several bad side-effects --- similar of what we are witnessing with the pharma industry and their beneficial, and yet harmful drugs.
- **Deconstructing the traditional culture.** Our old culture revered the environment, and people felt part of nature. When one feels that way it is hard to do harm to the environment. Unfortunately, most people now live in the cities surrounded by concrete, stone and steel that makes appreciation of environment and nature very difficult. The trend of moving to the cities will continue through the rest of this century and some experts project that as much as 80% of the population will live their lives in city environments, turning some metroplexes into megacities, which will have very negative effects on the environment and people. When people are isolated from nature, they ignore it (like all the other things that they don't see and feel). Anything that is ignored becomes immaterial and unimportant and over time it becomes irrelevant. The day that nature becomes irrelevant to the human race, that's the time that the real "end-of-times" will occur on this planet.
- **Creating a stroppy culture (to replace the traditional one).** Although cultures naturally change over time to reflect the latest habits and behaviors of a civilization or society, there are other several surreptitious cultural changes that have negative consequences on the entire society. The adaption of industrialism and capitalism have created a culture of:
  - Greed/Gluttony; Materialism
  - Consumerism

- o Self-Indulgence/Decadence
- o Hedonism/Narcissism/Egoism
- o Individualism
- o Eccentricity/Oddness/Bizarreness

Moreover, mindless technology[3], pathetic politics, a wretched justice system, and a damaged economy have added a few more negatives to the already impaired culture, such as arrogance and indifference towards leadership, role models, nature and God. Collectively they have formed a culture that is best described by these words:

- o Apathy/Indifference
- o Nihilism
- o Existentialism
- o Negativism
- o Pessimism
- o Skepticism, Cynicism
- o Distrust/Suspiciousness
- o Anarchism, Recklessness

It is difficult for any society to make a positive progress when it is suffering from a culture that is burdened with such a deleterious and toxic "package". Good and imaginative people do not care what the culture is as long as they are focused on creating new things that will benefit society and of course enrich their own pocketbook. However, this culture is very detrimental to the well-being of the entire society and the business world. One cannot build healthy enterprises with a culture that is full of apathetic, narcissistic, pessimistic and negative leaders and employees. No amount of innovation and creativity will save an enterprise that has a noxious and ugly culture. As **Peter Drucker** has pointed out *"Culture eats strategy* (and innovation) *for breakfast"*.

It is worth mentioning that from all of the aforementioned negative aspects of the culture, Consumerism poses a special problem for innovation not because it promotes the attitudes of *"buy-buy-buy"* and *"spend-spend-spend"*, but because it reinforces the attitude of *"forget the future"* and *"live for today"*. This attitude stimulates wastefulness and squandering of resources and goods of all types. It is well known that many people purchase "toys" just to make themselves feel good (by stimulating their self-esteem) and to deal with stress (by forgetting their troubles and anxieties). At a first glance all this appears to be harmless behavior, but it has a very dark side.

The dark side is all about *"Me, Myself and I"* and *"The hell with others"*, including ignoring nature, the environment, the planet and other people. Under this type of culture it is impossible to introduce the solutions of the future pertaining to sustainability, circular economy, lean, Conscious Capitalism, and other socio-techno-economic and business systems that are aimed at creating a brave new future for humanity and our collective civilization.

---

[3] **Technology has a dark side.** It was the rise of the movies that created the mass obsession with individualism and hedonism. It was primarily television that created the manias with consumerism, materialism, self-indulgence and greed. It was the collective impact of the media that has led to decadence, bizarreness, and oddities because they pay more attention to the misfits, outcasts and weirdoes rather than pay attention to the mainstream normal folks. Normal is not exciting and it is not news. The subliminal message to the brainless youth is that *"If you want to make news, do something insane and nauseating"*. Stupid and evil people will find bad ways to use robots, drones, systems and applications. Evil works overtime to find ways to destroy, manipulate, exploit and otherwise do harm to the world. It's all part of who we are.

It is also known that if all the people around the world raise their standard of living to the same level as Americans, the world would literally be out of resources overnight. **We already live in an unsustainable planet** and yet the population growth continues unabated. It is projected that by 2050 the population will surpass 10 billion people. As a reference point the **population** of the world reached **1B** for the first time in **1804**. Here is the rest of our progress:

- 2B – 1927 (123 years)
- 3B – 1960 (33 years)
- 4B – 1974 (14 years)
- 5B – 1987 (13 years)
- 6B – 1999 (12 years)
- 7B – 2011 (12 years)[4]
- 7.5B – in 2017 (when this chapter was written)
- 8B –in a few years

There are indications that our growth is slowing down, but the truth is that it may not be enough to avert ugly results in the future because we have already reached the saturation point --- we already have too many people on this planet, and we are already suffocating. Can one imagine how people will feel when 4-5 more billion people will be added to our total number?

Some experts project that the population growth not only will taper off, but even decline, but don't count on that, as most people lack the common sense of controlling their urges and understanding the big picture. Most people still live at the animal level. It does not take very much imagination to figure out what will happen on this planet when the population doubles in the next 100 years or so. Our problems are huge now, and they are expected to become even bigger in the next 100 years because simply this planet can only sustain so much life on it. To think that the number of people and animals can keep on increasing forever without a penalty is a major fallacy. All ecosystems have their breaking point and we are determined to find them ... the hard way.

In reality we are increasing our numbers at the expense of wild life already. WWF and many experts around the globe have raised the red flag, but very few people are paying attention because everyone is focused on themselves and their families. One cannot blame people for putting their focus there, but we expect that our governments would and should try to do more to protect the global ecosystems.

The issue of sustainability and developing sustainable communities, cities and societies is not a matter of wishful thinking or daydreaming, but a matter of absolute necessity. Society should not wait to reach its breaking point (which is imminent) in order to react and take the proper actions the last minute because it would be too late then. Smart countries and leaders leverage diagnostic and analytical tools in order to take the right actions before trouble erupts and people die. We need to be proactive and predictive, rather than reactive. It is the same concept that good corporations follow in maintenance and IT (incl. Systems and Communications) practices. It's called **Total Productive Maintenance** (TPM).

TPM = Predictive Maintenance + Preventive Maintenance +Remedial Maintenance

---

[4] World population reached 7 billion in October 2011 according to the United Nations Population Fund.

BTW, the words "Total" and "Holistic" are practically synonyms.

The Right Societal Culture Prompting New Types Of Innovation

The looming crises demand new solutions that will allow people to improve their standard of living, improve their lives and lifestyles, achieve their new goals and objectives, and create a better civilization in **The Age Of Limits**. The big question is: *"Is that possible?"* Can humanity continue its progress and achieve higher levels of development with all the negative factors against it? The answer is a crisp and clear "NO" because we collectively need to adopt a dramatically different **(new) culture, characterized by**:

- Togetherness ("We" instead of "I")
- Cooperation/Collaboration
- Empathy/Sympathy/Compassion
- Trust/Honesty
- Preservation
- Conservation
- Austerity
- Reliance
- Optimism
- Interest, Conviction
- Common Sense

The new culture implies that solutions must be aimed at conserving, preserving, maintaining, downsizing, economizing, reducing, reusing, rationalizing, and even rationing will be met with great skepticism, suspicion and resistance. Some people will even become belligerent and even violent against any proposed solutions that affect their perceived lifestyles and choices. The challenge for all governments around the world will be to introduce the new culture and supporting laws without appearing that they are curtailing and affecting the lives of their people. Business will face the same challenge, as they will need to offer products and services that support the new culture and lifestyles.

This is why governments and businesses need to start thinking today how they will handle the new challenges and massive changes. We will need innovation on all fronts:

1. New **education system** that supports the emergence of the new society (because it will take a few generations to fully implement all the proposed changes)
2. New ways of handling **mass transformation** with new generations (**The Great Transition**)
3. New **products and new services** for the new society (in the Digital Age)
4. New **laws and policies** to support all of the above

In other words, government, society institutions and business need to work together and support each other in every way and in every step of the transformation in order to achieve the desired results. From a business point of view, the main focus will be on the new products and services, with secondary focus on the transformation aspects, as they have to convince their own employees that they need to transform and change their ways both at the office/workplace and home. The point can be made that corporations have a better chance of transforming people and entire societies than governments can because companies can mandate to their employees the new culture that is acceptable at work, which eventually people adapt inside their own homes and families. That was true 200 years ago and it is still true today. For example, when a company implements the concepts of **Lean**, such as the **Five S's** or **7 Wastes**, it is hard for an employee to apply those concepts at work and ignore them at home. Habit alone takes over personal values and beliefs because eventually they become one and the same. It's the same with recycling and other Sustainability practices. Corporations need to step up their Sustainability and Going Green training, business practices and policies. Better yet, imbed them in job descriptions and performance reviews. That's when people will start really changing.

The New Society

Businesses will have to prepare for a new society that will have to **"do more with less"**. There is no such thing as "do less with less". People need to always reach for new plateaus of achievement and excellence in order to feel the sense of achievement that is so essential for people individually and collectively. We cannot afford to fall into another period like The Dark Ages. And that is exactly what humanity will face if the right solutions are not put forward in front of them today. This is exactly the purpose of promoting innovation! It's not innovation for the sake of business, profits, stock prices ... and jobs. It is **innovation for the sake of humanity**. Innovation is the main vehicle to save society from the looming crises (and itself) and improve (not maintain, and certainly not reduce) the standard of living of people. This may be the biggest challenge in the history of mankind because we never had such a challenge put in front of us before; and the truth is that today we have no idea how to handle it.

It is imperative to realize that certain solutions will need the cooperation and collaboration of several governments, businesses, academia, think tanks, NPOs, NGOs, and other institutions. The days of going-at-it-alone are over. No country, no government, no corporation or other entity will have all the money, talents and resources needed to produce the right solutions.

The new society will be characterized by these (sample list) traits and behaviors:

- New Demographics & Globalization Beyond Business
  - Massive Demographic Changes (as people are forced to migrate in order to save their families)
- High Speed
- High Anxiety
  - High Unemployment
  - Global Terrorism; Radicalization
  - High Complexity
  - Overwhelming Environment
    - Too much information (TMI); too much misinformation (TMM)
    - Too much choice (TMC)
    - Too much technology (TMT)
    - Too much of everything (TME)
    - Too many TLAs (three letter acronyms)
  - Polarization; New Class War(s)
    - The Have-nots against The Haves

- Localization and Tribalism (counter-reaction to Mass Migrations, Globalization and Oneness)
- Polarizing ideologies
  - Memory Loss (both personal and corporate)
- Conscious Capitalism (a kinder, gentler model)
  - Higher Purpose (beyond the Bottom or even the Triple Bottom Line)
  - Conscious Leadership (and Management)
  - Conscious Culture (and Core Values)
  - Stakeholder Involvement (and Integration)
- Advanced Sustainability
  - Sustainable Governments
    - Sustainable, Green and Circular Societies and Economies
      - Economic Empowerment
    - Sustainable Development And Growth
    - Sustainable Public Services (Energy, Water, Transportation, Waste Management, etc.)
  - Sustainable and Green Businesses
    - Corporate Social Responsibility (CSR)
    - Creating Shared Value (CSV)
    - Going Green
  - Sustainable and Green Families/Homes
  - Sustainable Education
  - Sustainable Agriculture
    - Hydroponics and Aquaponics
      - Vertical Farms and Gardens
      - Integrated urban and rural settings --- bringing nature into the cities

There are innovation opportunities behind each and every one of these traits and qualities. Some innovations will be aimed at improving life, while others will be aimed at eliminating or minimizing the pain points of society. There should no question in anyone's mind that **innovation is crucial to the survival of our species.** The new society represents a new world and a unique an opportunity to rethink the world and life itself. As was mentioned before, all previous major societal transformations were natural outgrowths of previous eras. This time we are facing a dramatic departure from all previous societies because we need to save the planet ... and ourselves from ourselves. The human folly is catching up with us. If this is not a call for major innovations then nothing is. People always worry about the big volcano or the big tsunami that may wipe out cities and kill thousands of people, but they forget that **the biggest tsunami is "us"** (similar to *"We've met the enemy and it is us!"*).

Unfortunately, we are faced with many obstacles and many challenges of which one of the biggest is that **The Age Of Limits** threatens to lead to degrowth, stagnation, unproductivity and ... tough times ahead. The challenge is to fuel growth in the middle of diminishing resources and limited funds. The innovators of the future have their work cut out for them.

There is no such thing any more as business-as-usual, conventional world, and traditional way of life. Convincing people of all that will be a major challenge by itself. Most people may be threatened by these realizations, but humanity has seen such major shifts before, especially when it moved from the Agrarian Age to the Industrial Age. It took well over 100 years for the shift to take place, but it did as people finally saw the benefits of the new era. But in order to move forward we must enable people to do so. Here are three such **major enablers for moving forward**.

1. **First,** we must **find the right name to call the new era**. Calling it **The Age Of Limits** (albeit true) is not the smart way to motivate people to transform. Several thought leaders have proposed several other labels for the new era, such as: The Information Age, The Technological Age, The Digital Age, The Conceptual Age and several others. We don't know which label is going to stick as we are still at beginning of this mass transition.

   We prefer the term **The Digital Age** for this reason:

   > Digital Technology is the real focus of our civilization today and for the centuries ahead. The word technology is much broader today than was defined in the Industrial Era because it covers systems, applications, communications, social media, the worldwide web, cloud computing and so much more. Digital Technology is replacing Manufacturing as one of the main mechanisms for creating real wealth in advanced nations

Note: Technology (in general) is driven by innovation. Without innovation the technology-based industries are helpless. Technology is equivalent to the monster depicted in the **"The Little Shop Of Horrors"** movie that constantly screams *"Feed me!"* **The food for technology is innovation.**

2. **Second,** we must **identify the right "vehicles" and instruments that will enable the transition from the old era to the new one is equally important.** So far, societies around the world have done very little for identifying such mechanism and investing the money to create them and/or enhance them. **Education systems** (for all ages) are the most important mechanisms, but our current curricula and seminars for the most part they have remained static and antiquated[5]. Other mechanisms include:

   - Proper and effective **laws and policies**
     - Regulating Growth (Reminder: Unfettered/Undeterred Growth and Growth For The Sake Of Growth are malevolent concepts and practices)
     - Taxing correctly and fairly (e.g.: no more loopholes for the rich and big corporations)
     - Taxing the right things (e.g.: taxing waste and harmful emissions)
   - **Tax incentives and tax breaks** to encourage investment in new advanced technologies and inventions
   - **Outreach programs**
   - **Social programs**
   - **Civic Engagement**

3. **Third, we must have very visible sponsors, champions and leaders that** <u>**continuously harp**</u> **on and tout the virtues and benefits of the new era.** Moreover,

---

[5] The current Education System is based on the Industrial Age model that among other things brainwashes people to become employees for corporations, rather than encouraging the entrepreneurial models. One must make a conscious decision to become an entrepreneur in order to enroll in the right courses at the college level.

the leaders need to present a unified front and avoid the silly and harmful politics that we see today.

There are several other factors that are important for an effective transition to the new era (incl. right speed, continuous communications and feedback, immediate response to problems and issues that arise from transitioning, and having focal points (with leaders, teams and budgets) that are in charge of critical programs). At this point we have only done baby steps, mostly in the areas of laws, policies and tax breaks. We need to pick up the speed and create the sense of urgency that is much needed in order to avoid major calamities in the future. The American government is lethargic by comparison to what other progressive countries are doing around the globe --- but we will not address it here.

Where Innovation Will Play A Role

Here are some examples:

- Transportation --- back to the future with supersonic planes, pilotless planes and drones
- Information Computing, Management and Sharing --- The Internet Of Things coupled with Big Data, Advanced Analytics, Sensor Technology
- Automation and Systemization of Things (incl. Artificial Intelligence and Advanced Robotics)
- Agriculture and Food Management
- Water Conservation, Restoration and Management
- Advanced Energy Generation, Storage, Distribution and Management
- Health Care (from Robo-Docs and Nurses to Stay-At-Home Health Care Services)
- Education (from Online Education to instant access to information/knowledge/wisdom)
- Government (from e-Government to online polling and voting)

Practically every aspect of our lives, every sector, every industry, every type of business and every type of product and service are ripe for dramatic innovation. The technologies that aid and enable transformations are mentioned in a later chapter.

Suggestion: It is highly recommended that you read the two books of a) **Home Deus** and b) **The Seventh Sense** as they both offer great insights pertaining to future societies, the human race and the role of innovation. **We must invent and architect the future now!** Here are four important quotes form those books:

"We do not become satisfied by leading a peaceful and prosperous existence. Rather, we become satisfied when reality matches our expectations. The bad news is that as conditions improve, expectations balloon." – **Yuva Noah Harari**, **Homo Deus**

"The most common reaction of the human mind to achievement is not satisfaction, but craving for more." — **Yuval Noah Harari**

"[Many people] *are happy to follow the advice of their smartphones or to take whatever drug the doctor prescribes, but when they hear of upgraded superhumans, they say: 'I hope, I will be dead before that happens"* — **Yuval Noah Harari**

"What is true for the machines all around us now is true for us too: We are what we are connected

to. And mastery of that connection turns out to be the modern version of Napoleon's coup d'oeil [stroke of the eye][6]*, the essential skill of the age. Centuries"* — **Joshua Cooper Ramo, The Seventh Sense**

In Conclusion

Innovation was always a key element of humanity's progress, evolution and growth. Humanity always reaches higher levels of achievement, advancement, development, excellence and consciousness through innovation, experimentation ... and trial & error. We have reached a new point in our human journey that innovation needs to be dealt with a sense of urgency, piety and utmost devotion as our collective future depends on it.

Key Reminders:
Innovation is the #1 Strategic Weapon!
Innovation is the #1 Sustainable Advantage!

It always was, and will always be!

---

[6] "Stroke of the eye" means having the gift of being able to see at a glance the possibilities offered by the terrain whether it is the battlefield or the business landscape.

2 THE EMERGENCE OF THE CONCEPTUAL AGE AND ITS IMPORTANCE TO INNOVATION

Phillip Andrews

Introduction

In the previous chapter it was mentioned that the preferred term for the new era is **The Digital Age**, but underneath that big umbrella there are several other terms and labels that offer additional insight and wisdom as to the massive transformations that are under way in our society. One of the great terms is **The Conceptual Age**, which was popularized in **Daniel Pink**'s book called **"A Whole New Mind"**[7]. The key points in his book are:

- **The Conceptual Age succeeds The Information Age.** This is another major transformation in our society that has been through these Ages:

  - Agricultural Age (farmers)
  - Industrial Age (factory workers)
  - Information Age (knowledge workers)
  - Conceptual Age (creators and empathizers)

  Note: Empathy is essential for comprehending the issues pertaining to sustainability and the looming mega crises and the derivation of appropriate solutions.

- **The right brain is finally awakened to new levels of capability and capacity.** The right brain is responsible for:

  - Big Picture Comprehension and Orientation
  - Imagination
  - Intuitive Thinking

---

[7] Pink's book contains some controversial points, which are not discussed in this book. Overall, Pink's book made the New York Times and BusinessWeek bestseller lists, and that has been translated into 20 languages. The book was named Best Business Book of 2005 by Strategy + Business, The Miami Herald, 800-CEO-READ, and Fast Company.

o Holistic and Integrative Thinking
o Synthesizing
o Artistic Views and Inspirations
o Emotional Sensations and Feelings
o Interpersonal Longings
o Meaning
o Philosophy and Spirituality
o Fantasizing, Daydreaming, Visioning
o Risk Taking

Note: All of those traits and functions of the right brain are super essential for innovation. Right-brained people are indispensable for creative work. Whole-brained people are even better, as they bring out the best of both halves of the brain.

- **Whole-brain people leverage these six essential senses (aptitudes, skills and abilities):**

  o **Design** – Moving beyond function to engage the senses and even the soul
  o **Story** – Narrative added to products and services - not just argument. This is the best of the six senses. Storytelling is a great skill (it always has been)
  o **Symphony** – Adding invention and big picture thinking (not focusing on details alone)
  o **Empathy** – Going beyond logic and engaging emotion, humanity and intuition
  o **Play** – Bringing humor and light-heartedness to business and products (integrating work-life habits and practices as well)
  o **Meaning** – the purpose is the journey, give meaning to life and work from inside one's self

  Note: All of these senses are equally essential for innovation. According to **Pink** *"the future belongs to a different kind of person"* with a different kind of mind – all of them creative, empathetic and rounded. **Pink** continues with: *"right-brain thinkers whose abilities mark the fault line between who gets ahead and who doesn't."* These new aptitudes are needed by both modern innovators, and those who want to be our leaders in The Conceptual Age.

- **The Conceptual Worker is the Advanced Knowledge Worker.** The conceptual worker is capable of leveraging the logical left brain with the emotional and inspirational right brain, thus becoming capable of deriving better and holistic solutions that are beneficial to more people and humanity as a whole. **Pink** claims we're living in a different era/age, where those who *"Think different"* will be valued even more than ever. Advanced knowledge workers on top of being whole brained, will have all the right tools and technologies to be able to be as creative, imaginative and productive as possible. It will be fun to be in such environments working with people like that. Every day will represent an opportunity to expand the mind, the soul, and the awarenesses of the true capabilities of the human race and human mind.

Pink's book represents the general movement in management literature (and even some business schools) to increasingly accept creativity and innovation as a major source of business value, differentiation and competitive advantage.

This may sound strange, but most business management books and schools took innovation for granted. The premise behind it was that companies naturally perform R&D (as a basic function of doing business) and come up with the next generation products, based mostly on four inputs: a) the geniuses that work there, b) inputs from key customers, c) competition, and d) research performed by leading universities, thinks tanks and other outside resources.

The notion that one must cultivate specific processes, culture, environment, and style of management to support innovation never occurred to most management teams and boards. The new attitude is to never take innovation for granted and moreover, and don't depend on the R&D Department for the best ideas. Those days are over. Some of the best ideas come from outside the four walls of the enterprise (this is one of the main reason for creating a robust Business-Innovation Ecosystem, which is addressed in later chapters).

Understanding The Six Senses And Abilities

1. **Design.** In the past design was something relegated to engineers that were educated and trained in the concepts of engineering designs using specific tools and techniques. Their normal pattern was to take existing designs and drawings and try to improve them in three areas: function, style, and quality. More than 95% of designs were done that way. The other 5% were focused on brand new designs aimed at creating the next generation products that were not just better than all previous designs, but were breakthrough products, such as the first **Apple** computer or the first **Polaroid** camera.

   The fascinating thing about those breakthrough designs is that the public accepted them as anticipated and expected products of our technological age. In other words, they were not noticed in a conscious way (as dramatic breakthroughs). They appealed immediately to the subconscious. There are designs that appeal to the senses only (through their choices of colors, shapes, typography, and even sex appeal), while other designs "speak" and appeal to the mind/intellect and soul.

   Thus, good designs are not superficial (like most of them today), lacking depth, value, meaning and purpose. They are designs that "sing to us" by elevating and improving our human abilities, capabilities, capacities, and/or allowing us to enjoy life in more meaningful ways. **Apple products** have become classic examples of this approach … and now the world is trying to copy both their designs and innovation approaches. Their designs are **"soul deep"** and represent the perfect product that is derived from holistic minds and holistic thinking.

   Daniel Pink makes this important point: "It is easy to dismiss design (and) to relegate it to mere ornament, the prettifying of places and objects to disguise their banality … but that is a serious misunderstanding of what design is and why it matters." The best designs are the ones that "marry" utility/functionality with significance. Value is not found in functionality alone.

> **Personal Anecdote:** It so happened that when I was writing this chapter I was in Paris surrounded by some of the most beautiful buildings in the world. I soon found out by asking my relatives and friends living there, that the most beautiful buildings are occupied by the rich and famous --- no surprise there. But what jumped at me immediately is that they selected to live in the old buildings that have style, class, character/personality, history and elegance. By contrast, most of the new buildings are just globs of steel, glass and concrete. Their emphasis is trying to impress people with size, functionality … and technology. They try to impress people with futuristic or trendy styles that are bold looking and eye-pleasing, but fail to appeal to the soul --- once again, they do not "sing" to the soul. In other words, their beauty is only skin-deep. They lack charm, warmth, and imagination that make people stop and admire, adore, and even think.

2. **Story.** We still live in The Information Age, where data, information, and knowledge are found in abundance everywhere. **The Democratization Of Information** has resulted into a phenomenal progress in understanding the world all around us and leveraging all those inputs to improve products designs along with socioeconomic systems, political systems, and all other types of systems and designs. But on the other hand, all this glut of information does not improve holistic thinking and big picture thinking, unless someone takes the time (as we are doing with this book) to **"connect the dots"** and put things in perspective. In other words, people need context and frameworks to fully comprehend what all that information means to them.

Daniel Pink said this: *"What begins to matter more (than mere data and information) is the ability to place these facts in context and to deliver them with emotional impact."* In order to understand the deeper meanings and big picture of the information surround us, we need the "translators". But we've found out that translations alone are not enough to fully grasp the important message. The best way to communicate is through storytelling. Storytelling is an ancient art that started with the myths and "holy books".

The story of **Hercules** is not about a single hero that achieved all those (12) labors/achievements. It was about setting the male role model in the ancient world. **Jason's** story was not about getting or stealing **The Golden Fleece** from the Phrygians. It was about describing an enlightenment journey … similar to what one reads in The Bible, if it is read right[8]. Of course other people find other meanings and metaphors behind the stories of Hercules and Jason, but the point is not which story is best, but which story makes the biggest and most positive impact to most audiences.

Mark Turner (a cognitive scientist) calls storytelling *"Narrative imagining"* and explains further that *"most of our experiences, our knowledge and our thinking is organized as stories"*. Narrative imagining is a key mechanism of thought and it helps put things in perspective. The best storytellers are old people that "have been there, done that" and

---

[8] The analytical minds freak out with such statements as they frantically lo

ok for evidence and references to back up such pronouncements and claims. Holistic minds, on the other hand, care less about data and facts and look for the essence of what an author is trying to convey. In this case the message is that metaphors, allegories and symbolisms are more powerful than all the data put together.

have the rich stories to tell. The richer the story is, the more impact it makes and the longer it stays in people's memory. This does not imply that young people are not good storytellers. It only implies they do not have the actual rich experiences to back up their stories and really hone their messages with real life examples.

Unfortunately, in our culture stories and storytellers have been downgraded as old people that reminisce about the past. Business and academia frown upon people that start telling stories, as if it is a waste of their time. Thus, it is not a surprise that so many old folks were forced to retire early and leave the business world behind them. The business world has not understood that by letting all that experience walk out their doors have lost a lot of knowledge, corporate memory and the ability to add wisdom where is needed the most[9]. The key to great storytelling is to wrap lessons learned, profound wisdom and warnings into the story itself. All businesses have stories that need to be repeated to the young upstarts.

Moreover, the best storytellers are the ones that know how to blend their own personality, character, experiences and insights into materials that exciting, revealing, enlightening, engaging, appealing, memorable and even haunting.

> **Personal Anecdote:** I noticed that when I gave presentations to students and professionals, they were more interested in my personal stories that I shared with them from my days at Ford, Deere, IBM and GE rather than the concepts that I was trying to convey. My stories make the concepts real, believable and the lessons learned end up offering more value than the theories by themselves. At the end, they remember more the stories that they've heard, rather than the theories and schemes.

3. **Symphony. Daniel Pink** states: *"Symphony...is the ability to put together the pieces. It is the capacity to synthesize rather than to analyze; to see relationships between seemingly unrelated fields; to detect broad patterns rather than to deliver specific answers; and to invent something new by combining elements nobody else thought to pair."* However, symphony is more than synthesizing and aggregating things, ideas and concepts together. It is also about harmonizing, synchronizing, balancing, matching and orchestrating. Once again, there is shortage of people that know how to do all that because it takes many years of "being in the trenches" and "cutting one's teeth" in order to achieve enough skills and capabilities in order to be able to help others in all aspects of Symphony.

Symphony is derived from the Greek word "symphonia", which has another important connotation: "agreement". Agreement implies peaceful co-existence, good relationships, and fruitful and mutually rewarding dealings --- all needed for our new societies.

And here is another interesting point: old people are generalists, young people are specialists. Generalists have a better grasp of associations, relationships (and the relationships between and underneath the relationships) and interactions, than specialists, which are trained to focus in one area only. This is one of the major faults of our current education system (a key remnant of The Industrial Age) that promotes specialization.

---

[9] To be fair, old people have the propensity of being conservative and resisting changes more than young people because they behave as the guardians of what is already there (invented and implemented).

Daniel Pink also mentions this important point: *"The most creative among us see relationships the rest of us never notice"*. It takes a very experienced and deep mind to see hidden relationships and associations. It is a fact that most people do not grasp all the relationships that are in front of their eyes, and even fewer people comprehend that all is interrelated, and all is part of a whole.

Thus, **Symphony promotes Holistic Thinking**, utilizing our whole mind, looking at the big picture … and even promoting Oneness. Here are two important reminders from great thought leaders: *"The part will never be well unless the whole is well"* --- **Plato**, and *"Whatever affects one directly, it affects everyone indirectly. I can never be what I ought to be unless you are what you ought to be. This is the interrelated structure of Reality"* --- **MLK**. Daniel Pink makes it very clear in his book that the ability to take seemingly unrelated pieces and form and articulate the big picture before us is crucial, even a differentiator. That's the essence of Symphony.

However, there is another aspect of symphony, which is captured in this formula:

Holistic Person → Holistic Lifestyle → Holistic Thinking → Holistic Innovation

4. **Empathy.** Empathy is another Greek word that means *"The feeling that you understand and share another person's experiences and emotions: the ability to share someone else's feelings"* (per **Merriam-Webster Dictionary**).

Moreover, Empathy is the ability of seeing with the eyes of another, listening with the ears of another, feeling with the heart of another, and putting yourself in the position of another. Empathy is an emotional trait of people that have such ability --- but not all people have it. This is an important trait for people that work with customers and consumers, designers that have to put products in the hands of consumers, and performers that have to be in front of audiences.

This is one of the human traits and virtues that is very difficult to teach to others as we know that many people among us are indifferent, callous, egotistical, narcissistic, and so on. Empathy is something that comes to some people naturally from their own genes. Others adopt it from their parents by emulating their behaviors.

> **Personal Anecdote:** In the last 5 years, I have devoted most of my time on matters of Environmentalism and Sustainability. One of the most important messages that I preach to my audiences is the need to **feel what Mother Nature feels**; they need to **see what Mother Nature sees**. It is clear that most people cannot do that. They lack that key capacity and ability --- or maybe an extra sense. And without it they cannot feel and see what Mother Nature feels and sees. Thus, they are happy to be just followers, rather than leaders that make a profound difference in life.

The unfortunate thing is that a lot of people are impervious to the needs and wants of other people and entire societies. For them empathy plays no role in the design of new products, services and solutions for the world. They are single-mindedly focused on delivering on what they want and feel is right for the world. They ignore the **"the white space"** (where unserved customer types and unarticulated needs exist) because they lack the intuition and empathy to "see" it and appreciate it.

Figuring out what belongs in the white space does not imply of taking the approach of "if you will build it they will come", but rather being sensitive enough to sense on what people/audiences need based on direct and indirect feedback from them --- going beyond logic and explanations/translations of raw data. Sometimes the obvious solutions are right in front of people's noses, but they do not see them. The perfect example of this is the invention of the mouse. Other people invented it and did not know what to do with it, but Steve Jobs immediately saw the value of it. History is full of examples like this.

Personal Anecdote: I've dealt with plenty inventors and entrepreneurs in the business world that had zero empathy for others. But it was not that alone. They had other traits that accompanied their lack of empathy, such as egoism, self-absorption, arrogance, indifference and even paranoia. I felt as if they were lacking the basic elements of humanity. They took the approach that they were smarter than everyone else and that it is the fault of others that they were not recognized and appreciated for what they had created. They forgot that empathy also means humility, self-effacement, and love. Yes, love! It matters in having good designs, inventions and innovations. **Soulless and unloving designs only serve the functional needs of people, while soulful and loving designs serve the total needs of people --- appealing to minds, hearts and souls.**

---

5. **Play.** Play does not mean play as most people think. The word play implies of not taking things so seriously as to become anal-retentive and neurotic to the point of being no fun. It is well known that people that are stress-free, joke, are playful and are also more inclined to be free-thinkers and creative. Daniel Pink makes the point that in the conceptual age work is not just about seriousness, but about fun and games (without taking them to the extreme point of being silly and becoming a nuisance).

It is a major misperception that serious and intense people are best suited for business and especially for managerial jobs. The truth is that serious and intense people are overwrought, making everyone around them anxious and stressed out, which hurts both productivity and creativity. The exact opposite is true (most of the time) as it has been proven that friendly and outgoing people boost both productivity and creativity.

Daniel Pink even quotes University of Pennsylvania professor, **Brain Sutton-Smith** who says, *"The opposite of play isn't work. It's depression"*. And this this true (for most people) as they have nothing better to do in life. Work puts meaning in their lives and sustains their livelihoods. Very few people have figured what to do with themselves outside work.

Pink goes further by pointing out that: *"Laughter is a form of nonverbal communication that conveys empathy and that is even more contagious than the yawn ..."*. It is not a surprise that the **Toastmasters Club** urges people to use jokes not only to break the ice with their audiences, but also to connect with their audiences as laughter is a form of empathy and intellectual connection. By the way, playing certain games at work and at home helps dramatically improve the communication between left and right brains, thus energizing the entire brain and achieving holistic-level intellectual proficiency.

Personal Anecdote: When I was working for **Ford** and **IBM** I worked for two fantastic managers that were a lot of fun, easy going, fostering a very nurturing environment, and had a great sense of humor. Those were the days that I've enjoyed in my career the most, and I still remember them very fondly. Interestingly enough, when my manager at IBM was replaced by a nasty, self-centered, and numbers focused manager (ex-accountant) the whole department suffered and all the best employees left the organization immediately. Two years or so later the IBM Robotic Assembly Institute (in Boca Raton, FL) closed its doors permanently. The amazing thing was that the man that replaced our good leader and founder of the Institute knew nothing about robots or manufacturing. He was the proverbial empty-suit that only knew how to manage the numbers. Thankfully IBM moved me to another organization that was even more exciting.

Lesson Learned: I have seen this story (with some variations) play itself again and again and again, at **Deere, GE, Deloitte, EDS, Century Business Services (CBIZ)**, and at several of my customers' organizations. Now that I am retired, I sit back and ponder why companies do such imprudent things. What in the world those CEOs were thinking when they made those horrible managerial changes? And then one realizes that their mental models (incl. perceptions) were very wrong. The perception that callous and nasty people are better managers is still very prevalent in our society today. In reality, this perception was always in play since the beginning of time. People tend to choose leaders that are uncaring, cold-hearted and ruthless because of the erroneous belief that those types of leaders will get better results and accomplish more than anyone else. Innovation struggles to thrive under such a leadership style.

6. **Meaning.** This is one of the most important senses/aptitudes that make a huge difference not only for innovation, but for the entire business and life itself, as we all are seeking to find the meaning of our lives, our work, our enterprises and us all. Life and work become a lot more meaningful, significant, valuable and enjoyable when one feels that there is meaning a higher purpose tied to them. It is the same message that the great professor **Joseph Campbell** used to preach to his audiences. People that work just for a living miss this point altogether. Campbell's message was ***"Follow your bliss"*** because your bliss is your destiny.

People that pursue their bliss and destiny automatically find meaning in both their lives and work. One does not have to explain anything to them in terms of meaning because they already know it or "feel" it. Others have to be taught what bliss is and how to put meaning in their lives. The best way to approach it is by asking people what they are passionate about. Some people feel passionate about certain things, while others have passion about meaningless things, such as playing cards and collecting dolls. The people that are passionate are usually more energetic, more enthusiastic/excited, more positive and more willing to share their ideas and views. Those are the right people for innovation. **Musk** and **Jobs** had passion and it showed in all aspects of their lives.

One can spot people like them immediately because when they talk and make presentations their enthusiasm comes out automatically. They are bubbly, happy, share stories, and ask others to share theirs. They feel at ease with what they are presenting, not necessarily because they have deep knowledge (although they usually do), but because they believe in the subject or topic that they are presenting. They encourage discussions and solicit questions because the feedback that they receive deepens their knowledge and broadens the meaning of their work and lives. Smart people know how to gain from dialogues to enrich their knowledge base. Arrogant (and dumb) people want to impress others with how much they know --- they are horrible listeners. They make everything one-way communication.

The concept of meaning has been adopted very successfully by **John Mackey** (co-founder of **Whole Foods**) that co-authored the famous book pertaining to **Conscious Capitalism**. He explained the value of having a **Higher Purpose**10 for companies that want to make a difference in our society. **Purpose-driven enterprises** and **purpose-driven lives** become one and the same thing. To John Mackey the words "brand" and "brand management" mean nothing if they are not tied to a higher purpose. Although Mackey does not mention Pink's book, the truth is that "meaning" is the connection point that both authors try to highlight in their own books.

We must add a seventh sense/ability. It pertains to:

7. **Wisdom.** There is a huge difference between knowledge and wisdom. Knowledge in The Information Age is readily available everywhere. However, knowledge without wisdom is crippled and in most cases useless. Wisdom is deep knowing. Knowing about God (or if one prefers The Force or The Source), Spirituality, the meaning of life, the value of innovation, that all things are interconnected and inter-related, that progress happens outside the comfort zone, that the cycle of birth-death is endless, that everything is a closed-loop system, that there is a hierarchy of systems (systems nested within systems), and so on.

Wisdom is one of the major sources of innovation because wisdom expands the mind and offers no boundaries set by society, upbringing, religion, education and society. It liberates the mind and liberated minds always think big brave thoughts. Here is an example of how people's brains get altered by parents and society without people realizing it:

Example: We as humans have the innate knowledge and wisdom of what is right and wrong, and what is good and evil. We see that when a toddler coils in the corner and starts shaking when s/he sees one parent hit and abuse the other. It's not just fear. It is the knowing of "This is wrong!" We automatically know that killing is not a good thing. And yet we send our kids to the armed forces to teach them that killing is acceptable in the name of God, country, and family. People don't realize that this is a form of brainwashing and distorted thinking. We accept it because logic tells us that killing is acceptable under certain circumstances. Logic, common sense, and several other "filters" distort wisdom, intuition, and insights. Thus, most people have no idea what wisdom really is, or what it is all about. Here are some simple questions for people to test their own wisdom:

1. Why is cultivating inner life important to cultivating wisdom?
2. Why is transcultural learning important to a better world?
3. Why does wisdom begin in humility?

---

10 Higher Purpose is more than Strategic Intent and Rallying Cry. It is the company's "calling" to be a "significant enterprise". It is life goal that commands one's thoughts, liberates one's energy, and inspires one's hopes.

4. Why is antagonism and competition healthy for innovation?
5. Why does Oneness produce better solutions?
6. Why do spiritual designs automatically appeal to people?

Here is an **example** of how to leverage nuggets of wisdom: People that have wisdom know that our separation from nature is a major mistake, and that technology pushes wisdom into the background, making the separation even more intense. Having this knowledge one must look for better options and inventions for our collective future and well-being. Wise people hear, see, and read such nuggets of wisdom and immediately start thinking of their implications on what they are doing or working on.

Wisdom has several inner/internal and external sources, including one's own virtues, intuition, experiences, innate and acquired knowledge, relationships, nature, crises, failures … and even destiny --- pretty much similar to the sources for innovation. Interestingly enough some of the sources can "cut" both ways. One of them is technology. It can increase wisdom by a great amount, but also can handicap wisdom and insights by giving them less importance. Information and knowledge glut is a major barrier to wisdom.

Personal Anecdote: In 2014 I was suffering from obvious blood flow restraints in my body. Everything on my left side was in severe pain (from my neck down to me groin). I was as pale as a white sheet of paper. I could hardly walk and I was ready to faint. I went to the ER room of the biggest and most famous hospital in Dallas to be examined, and their reaction was that there was nothing wrong with me! I went there for a second time and they sent me home again because their equipment said that there was nothing wrong with me. But, even the janitor could tell that I was ready to kick the bucket, but their equipment did not agree with that view. So, my wife took me to **Baylor Hospital** and immediately they admitted me to perform a triple heart bypass, which saved my life. Technology does not have all the answers … at least not yet. We still need people with wisdom … and intuitions … and common sense!

Conclusion

Daniel Pink's book mentions Conceptual or Holistic Thinking several times as it leverages the whole mind. Most people understand Holistic Thinking, but fail to understand how to enable it and how to use it properly.

Profound wisdom and great perceptions emerge from the synergy of both left and right brains. The higher the synergy is the higher the probability that emerging solutions will be beneficial to humanity, the whole world and the living planet.

3 ANALYTICAL VS. HOLISTIC THINKING

Phillip Andrews

Introduction

There is no need to get into a deep discussion here regarding the differences between Analytical Thinking and Holistic Thinking as numerous books and white papers have been written on this subject. The key point is that **Holistic Thinking** addresses the big picture and derives solutions top-down, as opposed to **Analytic Thinking** (Derivative of Scientific Thinking) that develops solutions bottom-up. Big Picture approach does not pay attention to details and does not worry about tearing things apart trying to understand the inner workings of things. Grasping the gist of things is good enough to make sense of the issues and requirements for possible solutions. In other words, Holistic Thinking goes against Scientific Thinking that was focused in dissecting everything to its finite elements in order to analyze and grasp how things really work.

Holistic brains usually excel in social and humanitarian issues and situations because they leverage their key traits of intuition, sensitivity, compassion and tact. This is important because that approach leads to offering more complete solutions to complex problems. **Holistic Thinking** opens people's minds to aspects of complex problems that most people miss due to their focus on the details. In most cases, the interrelationships between the components are more important than the components themselves.

Analytical Thinking and Holistic Thinking Comparison

Analytical Thinking (a.k.a. **Linear Thinking**) promotes serialized thinking viewing everything as a regimented (step-by-step) process, while **Holistic Thinking** promotes parallel thinking viewing everything as an integrated whole (a total system). We need both types of thinking to comprehend fully our world and to make solid progress. Thus, the issue is not choosing one over the other. The issue is understanding the value of Holistic Thinking, which was ignored for the most part in the last three to four hundred years. Interestingly enough, Holistic Thinking was prevalent in the ancient times, since people back then did not have the scientific skills or tools to pursue the scientific approach and methods to analyze the inner workings of all things that surrounded them.

Scientific Thinking has heavily influenced our current Education System by focusing almost exclusively on technical and analytical skills, and paying little or no attention to intuition, creativity, ideation, and imagination. Moreover, those analytical skills are reinforced when people join enterprises of all sizes because that's the key to their specialization.

The other skills are usually obtained through special workshops, OJT, or through personal efforts and natural instincts to improve one's intuition and creativity. However, the smart thing to do is to teach those skills in schools (as early as Middle School). Although some researchers proclaim that those skills cannot be learned or even be improved through teaching, the smart thing to do is find new ways to deliver the message about the value of creativity, innovation and intuition. These types of courses cannot be delivered through analytical methods and techniques, but rather through case studies, metaphors, examples ... and plenty of visuals (as it is known that holistic brains like and get stimulated by visual presentations).

The **differences between Linear and Holistic Thinking** are displayed below:

Linear Thinking	Holistic Thinking
Focus, specialization, analysis	Synthesis, generalization, imagination
Process Thinking	**+** Systems, Intuitive, Divergent and Lateral Thinking
Data, Information and Facts Driven	Insights, Patterns/Trends and Connections Driven
Experience and Know-How Matter	**+** Intuition, Insights, and Gut-Feelings Matter
Goal Oriented	Relationship(s) Oriented
Immediate Gains and Results	Benefit(s) Over Time; Long-Term Results
Fight Or Flight	Tend and Befriend
Competitive Spirit	Collaborative Spirit
Direct Approach	Indirect Approach
Point Solution(s); Tactical Focus	Total Solution; Strategic Focus; Overall Benefits
Focused Analysis	Complete Evaluation (incl. domino effect)
Partial Synthesis	Far-Reaching (Total) Synthesis
Physical & Intellectual Elucidations	**+** Emotional and Spiritual Elucidations

Horizon: Limited (bogged down in details and specifics)	Horizon: Unlimited (big picture, clear skies, "blue ocean" strategic thinking)
Capitalistic System	Blended or Hybrid System
My "whatever" (incl. religion and country) is better than all the rest	**Oneness is best** (NOTE: the world is craving for a new definition of Oneness --- one that appeases and beguiles the masses)

The advantages of Holistic Thinking are evident to everyone, and this is why several professions are shifting their focus to the right-hand column, thus promoting Holistic Medicine and Healing, Holistic Education, Holistic Consulting, Holistic Environmentalism, Holistic Sustainability, Holistic Innovation ... and Holistic Government.

Delivering Holistic Solutions

In the business world, the Holistic Approach and Thinking promotes the following principles[11]:

- **Continuous Learning**
  - Learning/Teaching Culture
  - Leverage Learning; Gather Ideas and Inspirations
- **Continuous and 360°Feedback**
  - From employees
  - From vendors, suppliers and partners
  - From customers and clients
  - From government
  - From the public
  - Gather Ideas and Inspirations
- **Continuous Scans and Discovery**
  - Own Performance
  - Competitors
  - Best Practices and Benchmarks
  - Sectors and Industries
  - Markets
  - Value Chains
  - Society/Societies
  - New Ideas (about everything)
  - Technologies and Systems/Apps
  - Intellectual Leaders
  - Think Tanks
  - Books, Magazines, Websites and Workshops/Webinars, etc.
  - Gather Ideas and Inspirations
  - Understand and Qualify the Challenges
- **Continuous Interpretations** (of what has been discovered)
  - Search for Meanings
  - Create and Tell "Stories"

---

[11] These Principles can be viewed as steps of a process. The main difference of these steps and the steps of a typical process is that these steps are happening in parallel and they all are interconnected, making it very difficult to portray them as sequential steps in a process. These steps should be viewed more as a mentality for innovation.

- o Create Scenarios
- o Frame Opportunities
- **Continuous Ideation**
  - o Generate Ideas and Inspirations
  - o Refine Ideas
  - o Prioritize Ideas
- **Continuous Analyses And Evaluations**
  - o Ideas and Inspirations
  - o Strengths
  - o Weaknesses
  - o Opportunities
  - o Threats
  - o Risks, Costs, Effort, Capabilities, etc.
- **Continuous Updating, Modifying/Tweaking, Improvement**
  - o Strategies
  - o Business Models
  - o Holistic/Total Enterprise Architecture
  - o Holistic Knowledge Management / Integrated Business Intelligence
  - o Product and/or Service Portfolios
  - o Processes
  - o Systems
  - o Operations, etc.
- **Continuous Experimentation and Prototyping**
  - o Analyzing results and make critical decisions of "Go, No-Go"
- **Continuous Evolution**
  - o Applying Continuous Improvement and Creative Disruption in a smart way (separated by periods of gestation so that the organization has time to absorb and institutionalize the changes)
  - o Applying Design Thinking and Creative Disruption

Note: Innovation applies to all of the above principles and/or activities.

Design Thinking

Design Thinking is the middle ground or intersection between Analytical Thinking and Intuitive Thinking. Some people despise the word holistic[12] and would rather use the word Design Thinking to express the same concept. However, Holistic Thinking is broader than Design Thinking as it goes further by integrating the best aspects of Systems, Intuitive, Divergent and Lateral Thinking[13].

Design Thinking is a methodology used by designers and inventors to solve complex problems, and find desirable solutions for clients, based on a specific mindset --- called **Design Mindset**. The design mindset is not problem-focused, but rather it is solution-focused requiring action(s)

---

[12] As they associate it with spirituality-related terms. This is silly bias. This is another blind spot of the Scientific Age that has demonized anything associated with spirituality. The word Design Thinking does not convey anything and is another "empty" term that has no value or "meaning". This is a perfect example of what Pink was trying to convey with his "6 senses". Some people are caught in semantics, politics and other superfluous influences rather than explaining the real essence of what is in front of them and what they are trying to say.

[13] These terms are defined in later chapters.

oriented towards creating a preferred future or a desired outcome. In other words, Design Thinking is solution-based, thus making it **Solution-focused Thinking**. This type of thinking usually starts with a goal in mind, (such as a better future, or an improved lifestyle) instead of solving a specific problem or issue. It takes into consideration both present and future conditions and parameters of the problem, while searching for alternative solutions and answers.

Design Thinking works best when it is human-centered because the proposed solutions are focused on the needs and wants of targeted audiences making them desirable right away. The notion that targeted customers don't know what they need or want is a fallacy because one must ask the right questions in order to get the right answers. But in order to ask the right questions, one must have a **deep understanding** of what is going on out there, what people feel and want (but cannot express in words yet), and what are the underlying assumptions (incl. perceived barriers, real and implicit limitations, and hidden opportunities). **Solution-Focused** and **Human-Centered Designs** are usually the big winners in today's marketplace.

Holistic Thinking incorporates all flavors and approaches to creating new designs. There is no such thing as a bad approach or a bad mindset because they all depend on the task at hand, the people involved, and the techniques or tools that they are using. Thus, sometimes it is best to work with specific goals in mind, while other times it's best to start with no specific goals at all. It all depends on the "collective understanding" of the people involved as to what they want to generate. **Understanding** is a tool of innovation that can provide visceral primary data that later can be "translated" or converted into products, programs, enterprises or anything else.

The primary issue for Design Thinking is that it is normally led by engineers, who typically want to turn it immediately into a crisp and clear process, which is a mistake in many cases. Innovation is NOT always a process. In many cases it becomes a process once the concepts, ideas, and theories have reached a certain maturity level.

Design Thinking is enabled by the **polymath mentality** because the more one knows, learns and experiences the easier it becomes to come up with fresh/new ideas based on the synthesis of a lot of different things. Synthesis is derived from **Abductive Thinking** or **Reasoning** (which is a form of logical inference). It starts with an observation, then it seeks to find the simplest and most likely explanation. This is a dramatic departure from the Scientific Thinking, which relies on specific conclusions and proven theorems or hypotheses. Abductive Thinking is content with best predictions, likelihoods, and best "guesses".

The reason why this is important is that Abductive Thinking opens up the "playing field" and the horizons of what is possible and doable. Of course there are risks associated with that type of thinking, but it fits perfect with people that want to take risks, experiment … and try different things (outside the norm).

Design Thinking usually starts by considering what people consider desirable, and then integrates the "inputs" of technology and business factors. So, the polymath mentality helps in both conceiving what is possible and also a) what affects it, b) what goes into "it", and c) what ties into "it". The diagram below captures the essence of all that.

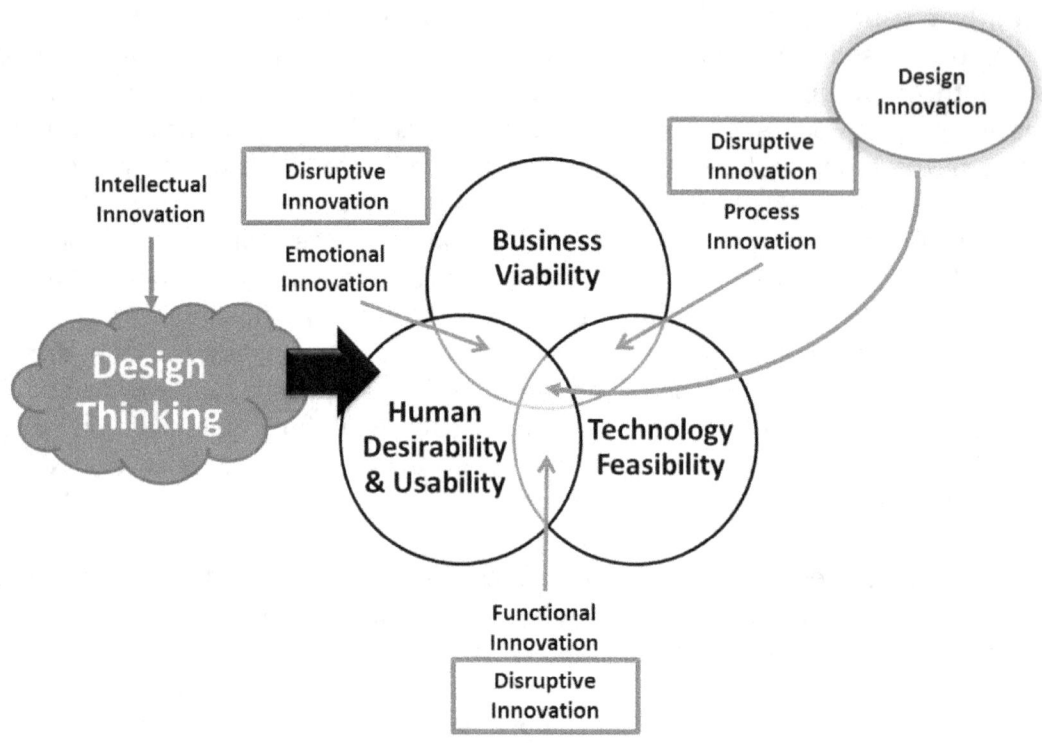

The Influence Of Needs and vMemes

Human Needs and vMemes[14] play an important role on how people see and translate the world. For example, the solution produced by a team full of Blue vMeme participants will be dramatically different from a team full of Yellow vMeme participants. Moreover, the Conceptual Age fits perfectly with both the Hierarchy Of Needs and Spiral Dynamics.

The **Abraham Maslow's Hierarchy Of Needs** explains how human needs "stack up". And although the original model was incomplete (because it missed some basic needs), it is now widely accepted as being an adequate depiction of human needs, and even human evolution[15]. In other words, humans collectively as a species put the emphasis on different needs as they progress from one stage or era to the next --- similar to the concept imbedded in Spiral Dynamics.

This is also the main theme of **Dr. Clare Graves, Dr. Don Beck and Chris Cowan's Spiral Dynamics** that describe society's collective progression through their identified vMemes (sort of value systems). The vMemes strongly correlate to the different eras in human evolution, but in Spiral Dynamics the main emphasis is on the human journey through the levels of consciousness rather than on human needs.

---

[14] vMemes (short for values-attracting meta-memes) can be thought of as broad orienting paradigms --- a schema through which we interpret the world. These vMemes fall into a series of eight levels (see diagram on next page) --- describing the evolution of our species in terms of ability to access and apply higher levels of consciousness. Each level has an awareness, peak, and decline phase --- similar to an S-Curve. People throughout all ages are spread across all 8 levels because all 8 levels co-exist --- not all people have the same maturity. Today, most people in the Western world fit in the top two vMemes.

[15] The Needs have changed through the ages. It is possible that all the needs were present from the start of the human race, but did not come to the surface and become predominant until people "matured", evolved, became civilized and changed the focus of their own personal lives and the focus of their societies.

The core principles underpinning **Spiral Dynamics** are that a) no one jumps levels[16], and b) everyone has access to all levels through their own learning and development. The truth is that some people do not migrate from one meme to the next because they are born with minds and abilities that other people do not have. For example, **Socrates, Plato** and **Aristotle** were always at the top of the pyramid with their holistic minds (see diagram below). They did not care where the rest of the society was. And that was the main reason why they were viewed as beacons of light for centuries. And this is true today as some people are able to hover at the top as holistic thinkers, while others are stuck in the lower vMemes.

Note: No advanced society around this globe is homogeneous ... and for a good reason. Not all people have the same abilities, senses and intellects. This is one of the main reasons why we have such a huge variety, not only of opinions, but views, perspectives, and understandings. People that have that extra ability and/or that extra sense to see and feel the world differently from the rest of the pack. Holism, globalization, Oneness, spirituality (beyond religion), eco-spirituality, sustainable cities, and a several other views do not appeal to all people. Not even Smart Cities and Smart Factories are acceptable to all people. As a matter of fact, many people feel threatened by such words and concepts. They see doom and gloom hidden behind each one of those words, not to mention dark conspiracies.

Thus, the hierarchies of vMemes and Human Needs serve not only as a tool to understand what drives people and the progress we have made as a society through the millennia, but also as a tool to understand why we cannot all agree as to what is important in life and in business. In other words, it is not easy to convince one that is stuck in the Red or Blue vMemes (see graph on next page) and exhibits behaviors of megalomania, narcissism, and authoritarianism to espouse the concept of:

One People, One Planet, One Future

However, as a species it is safe to say that we have collectively moved towards the top vMemes. There is a collective awakening going on right now in most Western societies --- and that phenomenon greatly is a huge part of **The Conceptual Age**.

Note: There is no job application form or interview process that can capture an applicants' mindset and vMeme level. Companies still make hiring decisions based on IQ and credentials, while ignoring EQ and SQ (that in a way reveal a person's overall maturity and total development).

Spiral Dynamics outlines how the human race has progressed from the bottom of the spiral to the top over several millennia; and our progress / journey continues with new views and perspectives made available by the awakening. The Conceptual Age leverages those new abilities, capabilities, skills and traits. The graph below intertwines all of them together.

---

[16] These principles apply to the masses and are generalizations about the human race. The truth is that society all had and always will have individuals that do not follow the norms. Some people were already in the Turquoise Meme since antiquity --- well before any authors even wrote a book to explain it.

There is speculation that both the Needs and the Memes will evolve even further through the next few millennia. Thus, this is only temporary snapshot of what we think we know and understand today.

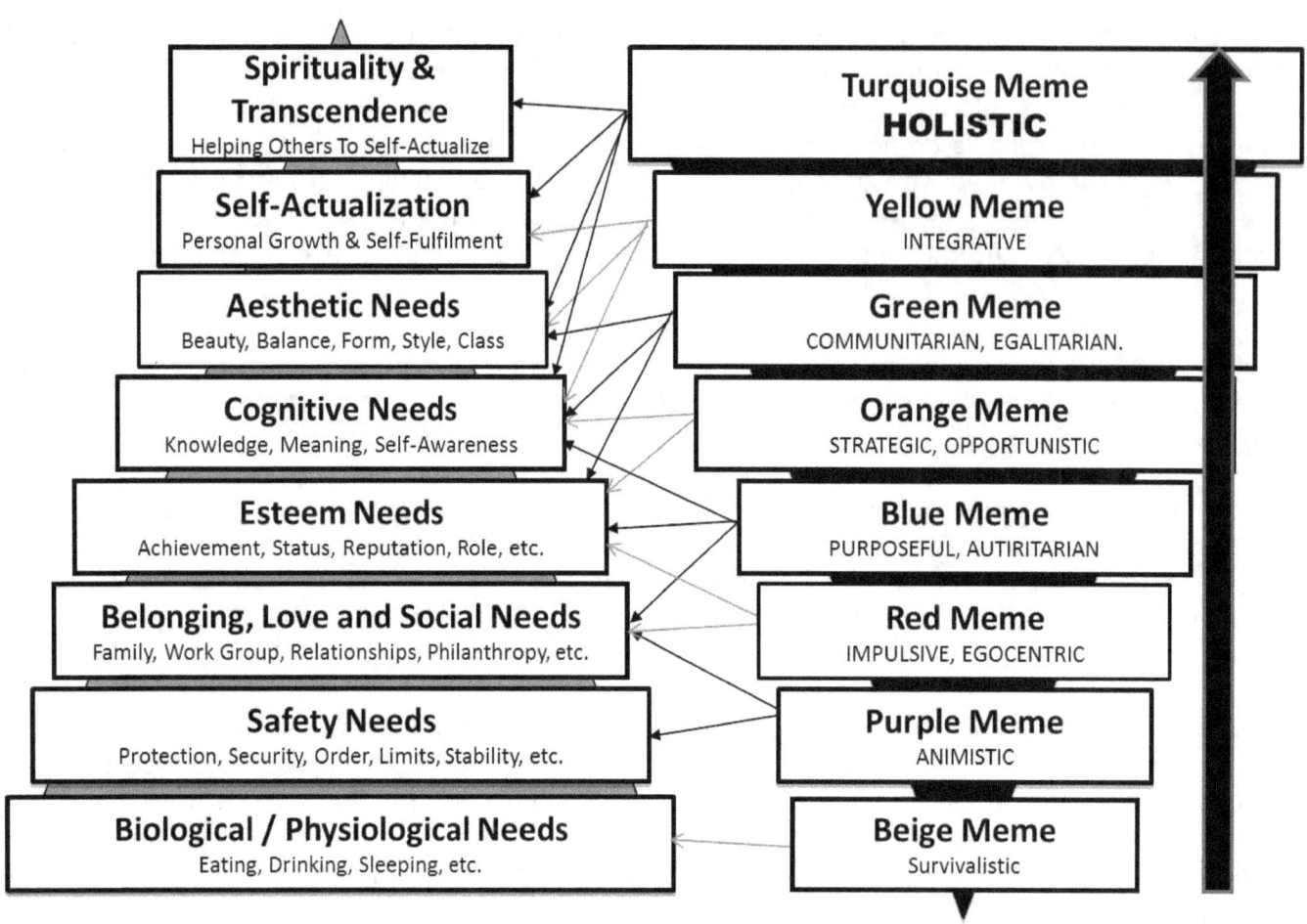

Note: The revised pyramid depicting the **new and improved Hierarchy Of Needs** is attributed to many sources, including **Tay & Diener** (2011) **Hoffman, E.** (1988) (*The right to be human: A biography of Abraham Maslow),* and **Kenrick, D. T., Neuberg, S. L., Griskevicius, V., Becker, D. V., & Schaller, M.** (2010) (Goal-Driven Cognition and Functional Behavior The Fundamental-Motives Framework. *Current Directions in Psychological Science, 19(1)*, 63-67).

Conceptual and Holistic Thinking is part of both the Turquoise Meme and the Transcendence Needs. In other words, both bodies of theory converge at the top where holism and Holistic Thinking become the essence of our existence, lifestyles, thinking, and behaving.

Three Important Notes:

1. Maslow's initial Hierarchy Of Needs was focused on the individual. Holistic Thinking and universal mentalities usually do not occur within that individualistic model. One has to reach the Transcendence level in order to understand that life is not about one's own life and personal needs. Life is about all of us and our **collective (= holistic) needs**. And that is exactly the essence of The Holistic vMeme. The so-called **Indigo Kids** are the ones that are focused on the big picture that includes the entire human race, all living things and the entire planet.

2. Each "Need" creates/generates its own innovations required to sustain it, maintain it, enhance it, and advance it. Thus, all innovations can be ranked according to the need they serve. The higher level needs usually produce the best innovations --- there are always

exceptions.

3. Most people still live life as "residents" of the lower memes, focused on their lower needs. Humanity does not move in unison, which causes all the problems that we see around us. In other words, the depicted hierarchy of needs does not apply to everyone --- some people do not have the full array. Moreover, where one puts her/his emphasis, that's exactly the type of lifestyle and level of existence they will experience in life. For example, if one is hungry and facing a civil war her/his mind will not be on the higher needs or worry about wisdom. In other words, deprivation, deficiencies, inequalities, enslavement, attachments, addictions, and many other negative factors blind or rob people of their top level needs.

Conclusion

Design Thinking is a formal method for practical, inventive resolution of problems and the creation of ingenious solutions aiming to improve future outcomes or results.

Holistic Thinking originates in the mind of the inventor or innovator. Understanding how one's brain works and reaches conclusions or generates ideas is very important because if the brain is not "wired" the right way then the outcomes and "products" of the brains functions will not be fruitful and valuable. Thus, the challenge for everyone is to figure out what is missing in their own minds. There are ways to climb up the hierarchies of Needs and vMemes. This is an extremely difficult task ecause everyone has blind spots --- they cannot see that which they cannot see. Secondly, very few people want to admit to themselves that their brains are not as "wholesome" and "wide-ranging" as they could be. Moreover, most people do not know how to engage their left brains because there are limited such workshops, seminars and books that can help.

The reason why one should and must climb to higher vMemes is that there are **more jewels or pearls to be found at the higher levels**. Thus, from a personal journey point of view, it is advantageous (in more ways than one) to get to the highest level possible.

Advice:
Find the pearls in your mind!
Share the pearls!
Help others reach higher levels!
Help others discover their pearls!

4 DISRUPTIVE AND RADICAL INNOVATION

Phillip Andrews

Introduction

The word "Disruption" suggests abrupt break in the action --- whatever that action is. In the business world the disruption can come in many forms, such as disrupting the business model, the products or services offered, the materials used to make the products, the supply chain, the markets, and everything else, including an entire industry. The examples are numerous and most people know them. Here are some examples:

- The fossil fuel industry put an end to the whale oil industry
- Alternative fuel sources are putting an end to the fossil fuel industry
- Online movies put an end to the videotape stores
- PCs and tablets are putting an end to the minicomputer industry
- Hand-held devices and smart phones are putting an end to the laptop computers
- Wearable technologies will replace all handheld devices (incl. laptops)
- Driverless vehicles are putting an end to transportation as we knew it

As a result of these disruptions, several industries and companies are finding themselves in trouble, including:

- Newspapers
- Bookstores
- Photofinishing
- Taxis
- Railroads

Technology has become the fourth major vehicle of creating wealth for nations and individuals (besides agriculture, mining, and manufacturing). Technology now is a form of a mania because it offers people the opportunity to use their imagination and creative juices and people like that. Technology has added so many new dimensions to human existence and new capabilities. Technology is also the Number One vehicle and force for change as Amazon, Uber and airBNB have demonstrated. Some people see this as a personal challenge to use technology to upset the established "Big Guys" (the incumbents), not to mention that it is also the best vehicle to make one rich the quickest way possible. Yes, it's always fun to trip-up the Big Guys and cut them down to size. This is a basic human need that is not as much about jealousy as it is about proving who is smarter and sharper. It is sort of an upmanship game.

In the past, people viewed Technology as being part of Manufacturing because the two of them were so interlinked that one had a hard time telling them apart. However, the digital revolution has made it abundantly clear that technology can stand on its own without manufacturing (although manufacturing can no longer exist without Technology).

However, Creative Disruption is not about technology alone. **Whole Foods and Wal-Mart** have shown to everyone that changing one's Business Model and focusing the enterprise on what is important to people can disrupt well established companies like **Sears/K-Mart, Woolworth, Tom Thumb and Kroger**. Now the **Krogers** of the world are slowly trying to become more like **Whole Foods** and **Wal-Mart** because they have lost so much market share to Whole Foods ... and their clones like **HEB, Trader Joe's and Central Market**.

The world is changing at a neck-breaking speed and very few people understand all the changes that are going on all around us. There is no question that the Digital Age has rejuvenated and even accelerated the innovation thrust --- one may even call it a movement. As was mentioned in a previous chapter, **innovation is essential in reinventing our civilization and societies.**

The Different Types Of Innovation

Enterprises and people in general see innovation under different lenses and have different labels to characterize it and explain it. In most cases innovation applies to all the areas listed below, requiring a different approach and a different type of innovation techniques and tools:

1. **Business Configuration Related**
   a. Business Model --- with 3BL[17] focus
   b. Business Ecosystem; Value Chain
   c. Business and Organizational Structure
   d. Business (Core) Processes
   e. Core Competencies/Capabilities
2. **Market Offering**
   a. Product Portfolio
   b. Service Portfolio
   c. Portfolio System (how products and services work together --- "feed" each other)
   d. Offering Performance (value proposition, distinguishing features, competitive advantage)
3. **Customer Experience**
   a. Brand (image, hidden/implied messages, higher purpose)
   b. Perceived Value (offering performance based on the value received or offered)
   c. Channels (number of them and convenience of accessing them)
   d. Customer Engagement (customer service, loyalty programs, other interactions)

---

[17] 3BL = Triple Bottom Line referring to People, Planet, Profits --- as preached in the early versions of Sustainability.

Others "bucketize" innovation according to these focus areas:

1. **Finance** (both external and internal)
2. **Processes** (both business and operational processes)
3. **Market Offering**
4. **Delivery**

At a higher level, there are **four types of innovation** that are crucial to understand because they set the tone for the company's culture and style of management. Here is a high level synopsis:

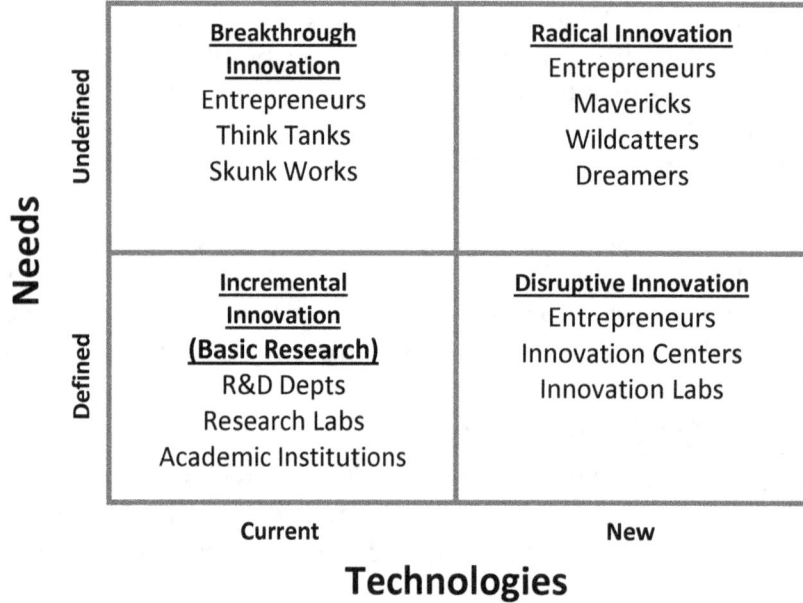

Most corporations in the past were putting all their emphasis in the **Incremental Innovation** (a.k.a. **Sustaining Innovation**) and were ignoring the other types because they did not understand that the other types even existed. That was the traditional role of R&D departments until the mid '80s when Apple introduced their Mac and showed the world their famous 1984 commercial declaring that *"On January 24th, Apple Computer will introduce Macintosh, and you'll see why 1984 won't be like "1984".*

Most people thought the commercial was making fun of IBM, which was true, but what they missed the point that Apple was also making a drastic switch from Incremental Innovation (IBM's old approach and culture) to Radical Innovation, which became Apple's mantra (sort of a Higher Purpose), brand image, and culture. While IBM at the time was retreating from robotics, sensors, vision systems, and even PCs, Apple was reinventing the computer business and getting closer to customers/consumers. IBM continued to retreat and become an impersonal entity focused on the big corporate clients, while Apple became a legend with consumers. IBM thought that sticking to its knitting was smart, while Apple was inventing new industries.

Personal Anecdote: When I was working for **IBM** in the early '80s, I was so proud of my company. When I was telling other people that "I'm an IBMer" one could see the glow on my face and the halo over my head. But then a seismic shift happened (under John Akers – a very bad CEO) and IBM pulled-in its horns, killed several great product lines and became a lame lamb with no vision and no ambition. It started losing key people, and the legendary culture of IBM took a severe beating. There was no halo anymore and no special pride. Apple was making history and IBM had nothing special to show the world except for its super-computers (that only 15,000 or so people in the whole world cared about).

We went from having the Pentagon contacting us to leverage our programming language for its robotic soldiers (because we had the most sophisticated robotic language at the time) to wondering if **Deep Blue** can beat **Gary Kasparov** in their now famous chess competition. Not exactly the thing that most people care about. This is a perfect example of what the value of innovation is all about. Apple did the smart things and became the most valued corporation in the world, while IBM struggled to survive (and some experts were even proclaiming its total demise at the start of the 21st Century). Who would have thought that the tiny and fledgling **Apple Computer** company would be valued several times over the value of IBM (by 2017)? But it happened, and now everyone knows why.

The Difference Between Disruptive Innovation And Radical Innovation

The difference is not really that important anymore because both types of innovation create dramatic results that are not worth debating as to the magnitude of their impact. Traditionally, Disruptive Innovation is focusing on defined needs, meaning that the markets and customers are defined to a certain degree because investors and venture capitalists are always looking for that in the business plans that they are willing to support. They are very leery and hesitant to fund something that has no potential customers. They have lost a ton of money chasing Holy Grails, mirages and ghosts. So, the expectation is that companies and entrepreneurs that are pursuing new technologies must have a good idea on how their targeted customers will benefit from the introduction of new products and services.

On the other hand, **Radical Innovation** is dealing with undefined or unarticulated needs. The companies and individuals pursuing those needs are actually "playing" in the "white sandbox" where not only the needs are not well-defined, but also the potential customers and opportunities. Very few people realize the risks that **Steve Jobs** took with the inventions of MP3, iPad, iPhone and all of his other inventions. He actually bet the company ... and to everyone's surprise the Board Of Directors went along with him because they believed his dreams and convictions. Most Boards are too lethargic and risk-averse to approve offerings that will jeopardize the company and everyone's job. After all, it does not look good in the resume to have worked for a company that went bankrupt, or worse yet, one was instrumental in bankrupting the company. The **Steven Jobs and Elon Musks of the world are a very rare breed indeed** --- not necessarily because they can think-outside-the box, but because they can sell their ideas to others and mobilize the entire company (and for that matter, the whole world) and have them behind them, supporting them. **The power of a good vision is imperative in becoming successful.** The key ingredients for a powerful and compelling dream/vision are:

- It serves the **Higher Purpose** (of both the company's and humanity's)

- **Big enough and broad enough** that people immediately see how it affects them
- The **value is self-evident**; no one needs to explain it or define it
- It **enhances the "user" experience** and/or improves QoL
- It offers **prodigious value** to a great number of people

The Differences Between Incremental Innovation and Disruptive/Radical Innovation

Incremental Innovation is also called **Sustaining Innovation** because its focus is to sustain the momentum that the company has with its current markets and customers. Here is a synopsis of the differences between the two kinds of innovation:

	Incremental Innovation	Disruptive Innovation
Problem, Issue or Challenge	Well understood and defined	Not well understood
Market Focus	Existing Markets	Some New Markets
Market Predictability	Very Predictable	Unpredictable
Types of Changes	Small to Medium	Extensive
Voice Of the Customer	It matters a lot	Nice to have, but not essential
Business Model Changes	Very few	Wide-ranging
Current Business Methods	Sufficient to proceed	Insufficient and may be detrimental
Customer Acceptance	Expected to be high	Unknown (despite Focus Group input)
Risk Level	Low	Medium to High

Examples of Disruptive Innovation include:

1. **Minimills** (replacing Integrated Steel Mills)
2. **Electric anything** (razors, toasters, clocks, ovens, washers, dryers, etc.)
3. **Latest electronic gadget** (MP3, flat screen TVs, tablets, wearable computers, etc.)
4. **Smart anything** (bombs, phones, toilets, roads, homes, buildings, etc.)
5. **Online anything** (movies, courses, news, email, music, etc.)
6. **Interconnected anything** (sensors, computers, systems, etc.)
7. **Driverless anything** (cars, trains, planes, submarines)
8. **Robotic anything** (from floor sweepers to CEOs)

Radical Innovation represents even more dramatic changes with totally new business models, new business methods, and a brand new offering that never existed before. Most people cannot tell the difference between Disruptive and Radical Innovation because in most cases it is unknown whether the needs were well defined or not. The easiest way to remember it is that Radical Innovations/Inventions change the world and alter life as we know it and experience it in a very dramatic way. Here are some examples that need no explanation:

1. **The Wheel**
2. **Paper**
3. **Printing Press**
4. **Indoor plumbing**
5. **Gun Powder and Guns**
6. **Electricity**
7. **Cameras and Movies**
8. **Refrigeration and Pasteurization**
9. **Air conditioning**
10. **Telecommunications (Telegraph and Telephones)**
11. **Radio and Television**
12. **Trains**
13. **Automobiles**
14. **Airplanes**
15. **Submarines**
16. **Computers, Software and Databases**
17. **Satellites**
18. **Atomic Energy**
19. **Space Travel**
20. **Credit Cards**
21. **Digital anything**
    a. Transistor & digital radios, replacing analog radios
    b. Pocket calculators, replacing desktop calculators
    c. PCs and home printers, replacing typewriters
    d. LCD TVs, replacing CRT TVs
    e. Cellular phones, replacing regular (landline) phones
    f. CDs and DVDs, replacing tapes and other analog media
22. **World Wide Web / Internet**
23. **Mobility** (from apps to systems)
24. **Nanotechnology**

And the best is yet to come! The innovations that are currently in the lab will blow everyone's mind in the years ahead. Here is a small sample of what inventors and scientists are working in their labs all across the world:

- **Capturing dreams.** One wakes up in the morning and presses the print button to capture the dream s/he saw the previous night, or press the save button to store it for future reference
- **Capturing memories.** Same as above. This is similar to what was depicted in the 1983 movie called **"Brainstorm"** (Natalie Wood's last movie). Memory bubbles will become reality.

- **Uploading memories.** To ensure that people totally lose sense of reality (like in the movie "**Total Recall**" (1990)). There are some good valid medical reasons why this is a good idea.
- **Personal Doctors at home.** Artificial Intelligence and new technologies will eliminate the need of running to the doctors' offices to perform most diagnostics (incl. MRIs) and certain treatments.
- **Online court houses and personal Lawyers.** Can handle your case online and having a robo-lawyer to defend you or go after the defendants.
- **Robo-teachers.** Going beyond online live workshops, webinars and downloadable files.
- **Augmented Reality.** Computerized information about everything. Just lift up your smart phone aim at a target and get instantaneously all the information you wanted for an intelligent and real time decision.
- **Brain Pacemakers.** For people that suffer from dementia or Alzheimer's illnesses

... and so much more. The future holds numerous (actually infinite) surprises for the human race. However, we all need a word of caution: people started believing that technologies will fix all the evils of the world. The so called **Technofix is NOT a panacea**. Technology can only fix so much. Many of the problems that humans have created the last few centuries, and continue to create today, CANNOT be fixed by technology. We need to apply additional fixes to our civilization, including social, political and economic fixes.

Understanding The Disruptive Innovation Model

The original model and term was Creative Destruction and was coined by **Joseph Schumpeter** in his work entitled **"Capitalism, Socialism and Democracy" (1942).** The intent of his work was to explain that Capitalism encourages a *"process of industrial mutation that incessantly revolutionizes the economic structure from within, incessantly destroying the old one, incessantly creating a new one."* He made the point that destruction and creation go hand-in-hand. In a way, destruction opens the door for creation. Sometimes it is necessary to clear the slate in order to start fresh with new concepts and new designs.

Schumpeter went as far as to say that the *"process of creative destruction is the essential fact about Capitalism."* We will go even further than that, by stating that destruction is a natural phenomenon --- as necessary as Evolution itself. Deep down it's all about craving change, wanting to improve, and reaching higher levels of excellence. This is a basic need that **Maslow** missed in his famous **Hierarchy Of Needs.** Self-Actualization and Self-Esteem explain some of the desire of wanting to improve, but the reality of craving improvement has very little to do with the "self" and more to do with inquisitiveness, curiosity and imagination. In other words, it is focused externally rather than internally; making improvements to improve one's world, and for that matter, everyone's world.

The word Destruction was eventually replaced by the word Disruption, which eventually became institutionalized in 1995 when HBR published a powerful article by **Clayton M. Christensen** and **Joseph L. Bower** called **"Disruptive Technologies: Catching the Wave".** Then, twenty years (2015) later, **Clayton M. Christensen** and two new co-authors **(Michael E. Raynor and Rory McDonald)** published a follow up article called **"What Is Disruptive Innovation?"** that reinforced the term and gave it more substance.

One of the main points that the authors made is that Creative Disruption is a process, not just an event. Here is what the authors wrote to explain the process:

"Most every innovation — disruptive or not — begins life as a small-scale experiment. Disrupters tend to focus on getting the business model, rather than merely the product, just right. When they succeed, their movement from the fringe (the low end of the market or a new market) to the mainstream erodes first the incumbents' market share and then their profitability. This process can take time, and incumbents can get quite creative in the defense of their established franchises. For example, more than 50 years after the first discount department store was opened, mainstream retail companies still operate their traditional department-store formats. Complete substitution, if it comes at all, may take decades, because the incremental profit from staying with the old model for one more year trumps proposals to write off the assets in one stroke.

The fact that disruption can take time helps to explain why incumbents frequently overlook disrupters. For example, when Netflix launched, in 1997, its initial service wasn't appealing to most of Blockbuster's customers, who rented movies (typically new releases) on impulse. Netflix had an exclusively online interface and a large inventory of movies, but delivery through the U.S. mail meant selections took several days to arrive. The service appealed to only a few customer groups — movie buffs who didn't care about new releases, early adopters of DVD players, and online shoppers. If Netflix had not eventually begun to serve a broader segment of the market, Blockbuster's decision to ignore this competitor would not have been a strategic blunder: The two companies filled very different needs for their (different) customers."

But **the process of Creative Disruption** is more than that. It involves all these steps[18] as well:

1. Inspiration, Ideation, Imagination
   a. Capturing the "Aha moment" or vision
   b. Capturing related insights, intuitions and gut feelings

2. Decision To Pursue (Judgement Call)
   a. Framing The Idea, Challenge or Opportunity
   b. Understanding the value, magnitude and thrust
   c. Identifying a starting point

3. Discovery
   a. Researching
   b. Getting grounded
   c. Gathering more inspiration and courage
   d. Making the decision to go to the next step

4. Interpretation, Initial Evaluation
   a. Rationalizing the idea
   b. Creating "the story" of what this is all about
   c. Search for meaning
   d. Reframing the opportunity based on new information and knowledge
   e. Re-igniting the imagination
   f. Evaluating the personal sacrifices and costs to one's own life and family

---

[18] In this book there are other processes and process steps mentioned as well. The purpose is to highlight the point that there are different views of dealing with Creative Disruption and Innovation.

g. Making the decision to proceed further

5. Ideation
   a. Building on top of the original idea; generating more ideas
   b. Refining ideas
   c. Weeding out ideas
   d. Prioritizing ideas
   e. Setting the course for moving forward (or delaying until further information becomes available)

6. Business Creation and Initial Funding
   a. Developing the Business Plan
   b. Soliciting funding; approaching investors; presenting the Plan
   c. Obtaining initial round(s) of funding
   d. Establishing a formal business entity; registering with the State

7. Experimentation
   a. Formulating the offering
   b. Designing/creating the detailed drawings
   c. Analyzing the original designs; performing a feasibility study
   d. Using simulations and other tools to test idea(s)
   e. Making mockups and prototypes
      i. Using 3-D Printing for Rapid Prototyping (if applicable)
   f. Finding and correcting the "bugs"
      i. Getting feedback
      ii. Reasoning and rationalizing the collected data
      iii. Refining original designs
   g. Productizing the offering
   h. Analyzing findings and making the decision if offering is still worth pursuing
      i. Re-evaluating everything

8. Build and Test Launch
   a. Preparing the initial production operation
   b. Initiating pilot production(s)
   c. Making initial batch
   d. Performing Test Marketing
   e. Collecting more feedback
   f. Making additional corrections (if needed)
   g. Making the decision to "go full speed ahead"

9. Funding The Venture
   a. Refining the Business Plan based on:
      i. Marketing Research
      ii. Competitive Analysis
      iii. Growth Strategy
      iv. Manufacturing Plans (in-house vs. outsourcing)
      v. Partner Plans and actual partnering agreements
      vi. More realistic financial projections
      vii. Final Management Team and Boards
      viii. The Deal (for investors), etc.
   b. Obtaining the required funding

10. Build The Business
   a. Recruiting the right people in all positions

    b. Setting up the initial organization structure and reporting lines

    c. Setting up the right initial business infrastructure

    d. Setting up the right initial technical infrastructure

    e. Setting up the right culture

11. Full Launch

    a. Setting up full scale production lines or giving the go-ahead to outsourcers to proceed with the agreed production volumes

    b. Allocating the right resources to evolve and refine the offering

    c. Initiating a Continuous Improvement Program and other programs that will cut costs and improve Customer Experience, etc.

    d. Tracking learnings

    e. Tracking funding

    f. Tracking metrics or key performance indicators

12. Pursue The Next Big idea

    a. Focusing on the next offering; thinking ahead

    b. Allocating resources to the next project

Personal Anecdote: Having worked with several startup companies and entrepreneurs it became very clear that everyone has their own idea as to how they want to proceed and what steps to take. Some of them have added steps to this process, others have skipped steps, and yet others changed the order of the steps. All of that is fine as there are several paths that would lead one to the "Promised Land". It is also worth mentioning that there are several ways one can fund her/his idea and there are several ways one can start a company. Some people started companies without even having a Business Plan, while others never created a formal company with a formal management team. Some people bootstrap everything and make-do with minimal help, resources and skills. Amazing, but all those versions work. This is part of realizing that *"where there is a will there is a way"*. People that have *"the right fire in the belly"* … and a little luck, can achieve just about anything. However, for every success story, there are at least 1,000 unsuccessful, futile and disastrous stories.

Other Key Points About Creative Innovation and Radical Innovations

From Clayton Christensen:

- *"Simplicity is always disruptive"*
- *"Disruptive innovations originate in low-end or new-market footholds"*
- *"Disruptive innovations don't catch on with mainstream customers until quality catches up to their standards"*
- *"Disrupters often build business models that are very different from those of incumbents"*
- *"Because disruption can take time, incumbents frequently overlook disrupters"*
- *"Some disruptive innovations succeed; some don't"*
- *"The mantra "Disrupt or be disrupted" can misguide us"*
- *"It is rare that a technology or product is inherently sustaining or disruptive. And when new technology is developed, disruption theory does not dictate what managers should do. Instead it helps them make a strategic choice between taking a sustaining path and taking a disruptive one"*

- *"When new technology arises, disruption theory can guide strategic choices"*
- *"Smart disrupters improve their products and drive upmarket"*
- *"First, researchers realized that a company's propensity for strategic change is profoundly affected by the interests of customers who provide the resources the firm needs to survive. In other words, incumbents (sensibly) listen to their existing customers and concentrate on sustaining innovations as a result. Researchers then arrived at a second insight: Incumbents' focus on their existing customers becomes institutionalized in internal processes that make it difficult for even senior managers to shift investment to disruptive innovations"*
- *"Those two insights helped explain why incumbents rarely responded effectively (if at all) to disruptive innovations, but not why entrants eventually moved upmarket to challenge incumbents, over and over again. It turns out, however, that the same forces leading incumbents to ignore early-stage disruptions also compel disrupters ultimately to disrupt"*

Quotes From Other Great Minds:

- *"We are here to put a dent in the universe. Otherwise, why even be here?"* – **Steve Jobs**
- *"If you are disrupting a market, you'll get many "Nos"* – **Unknown**
- *"One of the advantages of being disorderly is constantly making exciting discoveries"* – **A. A. Milne**
- *"Life is short. Build stuff that matter."* – **Unknown**
- *"(Disruptive) Innovation distinguishes a leader and a follower"* – **Steve Jobs**
- *"The entrepreneur always searches for change, responds to it, and exploits it as an opportunity"* – **Peter Drucker**
- *"Creativity is intelligence having fun"* – **Albert Einstein**
- *"Creativity isn't just about generating imaginative solutions to daunting problems. The most valuable people in today's workforce constantly challenge their own process and take a creative approach to everything they do --- from the way they observe, to the way they communicate, to the way they leverage their failures into successes."* – **Joel Jacobs** (Product Designed at MS)
- *"You can't use up creativity. The more you use the more you have"* – **Maya Angelou**
- *"Vulnerability is the birthplace of creativity, innovation and change"* – **Brene Brown**
- *"When the technology that has the potential for revolutionizing an industry emerges, established companies typically see it as unattractive: it's not something their mainstream customers want, and its projected profit margins aren't sufficient to cover big-company cost structure. As a result, the new technology tends to get ignored in favor of what's currently popular with the best customers. But then another company steps in to bring the innovation to a new market. Once the disruptive technology becomes established there, smaller-scale innovation rapidly raise the technology's performance on attributes that mainstream customers' value."* – **Joseph Bower**

There are numerous other great quotes on the internet that is worth for some people to review as part of the process of getting motivated and inspired.

... And A Distorted View of Creative Disruption

In the last decade or so, **the marketing industry,** which is always hungry for buzzwords to impress customers and consumers, has grabbed the term of Creative Disruption and has used it for their **"creative messaging"** as if they were not creative enough before. Creative Disruption to them implies breaking away from the normal advertising messages and techniques that bombard audiences on a daily basis and put more emphasis on:

- Offering contrasting and controversial messages which will be remembered and acted upon; exhibiting super-exaggerated presentations and claims (even shocking)
- Taking advantage of unusual or out-of-place presentation or placement (like posting ads on your email, search engine/browser), which are extremely irritating to most people and give the impression that they are being "spied upon". They euphemistically call this practice: **Intensely Targeted Messaging**
- Improving brand perceptions --- beyond the product itself
- Leveraging social media (such as: Facebook, Blogs and YouTube) to the max

Creative Disruption in Marketing helps businesses gain a competitive advantage by seeking tipping points for improvement before competitors get to replicate and improve upon the originator's approach and contact points. This approach of course has nothing to do with Creative Disruption. Outsmarting the "other guy" and being shrewder with ploys and gimmicks is creative, but not disruptive enough to really make a real difference in life or in business. Creating something unique and original that can be patented, trademarked, and copyrighted is what delivers true long lasting competitive advantage. Gimmicks, hype and trickery only offer ephemeral profits. Truly Disruptive models and approaches are sustainable over a certain period of time. In today's world there are no longer long lasting models (as they were in the Industrial Era). Business Models today are lucky to survive past 15 years.

Conclusion

The differences between Radical Innovation and Disruptive Innovation are very difficult for most people to discern and defend. Thus, it is best to combine them into one bucket. Moreover, the terminology has become confusing as people use words like creative, disruptive, destructive, strategic, radical, breakthrough, Big Bang, and others to describe innovation that is anything but traditional, incremental and sustaining. People should not get hang up on the words. It is the basic concept that matters. And what really matters is that there are basic two types of innovations: a) the incremental, and b) the disruptive. Holistic Innovation is the sum of the two because both are needed and should be leveraged.

5 DELVING DEEPER INTO CREATIVE DISRUPTION / CREATIVE INNOVATION

Phillip Andrews

Introduction

As was mentioned in the previous chapter, Creative Disruption or Destruction is not new concept. It was introduced by **Joseph A. Schumpeter** (1883 – 1950). He maintained that *"The fundamental impulse that … keeps the capitalist engine in motion comes from the new consumers, goods, the new methods of production or transportation, the new markets, the new forms of industrial organization that (the) capitalist enterprise creates."* He further maintained that *"This process of Creative Destruction is* **the essential fact about capitalism***. It is what capitalism consists in and what every capitalist concern has got to live in …"* In his view the kind of competition that counts has to do with *"… the new commodity, the new technology, the new source(s) of supply, the new type of organization … which strikes not at the margins of the profits and the outputs of the existing firms, but at their foundations and their very lives."*

He understood better than most modern executives and government officials that the capitalistic system is a *"… process of industrial mutation that incessantly revolutionizes the economic structure from within, incessantly destroying the old one, incessantly creating a new one."*

In other, words, capitalism by its very nature, behaves like nature. Everything must evolve to something bigger and better. There is no way to stop evolution (=progress) in nature … or in business. In a way, business is an ecosystem that fits within the other ecosystems found in nature and life itself. Smart leaders are finally finding out now (after 200 years of brutal exploitation of nature and its ecosystems) on how to coexist in harmony with nature and preserve the other ecosystems rather than destroying them.

Understanding Schumpeterian Logic The Right Way

Some people have translated Schumpeter's messages as promoting ruthless antagonism, and "take-no-prisoners" type competition in a doggy-dog world. But this is the extreme and myopic vision of capitalism because capitalism by its very nature is heartless, inhuman and cruel.

Schumpeter was only pointing the nature of the beast. This is one of the major reasons why thought leaders today are seeking to modify and improve the system because it is reaching its breaking point, giving rise to socialistic and other views that eventually will ruin the capitalistic system.

Schumpeter's views simply have to do with putting more emphasis on discontinuous improvement rather on continuous improvement. His mind never went to leveraging discontinuous improvements at undermining other companies, ruining the foundations of competitors or disrupting the livelihoods of others. He was simply stating the obvious: that discontinuous improvements and radical innovations happen! He did not invent discontinuous improvements --- he just highlighted them and brought them to the forefront of our consciousness; no different than what Darwin did with Evolution. Darwin did not invent Evolution; he just simply pointed out that it is there. It is happening!

Discontinuous or radical improvements that lead to large scale transformations of organizations and entire enterprises can be and should be simply aimed at creating a better and sustainable company --- a company that has a **higher purpose** aimed at improving the lives of many people and advancing our societies and civilizations. For example, the competition between **Apple and Samsung** so far has been healthy, benefiting all that seek the best smart phones. The breakup of the **Bell System** was also beneficial as it has allowed infinite amount of innovations by removing the cancerous monopoly.

Moreover, we all know now that no company can progress strictly on continuous or discontinuous improvement because they both lead to undesirable behaviors and consequences. One needs to have the right mixture of both. If one utilizes only continuous improvements, then s/he will find out the hard way that the interest for innovation dissipates and lethargy settles in, which is deadly. And if one only pursues discontinuous improvements, then one eventually will be faced with high levels of anxiety, frustration, stress, fear and even anger.

People and entire companies need time to absorb, internalize and otherwise digest the massive changes and transformations introduced by the new whatever (business model, organizational structure, style of leadership, partnerships, etc.). It's not easy for people to jump from one massive transformation to the next. Thus, it is smart to have the right blend of both continuous and discontinuous transformations --- and this is part of the art of great leaders. They know how to blend both and avoid the negative aspects of either one.

Another interesting aspect of leading organizations has to do with promoting and endorsing both the push and pull approaches of technology. For example, one can disrupt a value chain by "pushing" ahead with new technologies and inventing a new value chain, or one can help reinvent an existing value chain by leveraging a great technology, thus pulling it along to the next plateau of excellence. The same can be said for companies and people. Schumpeter was in favor of leveraging both the push and pull approaches. He saw the value of combining them both.

In a similar fashion, companies can either "push" people to appreciate unarticulated needs and wants (similar to what **Apple** did with the iPhone), or companies can be convinced to pay attention to (be pulled by) societal trends and wishes and respond accordingly (like **MS** usually does with their Windows products). This table captures the above point:

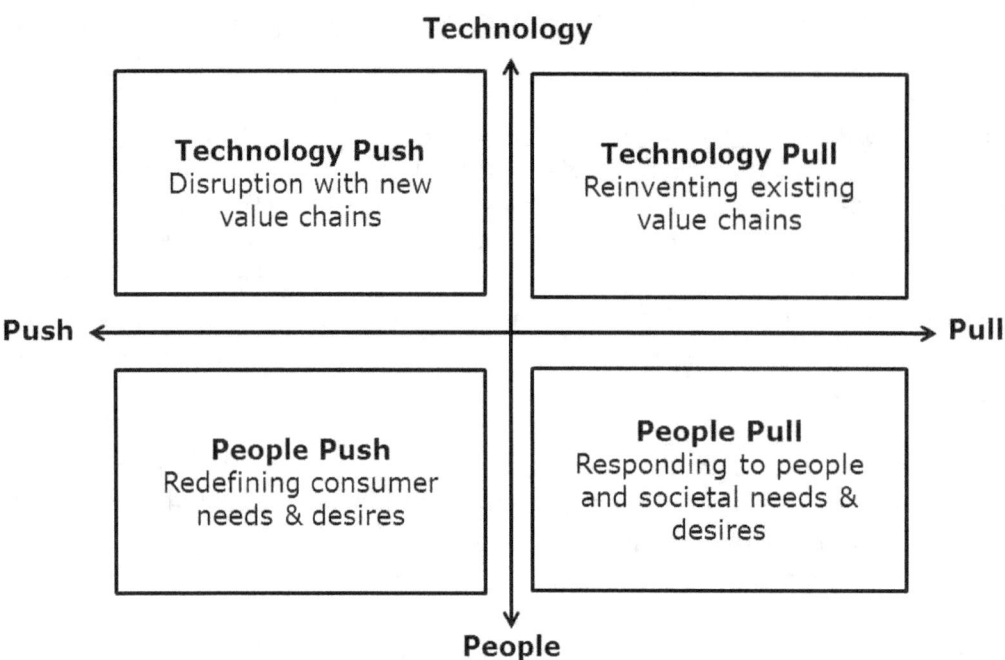

The word "destruction" is too strong of a word and it does scare many people because it has many bad connotations and also is counter to most people's culture and personal values as their mental models are geared towards continuous improvement, making things better and always keep adding and enhancing, not wiping the slate clean and starting all over again. Thus, it is not a surprise that very few people and companies are interested in considering or applying "destruction" to old cultures, paradigms, models … and products. Moreover, the typical Capitalistic System does not endorse the destruction of existing products because the mentality is focused on getting the maximum benefit of what is already there. In other words, "slaying cash cows" is not desirable. Most companies and executives would rather go down with their cash cows rather than abandon them. "Letting go" is indeed one of the biggest problems that everyone is facing, and this is exactly the very reason why startups always emerge replacing the old established companies.

When one analyzes the real reasons why companies like **Wang, DEC, EDS, Kodak, Xerox, Polaroid, Blockbuster, Borders, Yellow Pages, McDonnell Douglas,** and numerous others have failed, the real picture emerges of failing to invent and innovate. They were "married" to their cash cows and would not let go. So, it is very appropriate to analyze Creative Disruption, not from a process point of view, but from a management and culture point of view because they represent the main obstacles to moving ahead with it.

And although Schumpeter understood all of the aforementioned points, he was not correct on some other points pertaining to Creative Disruption. Here are two of them:

- He proclaimed that concentrated markets are more innovative because they can generate profits to fund R&D, but the truth is that the concentrated markets are disappearing as we are now faced with diffused markets, diffused industry borders and even diffused geographical borders.
- He also proclaimed that large firms are more innovative because they have the professional organizations, deep pockets, and well-established processes to scale up innovations and

ventures. That was true at his time, but this too has now become a passé hypothesis as small companies are obtaining funding from a variety of sources (incl. big corporations) that enable them to invent and innovate.

The Main Principles And Tenets Of Creative Disruption

The principle/tenets of Creative Disruption are important to understand and apply as they become the foundation for both the style of management and culture that will aid the process. Here are the main ones:

1. **Be willing to perform "surgery", even if it means "amputation".** It is mental state that very few people can pursue and exercise as most people are scared or turned off by the ugliness of the operation (no different than performing real surgeries). Most people cannot handle the "blood, guts and gore" of surgeries. It is appalling. Companies must very carefully choose the people that put in management positions in order to perform such operations. Once again, this is no different than a hospital situation. One would not put a pediatrician or an ENT doctor in charge of the surgery department.

2. **Having the courage and mental strength** to put up with all the negative aspects of the "surgery". While one is going through the Creative Destruction process, s/he will encounter many hostile people, negative comments, personal attacks (sometimes more than verbal attacks), and insults. One's character will be questioned, along with the person's values, beliefs … and even religion. It's not a pretty picture.

3. **Having the right reason for applying Creative Disruption.** Several executives take credit (and Wall Street is all too eager to endorse them) as great disruptors --- **Jack Welch** comes to mind. Jack performed one of the most serious "surgeries" in the corporate world and was hailed as one of the best executives ever. However, his motives and main intent was not driven by innovation or Creative Disruption. His motives were based strictly on financial gains. He knew how to manipulate the bottom line and he did a fantastic job with that. But when it came to innovation he cared less. He "nuked" many great divisions (including practically all of **RCA** and the famous **Sarnoff Labs**) because they did not fit with his financial goals. That is not what Creative Disruption is all about. So, having the right reason and right goal in mind is imperative in this "game".

4. **Having the right business vision and business philosophy.** The correct visions drive innovation. The bad ones only have fluff for public consumption and marketing hype. Innovations need to support and advance the vision of the company. Having worked for several major corporations, I can testify to the fact that I did not meet one employee that knew her/his company's vision or philosophy. For example, 99% of the employees of an automotive company know that their company's product lines are cars. They have no idea that the company's vision statement declares that they are in "the transportation business" (not automobile business). So, where are the other modes of transportation? Where are the innovations pertaining to other products outside their automobiles? Everyone knows the answers to these questions. The disconnect between the vision statement and what the company really does is a major handicap to innovation. When a company's vision statement is fluff, employees know it and care less about the company's future. Maybe this explains why **GM** struggled to survive the last forty decades. Their version of innovation for all those decades was Sustaining Innovation, not Creative Innovation. The new management team has changed all that.

5. **Paying attention to the brand and what it stands for.** In a similar fashion as the Vision Statement, brand legacy, reputation, recognition and "personality" gives clues to

employees about generating new ideas that will lead to new products and services. This does not imply that one needs to "stick to the knitting" and never stray away from that which made them famous. Dumb consultants advise companies to stick to their knitting and avoid differentiation. Their advice is harmful. On the contrary, differentiation should be encouraged as long as it makes sense and it complements the basic brand. For example, the acquisition Of **RCA** by GE made a lot of sense because they had so many complementary product lines --- too bad GE destroyed all that. On the other hand, the acquisition of **EDS** by GM made no sense whatsoever --- and that is why GM got rid of EDS only after a few years. Thus, one must pay attention to the brand (as well as company's vision) and ignore the bottom line. Improving the bottom line does not drive innovation or fuels employee motivation. Companies that are driven by the bottom line, sooner or later suffer the business version of heart attacks.

6. **Always performing internal and mostly external scans.** It has always been smart to perform scans in order to stay abreast of the latest trends, technological advances and social changes (including tastes and preferences). Smart companies have teams of people that do exactly that. For example, the emerging technologies of IOT or IOE, Big Data, MEMs, Smart Sensors, Smart/Sentient Robots, 3-D Printing and several others create practically infinite possibilities for new inventions. We are at the cusp of a huge technological revolution that will affect our society in very profound ways (as it was explained in a previous chapter). One cannot afford to miss this opportunity of creating the next generation of product and services. However, it is not just technologies that transform our world and societies. There are systemic changes in every sector, in every industry, in every profession and in every system. Here are two recent examples:
   a. Who would have thought that Amazon will be Wal-Mart's biggest competitor?
   b. Who would have thought that Wal-Mart would be a threat to financial institutions?

7. **"Seeing the glass always half-full".** This normally does not fit with the traditional cultures because there is no way that one can teach or even demand that of employees see it that way, as this is a deeply ingrained trait. There are some ethnic groups (like the French) that are naturally not happy with anything in life. They always have to find something wrong with whatever they are facing. Americans slowly and steadily are becoming that way as well. In a strange way this is a good attitude for a company that is seeking continuous improvements and Disruptive or Creative Innovation. As strange as it sounds, pessimists are more likely to change a product (and the world), than optimists because they have the motivation to create or reach for something better --- within limits of course. But one must have the right leaders at the helm to turn all that skepticism, griping and fault-finding towards positive outcomes. If one is not careful all the "pissing and moaning" could turn into a negative energy that can destroy a company (or for that matter, could destroy a whole country).
   - **Important Note:** "Pissing and moaning" most of the time is a manifestation that people in a company (or country) are internally focused and have nothing better to do than analyze everything, debate everything, criticize and nitpick every little thing. The best medicine for changing this attitude is to create a goal that forces people to become externally focused. When people are focused on conquering new "targets", achieving new goals, and getting into uncharted waters, they forget all the internal problems because the external focus is a lot more important. Griping stops when people are busy deciphering, solving, creating, generating, achieving and triumphing. This too is another "gift" that great leaders have. **Lee Iacocca** is a perfect example with the invention of the **K-car** that helped Chrysler avoid chronic glumness ... and

bankruptcy. BTW, declaring wars has always been one of the favorite tricks of evil politicians to avoid internal strife and potential uprisings. In the business world, we don't have wars, but we have competition. The challenge is how to compete in such a way that it is spirited and aggressive enough to keep employees externally focused, and yet it is friendly enough to be civilized and beneficial to society and the world.

8. **Systematizing Innovation.** It can be done by imbedding innovation in the culture and style of leadership, by having the right processes, and by utilizing the newest and greatest tools and techniques.

Conclusion

Creative Destruction or Disruption is not for everyone. It does require special people (like **Lee Iacocca and Steve Jobs**) that know how to blend vision, dreams, passion, competition, style of leadership and culture (both personal and business) the right way. It does take guts, courage, perseverance, outside-the-box thinking and other personality traits (which are outlined in a later chapter) to lead Creative Disruption initiatives and transformations. Most of the workshops on transformations and change management do not address personality traits and styles of leadership because they are afraid of insulting members their audiences (as most of them do not have what it takes to play this "game").

"A company's success hinges upon its ability to adapt, innovate, and overcome. Creative people are nonconformist in nature and thought, they will leapfrog the status-quo in imaginative bounds and offer up groundbreaking ideas." – **Ryan Ringholz** (Designer at Plae)

6 TRIGGERS AND OBSTACLES FOR CREATIVE DISRUPTION AND INNOVATION

Phillip Andrews

Introduction

To better understand Creative Innovation and Disruption one needs to understand what some of the triggers and obstacles behind them are. Without that knowledge it is difficult for one to be successful in introducing significant innovations. This chapter only addresses some of them as one can write a whole book on this topic. The big picture for triggers involves all the elements shown in the schematic below:

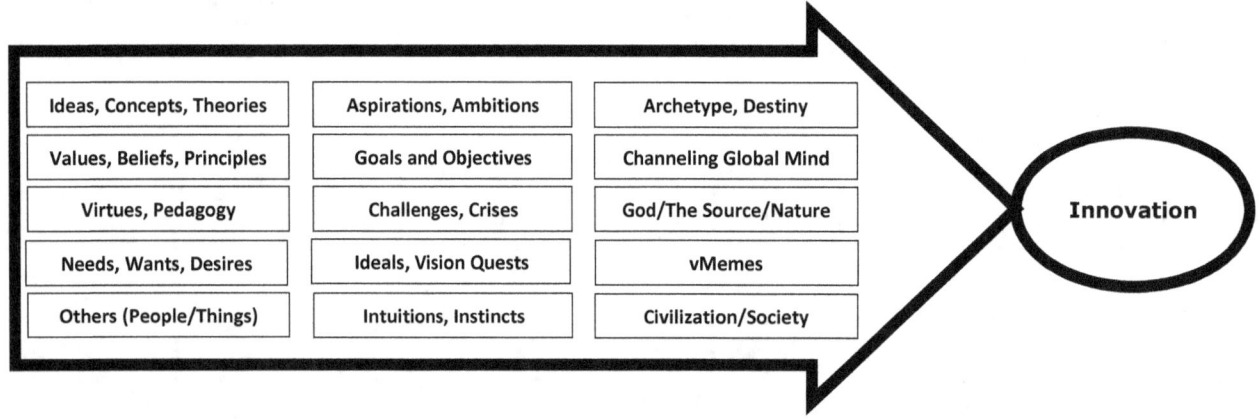

Key Points:

1. Some of those triggers and factors cover an array of secondary triggers and factors, such as feelings. For example, euphoric feelings (like happiness and love) as well as ugly feelings (such as anger and frustration) can trigger inventions and innovations. They are captured in the above schematic as Needs. Feelings are viewed as expressions of Needs.
2. Some triggers and factors are more important than others, but no one can really prioritize them as they all play a different role in people's minds. From a holistic point of view they

all matter equally.

Furthermore, we have the "sparks of innovation" that are outlined in a later chapter. Sparks and triggers can be one and the same thing, or sparks can be viewed as the aids and mechanisms that enable the triggers to take off.

Main Triggers

Here are some **key technologies that aid and enable transformation**s across several sectors and industries:

- **Internet Of Things** coupled with **Big Data, Advanced Sensor Technologies, Cybersecurity, Virtual Reality, Augmented Reality, Artificial Intelligence, Virtual Computing, Virtual Networking, Social Cloud,** and other Technologies and Systems. Eventually we will have the **Internet Of Everything**

  Here is a small sample of the new professions that the web and IoT have already created:

  - **Online Brokers (incl. real estate, travel agencies, financial services)**
  - **Online Retailing**
  - **Online Book Publishing (and Digital Printing)**
  - **Online Education**
  - **Online Legal Services**
  - **Online Medical Services**
  - **Online Security Services**

  Note: These industries and professions only started in the early 21st Century. And this is only the beginning!

- **Advanced / Sentient Robotics** (also coupled with AI and other Systems). Advanced Robots will replace many professions from lawyers to food servers and even certain teachers/professors
- **Advanced Drones** (for farming, policing, firefighting ...)
- **Enhanced Humans** (with powered exoskeletons, artificial body parts, enhanced brains and senses ... resulting into having Hybrid Humans and/or Cyborgs)
- **Data-driven Manufacturing**
- **Microelectromechanical Systems** (MEMs)
- **Biotechnology** (incl. Biosensors)
- **Nanotechnology** (incl. Nano-Materials)
- **Terahertz Imaging**
- **Virtual Reality and Holographic Imaging**
- **3-D Printing** and 3-D Displays
- Next Generation **Wireless Communications and Social Media** (incl. Smart Mobility)
- Next Generation **Desalinization**
- **Super-Vision**
- **Brain-Controlled Computers** ,Robots and other Devices
- **Sensors** (and Sensor Technology) will be omnipresent/ubiquitous, pervasive and omniscient
- **Flexible Intelligent Screens** (beyond Wearables and Implantables)
- **Smart Products and Smart Objects** (from smart streets and signs to smart toilets, tables

and clothes) (We may also get smart Barbies for a change --- and in the future Barbies will smarter than the kids themselves)

- **Driverless Vehicles, Airplanes and Ships**
- **Intelligent Medicine and Intelligent Diagnostics** (such as MRI) that can be applied at home
- **Telemedicine**
- **Precise Genetic Engineering Techniques**
- **Neuromorphic Technology**
- **Tricorder** (yes, like Star Trek, checking vitals)
- **Advanced Cyber-Security** (incl. Biometrics); Homomorphic Encryption
- **Fog and Quantum Computing**
- **Digital Genome** (Genome Editing)
- **Hydrogen Fuel Cell** s(for Batteries and Vehicles)
- Next-Generation **Educational Systems** (online degrees for all levels)
- **Recyclable Thermoset Plastics**
- And many more

The above list is only a partial list of what is already being developed in labs all across the world that will drastically change everything we are dealing with today in all aspects of our lives and business. Smart companies are making the right investments in new technologies because they know that they affect their business models and offerings in the future. Moreover they watch very carefully certain megatrends that will further influence their direction, decisions and character of their companies. Here are some of the **megatrends** that affect innovation:

- **Omni-Convergence and/or Hybridization of:**
  - Industries and Technologies
  - Systems and Applications (such as ERP, CRM, SCM, and thousands or even millions of applications)
  - Strategic Enablers (such as Going Green, Sustainability, Lean and Conscious Capitalism)
  - Governments and Political Systems
  - Cultures and Socioeconomic Systems
  - Everything[19]
- **The Digitization/Digitalization of:**
  - Life (everybody will have a digital footprint --- whether they like it or not)
  - Money and Commerce (incl. Medicine and Health Care)
  - Capitalism (Intelligent Capitalism)
  - Most Industries (Industry 4.0)
  - Everything (imbedding microchips everywhere and connecting them through wireless and virtual networks)[20]

  Note A: Digitization of everything implies that digital technology is embedded and inserted everywhere (replacing analog technology in just about everything). All the products that are or will be coming out are characterized as being smarter, faster,

---

[19] This is one of the **hidden megatrends** that has always been part of life (hidden behind evolution). Things (from cells to robots, to databases, to systems to societies) have the tendency to aggregate, accumulate and synthesize in order to create more advanced, smarter and more multifaceted and intricate entities.

20 Moore's Law continues. By 2025 microchips will only cost a penny allowing their use and application everywhere.

better, cheaper, as well as connected, augmented, analytic, predictive, virtual and ultra.

Note B: Technologies will allow the concept of **Big Bang Disruption** to become a reality. A defining feature of this type of disruption is the ability to allow experimenters to combine cheap component technologies into new products and services and launch them with little or no risk. Most experiments and inventions will fail, but at little cost. The benefit of this approach is that it usually produces worthwhile insights for the next iteration of experiments.

- **The Miniaturization of Everything**
- **Infrastructure Invisibility** --- making the infrastructure invisible and immaterial to the users. There is no good reason why users need to know the operating systems, programming languages, editing features, and other system idiosyncrasies. Making all that transparent to users will finally liberate the users from the slavery of the "experts". People do not have to experts in order to run a machine and realize the benefits of that machine. "Click Here" and "Click There" is the only expertise that people will need in the future.
- **Moore's Law (the Uber-Disruptor)** --- affecting price, performance, size, and computing power in a relentless improvement mode.
- **Shared Economy** --- affecting the way we share all (natural, social, and business) resources. Although the Shared Economy has been in existence for a while with services such outsourcing and community services, there is a new wave emerging with services for Shared Manufacturing (based on 3D Printing), Shared Purchasing, Shared Logistics.

Obstacles and Roadblocks To Creative Disruption
Some of the obstacles (mentioned in earlier and other chapters) are:
1. Learning to let go
2. Bad culture --- bad habits
3. Lack of vision
4. Lack of ambition
5. Stagnant atmosphere / environment
6. Lack of good (high performance) people
7. Lack of a catalyst and a rainmaker
8. Lack of knowledge or pertinent information

Here are some additional obstacles:
1. **Government regulations** designed to protect the status-quo and stack in past paradigms
2. **Politics inside the company**. Major Creative Disruptions can dramatically affect one's career, total compensation and advancement opportunities inside and outside the company where one works. This usually generates envy of the worst kind. Many people do not want the peers to overshadow them and see them advance.
3. **Marketplace is not ready for the new product or service.** There is such a thing as "getting ahead of one's self" or not being appreciated by the public and marketplace. There are numerous examples of inventors (incl. **Joseph Swan, Edwin Armstrong,** and **Dr. Royal Rife**) that died penniless and unrecognized because they were so far ahead of their time. Yes, one can be too smart for her/his own good. Many entrepreneurs "ate dust" for getting way too far ahead of the curve. Seeing the future ahead of others sometimes has its drawbacks. One must be as keen as "selling the future" as "seeing the future".

4. **Financing is not available.** Major transformations and Creative Disruptions require hefty budgets. They cannot be done with heroics alone.
5. **The Right Project Manager(s) is not available.** Major transformations and Creative Disruptions require good Project Managers that not only know how to implement the proposed changes (Project Management and Budget Management), but are also experts in Change Management, Relationship Management, People Management, and Migration Path Management.
6. **Technofix Mentality.** Believing that technology is the answer to everything and that technology can fix everything. Such a mentality creates mental blocks as to what is really needed to fix a problem, not just the symptoms.

Technofix's Major Drawback

The aforementioned discussion about triggers for innovation is saturated with technologies, leaving everyone with the impression that very little else matters in our future except technologies. Believing that technology will solve all of civilization's problems and ills is wrong, as **Michael and Joyce Huesemann** point out in their very astute book called **"Techno-fix"** (2011). In other words, we cannot Techno-fix our way to a sustainable future because **technology cannot fix:**

- Poverty; inequality of income
- Inequality of classes and the demise of the middle class (a.k.a. the gap between the haves and have-nots)
- Bad behavior and criminality
- Decadence, depravity and corruption
- Idiocy intricate
- Man's proclivity to conflicts and self-destruction
- Climate Change (incl. slow rising seas)
- Threatened species
- Threatened languages, cultures and civilizations
- Many other societal ills and human follies

The above societal ills will require other solutions beyond technologies and computerized systems. To believe that humanity will be in the clear once technology resolves our issues with energy, food and water would be foolish and irrational. Moreover, the magnitudes of some problems are such that no technology would be able to fix in a complete, economical and efficient way. For, example, **Solar Technology** has not been proven (so far) to be a satisfactory substitute for fossil fuels, no matter how hard companies and entrepreneurs have tried in the last thirty years. Electrifying entire cities with solar energy is still a pipe dream. But even if it were a viable solution, one has to question the cost of such implementations, including the ongoing maintenance costs.

In addition, previous attempts to increase food production through genetically modified crops and organisms has met with great resistance, and in some cases with fury as people are afraid of anything that is not natural and wholesome. It is not only that **GMO-based foods** lack taste, but also that they lack all the health benefits that one expects to get from grains, fruits and vegetables. It feels as if eating GMO foods only serves the purpose of fooling hunger, rather than having a wholesome, healthy and tasty meal. This defeats the very purpose of eating food, which is expected to be a pleasurable experience coupled with many health benefits. Understanding life and the purpose of our existence is paramount in developing new innovative products, services and solutions.

The false prophets and pseudoscientists that let people believe that science and technology will save humanity's and planet's future do as much harm as the apathetic and deceptive political leaders that try to assure people that everything is great, normal and copacetic. On top of all that we have our culture that fuels **technomania**, which further distorts the real picture and reality itself. It is sending subliminal messages to people that technology is all that matters now.

However, there is no need to sound the alarm yet or push the red button, but it is time for our leaders to quit gazing at their navels and look up to see the yellow (caution) light as the critical time is approaching fast. The good news is that we still have time to plan and properly prepare for the future. This is the time for everyone to prepare for a challenging future. This is the time to prepare businesses and entrepreneurs the right way for handling innovation the right way.

Other Red Flags (Besides Bad Culture and Technomania)

Red Flag 1: The rich. The truth is that the rich always did and will always have a different lifestyle from the rest of the folks, which will make it very difficult for government and business leaders to explain why there is such a huge discrepancy between the behaviors and habits of the rich and the rest of the population. It is extremely difficult for one to ask some people to tighten their belts, while others continue to be wasteful and careless. If the rich do not comply with the same fervor and zest as the rest of the society in achieving a **sustainable society** then the transition to a sustainable world is in peril … and the resentment towards such people will reach its boiling point. Moreover, innovation will create many new rich people and that will add to stress and friction between classes.

Red Flag 2: The resistance to change will be overwhelming. Without a master plan, dynamic leadership and the right budgets to support the transition to a sustainable society the transformation not only will struggle, be delayed and even derailed, but end-up into a major mess, that will result in having many angry people around the planet. Anger can be easily converted into all kinds of bad reactions, such as civil wars, revolutions, crime and total chaos.

> **Note:** The disrupted people have already started fighting back and badmouthing any new "systems" or new ways of doing business. As one CEO once proclaimed, *"If technology is the Hare, then employees are the Tortoise"*

Bad human habits are hard to break. As **Mason Cooley** has vary accurately pointed out: *"Human society sustains itself by transforming nature into garbage"*. This implies that we still have long way to go to learn about sustainability that goes well beyond: reduce, recycle, and reuse (garbage). We also have to learn to replenish, restore and substitute. All previous generations have lived on this planet thinking that abundance will be with us forever. This is the first time that we need to face the fact that abundance is a myth because we finally are coming to grips with the fact that we live on a planet of dwindling resources. The new mental frames, habits and behaviors are not properly explained to the masses, which makes the transformation even harder.

Red Flag 3: Fear to tell and face the truth. Most politicians are afraid to be harbingers of bad news for the fear that they may be labeled as alarmists and false prophets. On top of that, they may be proven wrong, which will mean the end to their careers. They would rather promote the

"Never Ending Scenario" pretending that all is normal. The "steady as she goes" approach is a safer way for them to take. They would rather repair the damage done in a reactive mode than be proactive. Proactive and predictive approaches are not part of the political culture. And all that is very understandable as most people do not comprehend or even want preventive and predictive solutions. They have to see, experience and feel the disaster prior to taking action. Moreover, it is easier to justify the budget and expenditure for the actual repairs.

Red Flag 4: Many Education Systems do not address key topics, such as innovation, breakthrough thinking, outside-the-box-thinking, systems thinking, holistic thinking, entrepreneurism, sustainability (sustainable living), collaboration approaches for co-creating, co-shaping the future, and several other pertinent topics needed for our new society. Moreover, schools need to teach courses regarding: social skills, cognitive skills, decision making skills, life skills, and other necessary skills necessary for the future --- and very little is done today in these areas. So, it is not a surprise that most students lack the needed skills for The Digital Era.

Finding The Sweet Spot For Creative Disruption and Innovation

The best designs are found in the intersection of **Human Desirability and Usability, Business Viability**, and **Technical Feasibility**. It is difficult to find solutions that fit in the intersection, but that's exactly what makes them successful, fruitful, attractive and prosperous.

The problem that most companies have is that they don't use this model as a key criterion prior to introducing their new products or services to the marketplace. As a result they keep introducing subpar designs that are destined are destined to marginal results, such as **Pepsi A.M., Apple Newton, RJ Reynolds Smokeless Cigarettes, Microsoft Bob and Zune**, and thousands of others.

It should be noted that the people involved in those decisions to introduce "abortive" products convinced each other that their ideas were brilliant. And probably they were. However there is a fourth component that is not included in the diagram below; and that is **Market and Societal Readiness.**

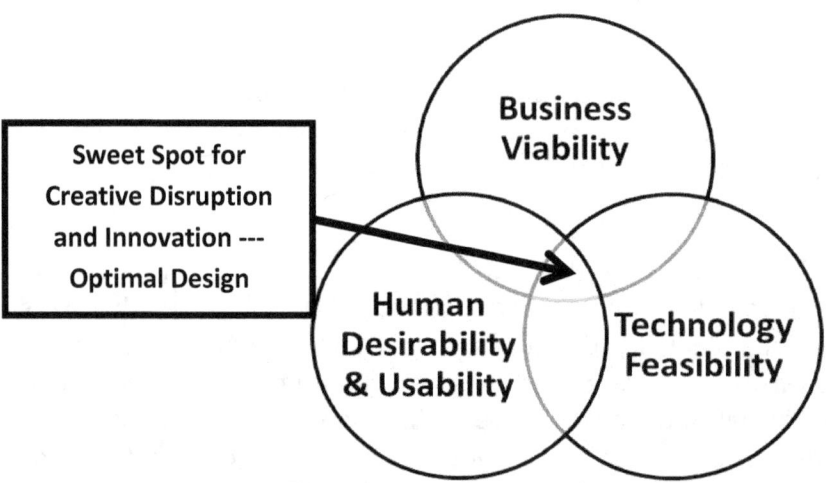

The inputs from all three domains are numerous and varied. That is where the secret sauce resides for each company because the inputs or ingredients are the ones that will differentiate one company from the next. Each company should produce their own version of a preferred solution that integrates what it perceives as the best mixture of viable, feasible, desirable and usable designs.   For example: How many companies consider Psychology, Sociology, Ethnography, Ergonomics, Phenomenology, Human Factors, Artistic Considerations, all Engineering Disciplines, Architectural and other inputs, in formulating a new design?   One can easily see that the options and solutions are infinite and it takes the right individuals to make the right choices.   The right secret sauce is equivalent to Merlin's magical wand.   And no one can offer you the recipe of the secret sauce because it is always dependent on those who are involved.   This is why most Venture Capitalists today pay more attention on the management team leading a startup company rather than their financials.   For existing enterprises, the secret sauce is also dependent on their senior management executives.   They are the ones that can make either a great sauce or a deliver a poison.

Conclusion

The triggers and obstacles for Creative Disruption explain the opportunities and the difficulties that we are facing in our society today.   Dealing with the triggers is a lot easier because people like both the challenges and the wealth that will be generated from them.   Dealing with the obstacles is the difficult part because it requires **major changes in our thinking, lifestyles and behaviors**. People naturally resent being told how many children they are allowed to have, how many and what type of vehicles they should drive, what type of foods they are supposed to eat, etc. Resistance to change will be the biggest challenge of them all, and this is exactly where a coalition of governments, businesses, education systems and civil institutions will be needed to step in and set the guidelines and new norms for a promising future.

"With this mobile era we have very new, very different media. It's a paradigm shift into a non-linear era of great complexity. Creative individuals see realistically, holistically, and aren't tied to a linear mindset. Creative practitioners play a critical role in creating and improving products, services, and policies in a mobile, Digital Age." – **Linda Holliday** (Founder of CITIA)

7 THE ESSENCE OF HOLISITC INNOVATION

Phillip Andrews

Introduction

Previous chapters already painted several aspects of Holistic Innovation, but there are other aspects that are worth mentioning in this chapter. Innovation itself is undergoing dramatic transformation, along with everything else in our civilization. Innovation no longer is the domain of enterprises and entrepreneurs. Even in large corporations, innovation no longer is driven by R&D Departments. That R&D monopoly and ivory tower mentality have ended. We have entered the era of everyone participating in the innovation "game" and everyone being capable of benefiting from it.

The point can be made that The Industrial Revolution introduced numerous great things to society and has catapulted humanity into the Modern Era, and even opened the door to the Post-Modern Era, but on the other hand there were some problems with the original models and thought processes that resulted in hierarchical and control-based structures and styles of leadership that reflected old remnants of the feudal world that dominated societies for millennia.

The 21st Century represents a **New Renaissance** that gets rid of the old models, concepts and precepts and introduces new ones based on new business models, new approaches to doing business, new technologies ... and new major forces, such as Sustainable and Smart Societies ... and Oneness.

Some Of The Problems

The Holistic Approach is a great concept that applies to many things in life, from medicine, to brain, to thinking, to learning. Although the term is greatly overused, it is still smart to use it in conjunction with innovation because it puts a new perspective as to how it needs to be viewed and treated. It is the perfect word to describe what is going on with innovation. First, we need to revisit how most companies operate and behave. Here are the typical patterns:

- Traditionally most companies look for ideas **inside their own four walls**. They expect that their own employees will produce the ideas that will open new markets, reach higher levels of excellence and dazzle their world with their brilliance. After all that's why they pay their salaries. Some employees are tasked with inventing and innovating the company's products and services.

- Most companies still have **high walls between organizations** (creating the infamous "silos"), especially between R&D and Manufacturing. The manufacturing staff was usually treated as the second rate citizens inside the enterprise that knew very little about the product, the marketplace, or the customers. Their main role was to just make the product and ask very few questions. The prevalent mentality about manufacturing was that those pour souls don't need to know anything else outside the manufacturing floor. Manufacturing might as well have been in a deep basement, or another planet. This is one of the reasons why manufacturing became such an easy victim to the outsourcing craze.

Personal Anecdote: When I worked in the Automotive Industry in the 70's I was part of a **Ford's Manufacturing Engineering team** for the Transmission and Chassis Division headquartered in Livonia (a Detroit suburb). Our Design Engineering counterparts were in a Dearborn, and we were not allowed to visit them or even call them (back then there were no emails). We saw several problems with certain designs, but we could not communicate them directly to our design engineers to solve our manufacturing problems. The rules and protocols were so complex and painful that we all took the approach of *"Good luck with that"*. It was not worth it to go through the steps of escalating a manufacturing problem because the typical design engineer's attitude was *"Who are you to tell me?"* As one can imagine, there was no relationship between Manufacturing and Design Engineering at that time, which hurt the company badly, and quality took a major hit (at that time). The joke out in the marketplace was that **FORD** stood for "**F**ix **O**r **R**epair **D**aily". That's was the typical penalty for having silos. It took Ford well over a decade (and a lot of pressure from Japan) to change their business practices and processes.

By the way, the design engineers at Ford and other manufacturing companies where I worked seemed to have this arrogant attitude that they were better engineers than the rest of us, and dealing with us was a total waste of their time. The culture was just as a big of a problem as the silos and foolish policies and procedures.

Today's recommended approach is to have all the engineers work together in the same building; and organized around a product or a specific goal. Thus, the right structure and style of leadership (that empower employees to come up with innovative ideas that are sounder and better solutions) have replaced the old hierarchical structures and controlling styles of leadership.

The focus today has shifted from individual and organizational heroics to teamwork and collective efforts. Moreover, the focus shifted from individual roles and responsibilities to the offering itself, along with focusing on the processes and procedures that directly affect that offering.

- Most companies still follow the **hierarchical model of command and control**, creating more "floors and ceilings" that hamper communications and clip people's urge to invent, innovate or try anything different. Big corporations have very regimented processes, very specific roles and responsibilities (captured in job descriptions) that employees have to sign in as a form of a contract with their employers. After all their performance measures/metrics, bonuses, merit raises, and promotions are based on those job descriptions and subsequent evaluations. On top of that, there are strict channels of communication that either explicitly or implicitly are restricting employees from working outside their little "boxes". In the forty plus years that I have been working either as an employee or as a consultant, I have yet to see one job description (outside the R&D Department) that encourages employees to invent and innovate.

- **Most companies do not listen to their employees.** Most **Suggestion Programs are shams** that do very little to either encourage employees to bring forward their ideas or get rewarded properly for their ideas. Thus, it is not a surprise that most recommendations are about changing lightbulbs and wall colors. Companies do not offer training programs that explain to employees how to think outside-the-box, offer brave new ideas, submit them properly and get rewarded accordingly. In other words, they send the subliminal message: "We care less about your suggestions and ideas". No wonder then that employees that have great ideas quit their companies and start their own.

Personal Anecdote: I used the Suggestion Box at **Ford** one day, and in no time flat my idea was rejected although it would have saved the company money by improving productivity and efficiency in their tool cribs. That was one of the major trigger points for me to quit the company and go work for **Deere**. This is a typical reaction and explanation why some employees are leaving their companies. Deaf ears produce unhappiness.

Personal Anecdote: When I left the corporate world and became consultant, six of my customers asked me to join their organizations as an employee because they liked so much my work, ideas and work ethic. I gladly accepted their offers because I was very wary of being an independent consultant always searching of the next engagement and revenue. I craved stability. I learned the hard way that once you become an employee you lose your status as a subject matter expert, guru and brainiac. After a year or so working for each one of them, I became just another employee that his voice carried no weight or value. It's amazing how companies treat their own employees. It is true that if one wants to be considered an expert s/he has to be an outsider ... at least 50 miles away from the employer's location.

The Solution

The ideas of "tearing down" the four walls of the enterprise (per the **Extended Enterprise, Business Ecosystem,** and **Partner Relationship Management** models), blowing up the silo walls (per the **Horizontal Organization, Business Process Management, Reengineering,** and other strategic enablers), and flattening organizations (based on the **Flat Organization, Networked Enterprise, MBWA, Touchy Feely,** and several other organizational designs and styles of leadership) have been around since the '80s. But unfortunately, most corporations have not been able to implement those concepts properly for several reasons. Here are some of them:

- **Stuck in their old bad habits and patterns.** The old model is easier to manage, thus making the migration to new models very difficult to master. Companies and people in times of stress and crises tend to go back to what they know best and feel comfortable. Since most companies are always in crisis mode and the stress is always high, it is easy to see why the new models and styles are shunned.

- **Unable to perform Change Management the right way.** Change Management requires a focal point (a champion), courseware, specific tools, techniques ... and a budget. Unsurprisingly, most corporations believe that every department/functional manager will automatically perform Change Management in her/his organization because it is part of their responsibility --- but it ain't so. Even worse mistake is to place Change Management in the hands of the HR Department. Change Management requires special personalities and skills that very few people have. **John Sculley** (failed ex-CEO at Apple) proved that point well beyond any doubt.

- **Unwilling to train people the right way or spend the money for it.** The smaller the company is the higher the probability that there is no training of any type, as it is viewed as a cost to be contained, rather than as an investment to advance the company to the next plateau of excellence.

- **Fear that business partners will take advantage of them.** There is still plenty of paranoia of trusting people and organizations outside one's own company. This is a remnant of the Industrial Revolution where competition was nasty, mean and in many cases unethical. And although some of that is still going on, the smart companies realize that those paranoias need to be set aside in order to manage relationships and partnerships the right way. Unfortunately, this is another weakness that most enterprises of all sizes possess, as they are unwilling to make the investment to manage relationships the right way because it requires additional resources and budgets. They believe that contracts and legal documents is all that they need to manage partnerships; and this could not be any further from the truth.

- **Fear that employees will become difficult to manage and control.** Flat and empowered organizations with **self-directed and self-managed** (SDSM) **teams** are viewed by many managers as a threat to their authority and status. It is easier to pursue the command and control model as most managers are scared of being fired for not meeting the company's performance goals, targets/results, and metrics. Not meeting expectations means losing money and promotions. So, it is easier to dictate rather than encourage and motivate employees. The sad reality is that the authoritarian style usually kills innovation. Very few managers are touchy-feely today and they are not viewed in favorable ways by their own superiors that supposedly endorse that style of management. It is also true that most Boards and stockholders prefer psychopathic leaders (like **Ken Lay** (ENRON), **Angelo Mozilo** (Countrywide) and **Jack Welch** (GE)), rather than the warm personalities of kind-hearted people. Recent studies have confirmed this view (Forbes Magazine, Jan 5, 2013).

- **Fear of a backlash by eliminating certain positions and perks.** By delayering the organization some people always get hurt by being demoted or even eliminated from a company's roster, leaving salaries stagnant or even reducing pay, and losing the status of holding those positions (and the power and authority that goes with them). It is impossible to eliminate the hard feelings, resentment and disenfranchisement from the company that undertakes such a task. The hard feelings result into apathy, lack of motivation, doing the minimal work, and even quitting the company. Alienating one's own employees is never smart. After all employees are (or should be) the enterprise's most important asset. Innovation depends on them. So, is there a good way to delayer a company? The answer is "Yes", but very few companies are doing it.

The net result of all those factors and fears is that very few corporations look any different today than they did 20 - 30 years ago. And when it comes to small size enterprises the situation is just as bad or even worse because:

- Most SME owners are even more afraid the delegate authority and power to their own management leaders as they do not have top talent that they can trust
  - Most of them do not even have full management teams
  - Most of them have unqualified people in management roles
  - Nepotism is still prevalent
- Most SME owners do not empower their employees and do not involve them in any ideation or brainstorming activities. The business owner automatically assumes the role of **Chief Innovation Officer** (a one-person department), not realizing that s/he is not as smart as s/he thinks. No wonder then that the attrition and employee turnover rate among SMEs is horrendous.
- Most SMEs have minimal training programs even for their own management teams. **Leadership Development** is cursory, and **Organizational development** is only focused on specific skills and government mandatory training (incl. compliance issues) --- such as the case with Environmental Health & Safety training.

Thus, one can very quickly see that the "landscape" (in the SME world) is not conducive to innovation and breakthrough thinking. It is easy to understand that most SMEs are holding themselves down, but they don't see that. This explains the high failure rate among SMEs, which according to Forbes, Bloomberg and other publications exceeds 80%. This also explains the boom in startup companies because smart people want action, movement, challenges, and opportunities. It is no secret that **startup companies** are afflicted by **Innovation Mania** and that is a good thing.

So, Let's Take a Look At the Startup World

Startups are not encumbered by the dos and don'ts of larger enterprises or the rules of despotic leaders that believe that they have all the answers. They have very little fear of failure, and as a matter of fact they deal with risk as if it were a challenge. There are several other factors (outside being disenchanted working for SMEs) that drive up the volume of new companies and inventions. Here are some of the key factors that affect the volume of inventions that we see today:

1. More people have degrees now than ever before and they want to patent every little thing. They are more familiar with the process and the value of patents.
2. More people realize that the entrepreneurial field and career path is open to all, at any age and any background. Moreover, many educated engineers and scientists have realized that it is more fun and a quicker road to riches to work on one's own ideas rather than to work for larger enterprises (which in a way, they "steal" their employees' ideas and inventions to enrich themselves and their stockholders). This is one of the quiet, but very profound transformations in our society because up to this point in time, the Industrial Revolution had dictated that universities and colleges prepare students to be employees, not entrepreneurs.
3. We are witnessing now is the **mushrooming effect of innovation**, which results from having:
   - **A broader base of innovations** (to work from and with, as a baseline).

Each innovation creates or opens the doors to a minimum of 2-3 other new innovations. Thus, the exponential explosion of innovations is easily explained. This is one of the advantages that major corporations (like **IBM**) have because they are able to build on top of what they already possess.

- o It is the same phenomenon observed in books. Each book becomes the seed for two or more books in the minds of people that read that book --- and we certainly hope that this is the case with this book.

- **More and better tools.** The advent of the computer has dramatically revolutionized everything. Computers rank among the top ten most important inventions in human history (along with inventing the telephone and steam engines).

- **More capital available than ever before.** New mechanisms, (such as crowdsourcing, crowdfunding, microfinance, peer-to-peer lending, and a plethora of ways to obtain government grants).

- **More knowledge and information.** This is the major benefit of the worldwide web that has democratized information and made billions of reports, data, nuggets of wisdom and contact points available to those who dare to "mine" and explore.

- **More Innovation Centers** (incl. Incubators, Accelerators, Makerspaces, etc.). In previous centuries a city was lucky to have one Innovation Center. Now major cities have several of them[21]. Moreover, great universities, high schools, middle schools, and ambitious suburbs (as opposed to the lethargic ones) have their own Innovation Centers because they do understand that **Innovation Centers are**:
  - o Helping the local economy
  - o Helping students hone their skills and find better jobs
  - o Creating jobs, which improve the tax base
  - o Improving the public image of the community, which attracts entrepreneurs and other business leaders, which in return help improve the culture and arts of that community, which in return they improve the quality of life
  - o Encouraging the community to become even better in all aspects of living and working

This explosion of innovations will continue well into the future as the above **triggers** will become even more prevalent and better institutionalized. We are only at the beginning of this phase, which started in the latter part of the 20th Century. However, we must not lose sight of **two other important phenomena in the business world**.

1. The first one is pertaining to the fact some of the best innovations emerge from startup companies like **MS, Apple, Whole Foods, Uber, AirBNB, Facebook, Google** and infinite others. Unfortunately for every big name that everyone recognizes there are thousands of other companies that didn't make it either because the competition wiped them out or they were gabbled up by bigger companies that are always looking to grow through mergers and acquisitions. Smart companies have their eyes open as to who is doing what, and they are always ready to absorb smaller companies that

---

[21] Here in the DFW Metroplex, at last count, we had over 35 Innovation Centers, not counting the ones inside big corporations like AT&T and TI. The L.A. Metroplex has over 150 of them.

have the right innovations. They play the "Corporation Games" (and yes, they are always changing corporation names, as well, as that **Jefferson Starship** declared in their great song **"We Built This City"**). Many entrepreneurs and startup companies are all too willing to sell off their enterprises to the big ones, so that they can make enough money to start a new venture. They call it **Serial Entrepreneurism**, and that is smart as most entrepreneurs are not seasoned professional managers that know how to grow their companies, or even stabilize them.

2. The second one pertains to the trend of major corporations having their own **in-house Innovation Centers**. One of the most famous one is the **AT&T Foundry** (Innovation Center) that is currently spread in four cities (Plano, Atlanta, Palo Alto and Ra'Anana, Israel) so far and the speculation is that there will open others in Europe and Asia. AT&T and its sponsors (Ericsson, Alcatel-Lucent, Amdocs, Cisco, Intel, and Microsoft) collectively have spent over **$100M** to introduce those centers. This is how serious they are about the value and benefits that they receive from their Innovation Centers. These types of Innovation Centers represent a new for form of **Intrapreneurship** because the original concept was a major failure. The basic reason for its failure was that most companies either gave it lip service, or their reward system fell short of expectations in the intrapreneurs' minds. They expected bigger payoffs and rewards, which did not materialize. These new Innovation Centers offer:
   - Bigger rewards to their own employees
   - A (big) stake in the outcome
   - Invitation to outside entrepreneurs to join in and benefit from their participation. In a way, this is another mechanism for entrepreneurs to get funding for their ideas. These types of Innovation Centers are also key to:
   - Expanding a company's Business and Innovation Ecosystems ----making them organic and dynamic
   - Helping the local economies
   - Being part of Innovation Zones and becoming key players inside those zones

This concept is so exciting that Consulting Firms (e.g.: **Deloitte Global In-House Center**) are doing, and so are major newspapers (e.g.: **The San Francisco Chronicle Incubator**) and hospitals (e.g.: **Cleveland Clinic Innovations** and **Baylor Global Innovation Center**) and so are all good universities. It is a given that this trend will be expanded to all sectors, industries and many enterprises of certain size and influence. Moreover, many international companies will follow AT&T's example by installing Innovation Centers in all the innovation hot spots around the globe (e.g.: **BMW** building its Innovation Center in Mountain View called **Future Lab**). It is apparent now that **Innovation slowly and steadily is becoming an industry**[22] **on its own merits** (similar to the Outsourcing Industry and several other "horizontal" industries that serve vertical industries).

Caution: The AT&T Foundry calls its innovation partners "Technology Suppliers". That is not the best term to use, as the word "suppliers" demeans the value of the partners and implied the relationship with them. Psychologically and subliminally it makes a huge difference.

Interesting Note: Several leading Universities, High Schools and even Middle Schools have

---

[22] Composed of Incubators, Accelerators, Coworking Spaces, Entrepreneurial Dens, Genius Dens and dozens of other versions, including the online communities. The problem is that companies do not know how to leverage all that yet. The business world is awaiting for the right formula on how to leverage this new industry and enhance their innovation ecosystems.

started implementing **Makespace labs** that allow students to learn from experimentation and hands-on learning (or project-based learning). This approach will take off and eventually emulated by all schools because, not only is one of the best ways to learn, but also it is the best way to develop then next generation of entrepreneurs that have the right foundation, skills and culture.

Why The Innovation Ecosystem Is A Great Idea

Its value is more than adding potential partners and making deals. This is a strategic shift that makes a profound difference in how companies ideate, innovate, access and utilize ideas, concepts, information and content. Innovation Ecosystems represent the combination of Enterprise Entrepreneuring, Intrapreneuring and Extrapreneuring[23] (External Entrepreneuring) all at once. In a way, the in-house Innovation Centers represent **Total Entrepreneuring**. This is smart and it represents the **Holistic Approach** and thinking of what innovation effort is all about.

This is similar to what we are witnessing in the cooperation of governments, institutions of all types (incl. government agencies), NPOs, NGOs, Think Tanks, Academic Institutions, and businesses. It is evident that as the human race progresses and advances to new (higher) levels of existence we learn to do what nature and the universe have been doing since the beginning of time, which is aggregating simple life forms into more complex and synthetic forms capable of doing more things than ever before. In other words, evolution is forcing us down a certain path that very few people are capable of comprehending yet. This path is unavoidable because there will be a day that we all will have to cooperate and collaborate in order to survive. Wars are not the answer, and neither are ugly competition and nasty antagonism. **Our collective survival and advancement depends on synergy, harmony and banding together.**

> **A Hypothetical Example:** Let's pretend that a shepherd in New Zealand, while herding his sheep, comes with a brilliant idea how to replace rubber tires with new materials (that have nothing to do with sheep or wool). The shepherd's dilemma is how to get his idea commercialized. The traditional way is to create a patent to protect his invention and then either sell his patent to a corporation, or become an entrepreneur that will lead to having his own startup company. However, the shepherd does not want to become an entrepreneur or start a new company. And he does not have the money for lawyers and patents. What are his options then? One approach is to contact directly the automotive companies around the world and ask them if they are open to discuss his idea with him. Let's also pretend that **Ford** in Detroit has accepted his idea and officially declared him to be one of their people in their Innovation Network or Ecosystem. This implies that they will take it upon themselves to patent the invention and compensate the shepherd the right way. Next time the shepherd has any additional ideas (like cleaning windshields without the use of wipers) the shepherd does not have to go through legal departments and contract signing. All he has to do is submit his idea to the **Online Suggestion Box** and have money going directly to his bank account.

Thus, the **Holistic Approach** delivers these **benefits**:

- It integrates the Business and Innovation Ecosystems into one
- Allows ideas to flow into the enterprise from anyone inside and outside the company
- It eliminates walls, silos, ceilings, floors and other barriers that typically thwart and

---

[23] Similar to having Extranets.

frustrate innovation
- It encourages collaboration and synergy which are great virtues of the global village
- It spreads the wealth in equitable and just way

The Role Of The CEO In Holistic Innovation

Another aspect that is changing by the Holistic Approach is the role of the Chief Executive. The CEO must willingly and happily view her/himself as the **Chief Innovation Officer** because someone needs to be in charge of the innovation effort, which goes well beyond introducing new products and services in the marketplace. The innovation effort is actually a **socioecological system** (on top of being a business system) that involves the alignment of: Business Culture, Corporate Social Responsibility, Environment (with focus on the Sustainability principles), Corporate Strategy, Organizational Structure, Leadership Style (Governance), Measures, Motivation, Relationship Management, and Strategic Alliances. The old style of management, where CEOs like **Jack Welch** (GE) and **Roger Smith** (GM) only cared about the financial strength of the company (along with acquisitions and divestures) went away. The new CEOs better be on top of the game and leading the innovation efforts ala **Lee Iacocca** and **Steve Jobs**.

Lesson Learned: If one wants the CEO to also be the **Chief Innovation Officer** then one need to select a chief that knows the business, customers and the product at an intimate level.

Personal Anecdote: I had the privilege to work in organizations that were led by **Henry Ford II** (Ford), **Lee Iacocca** (Ford), **John Opel** (IBM), **John Akers** (IBM), **Jack Welch** (GE), **Ross Perot** (EDS), **Les Alberthal** (EDS), and **Mike DeGroote** (CBIZ). Observing their leadership styles and impact on the business world and society in general, it was clear to me that the best leaders were the ones that focused on innovation and growing the company, while the despised ones ignored innovation and strategic planning as if they did not matter.

Lessons Learned: Innovation is the best fuel for a strong culture and an energized organization. Innovation gives the organization the pride of *"We are special!"* and the necessary optimism that the future is bright. Optimism is a key ingredient into fueling continuous and exciting innovation. When **John Akers** pulled the plug on IBM's robots, sensor technology, vision systems and deemphasized PCs (among several other faux pas) one could feel the air coming out of IBM's tires. And although GE did very well financially in the marketplace, internally **Jack Welch** was never admired by most of his employees and the culture was one of the worst of all the companies that I've worked for as an employee, or have experienced as a consultant by visiting over 200 companies of all sizes. Fear and intimidation were his primary tools of getting the results that he wanted. As a result innovation at GE suffered under his regime. Unlike **Roger Smith** that was an empty suit, Jack Welch was involved with R&D, but his approach was asking questions of progress, instead of prompting the different Business Groups (Divisions) for fresh new ideas. As one of our GE VPs mentioned to me, *"Jack behaves like a thermometer, while the company needs a thermostat!"*

Good chiefs do not go to the R&D Department and ask the executive there, *"So, what new do you have for me now?"* or *"What is your department working on now?"* Good chiefs work shoulder to shoulder with the R&D departments to create and mold the future.

Having the CEO behave as the Chief Innovation Officer reinforces the Holistic Approach and sends subliminal messages to all employees that **innovation is anyone's and everyone's job**. Our future depends on this approach.

Smart CEOs also understand another important aspect about innovation. It is the fact pertaining to the Earth and our **Global Biosphere** (a.k.a. **Ecosphere**). In past centuries people recognized the importance of the Biosphere, but since they created the **Technosphere** people started forgetting and ignoring the Biosphere, as if it does not matter anymore (Oh, the arrogance of man!). But it does matter! And one can tap into it to gain additional insights for innovation.

Some **pharmaceutical companies** are already doing that. They are visiting indigenous people around the world (representing the biosphere), interviewing them, and literally stealing their ideas regarding healing remedies based on old wisdom and secret recipes, and then introducing drugs (incl. homeopathic meds) as their own inventions. It is a pity to see the unethical practices of such companies, but on the other hand they get credit for being smart enough to recognize that there is a lot of value hidden in nature and in old knowledge.

But the biosphere is not a source for the pharma industry alone. It holds a lot more ideas outside healing and soothing. In reality, everything we try to introduce in aviation, computer systems, AI, microbiology, nanotechnology and so many other fields, are imitations of what nature and the biosphere have already been doing for ages. Nature is indeed a great source for innovative ideas. It took eons for nature to create its own "devices" and mechanisms that work well in our world.

Smart CEOs know how to **get maximum value from all three spheres** and more importantly they know how to balance, synergize and harmonize all of them.

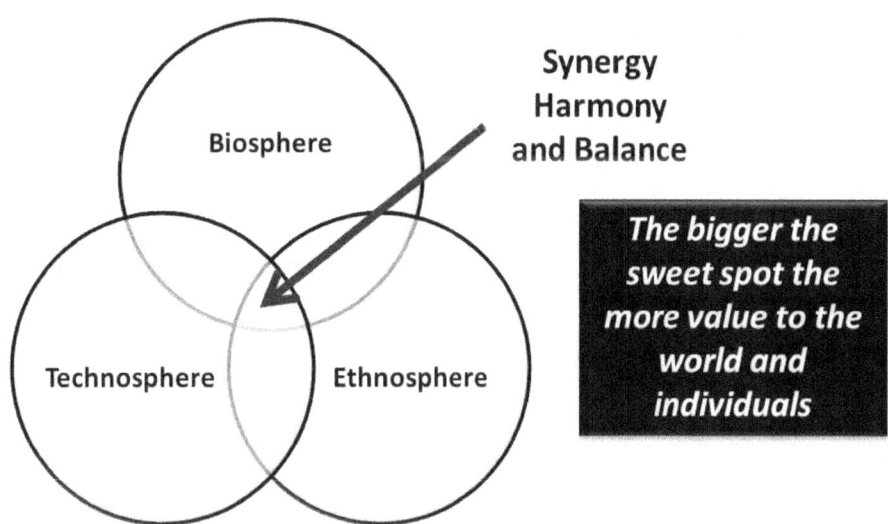

This is similar to what **Sustainability** preaches with its **3P's: People** (= Ethnosphere), **Planet** (= Biosphere / Environment / Ecosystem), and **Profits** (= Business --- mostly driven by new technologies and sciences ➔ Technosphere). Executives only recently started realizing that **the Holistic Approach also has to do with paying equal attention to all three spheres.** There is tremendous value not only addressing all three spheres, but also looking at the big picture that together address humanity, the planet and all its ecosystems. The solutions for **a better, brighter and sustainable future for humanity reside in the big picture**.

Here is one example how the three work perfectly together:

Biosphere ➔ Technosphere ➔ Ethnosphere

Solar Energy ➔ Alternative Energy Source ➔ New Solutions; New Products for People; Less Pollution; Smaller (or Zero) Carbon Footprint

Reminder: The overlap of spheres naturally produces collisions and frictions. **Organic collisions** produce ideas. So, don't be afraid of conflicting and diametrically opposed ideas. Organic collisions are part of having an **organic (= dynamic, lively, vibrant and energetic) ecosystem**.

The Main Infrastructure For Holistic Innovation

The Innovation Ecosystem, like all ecosystems, needs a robust and healthy infrastructure. Without infrastructure the ecosystems fall apart. **The internet is part of it because it democratizes not only information, but also innovation as well**. Thus, the Internet of Things (IoT) is part it. But that is not enough. The additional pieces of the infrastructure include **Big Data** with all the advanced analytical tools that go with it, and **The Cloud** for sharing information, knowledge and progress. But all that still may not be enough to have a vibrant infrastructure. What one needs to add is a robust and dynamic **Knowledge Management System** (KMS) that empowers and allows the participants to find the right (up to date) research info, knowledge, forms, tools, techniques and case studies that shorten the time, effort and cost of innovation. The right infrastructure is imperative to having all the partners in the ecosystem move in a synchronized mode and in the same direction.

Unfortunately, mastering the infrastructure the right way is still in its infancy level and will be a few more years to set it up the right way, where all the participants on it benefit the right way. Of course consulting and technology firms will pretend that the infrastructure is ready today, but no one to our knowledge has designed a robust and successful innovation ecosystem infrastructure yet. However, progress is being made on a daily basis.

Conclusion

Holistic Innovation represents to convergence of many ideas and practices that allow innovations to emerge from anywhere within and outside the enterprise. The bigger an enterprise's boundaries are, the higher the probability that more and better ideas will emerge that will benefit all of those involved. This is one of the main reasons why enterprises do not simply talk about their extended enterprise any more, but focus on the business ecosystem that actually contains several sub-ecosystems. The larger their ecosystems the more energetic and powerful the enterprise becomes.

Corporations like **Google, Apple** and **Microsoft** have some of the best and most robust ecosystems on this planet and the results speak for themselves. Companies like **Kodak** and **Xerox** have the most anemic and unimpressive ecosystems and their results speak volumes as well.

Business ecosystems need strong infrastructures and IoT will serve that purpose as it is fixing to become the **Internet Of Everything** (IoE) (by integrating or incorporating Big Data, M2M Learning, The Cloud, KMS, and other technologies into one cohesive whole). The future looks very exciting for those that understand what really matters.

"Fools act on imagination without knowledge. Pedants act on knowledge without imagination"
– **Alfred North Whitehead**.

8 THE INNOVATION ECOSYSTEM

Phillip Andrews

Introduction

Like everything else in life, the definition of the enterprise has evolved. We went from isolated entities (the 4 walls of the enterprise), to the extended enterprise, to the networked enterprise to the business ecosystem. One can see the same evolution in everything. For example, we migrated from standalone robots, to robotic cells, to robotic multiple and interconnected cells, to robotic lines, and then finally to all-robotic factories. One can see the same thing with data bases, and computerized systems, and sensors, and networks. The tendency is to connect things and to leverage the joined capabilities of what is out there. Isolated entities provide very little value … and future.

The integration of entities, not only provides the combined power of all the constituents, but also adds unique new capabilities that no one could even comprehend before. Thus, it is not a surprise that the **World Wide Web** is more than the aggregation of networks and websites. Now it is becoming the **Internet of Things (IoT)** that is exponentially more powerful than what it was originally perceived in the form of **ARPANET** (The Advanced Research Projects Agency Network), which was an early packet switching network, and the first network to implement the TCP/IP protocol suite. Both technologies became the technical foundation of the Internet.

As everyone knows the IoT slowly and steadily is becoming the **Internet of Everything (IoE),** which will revolutionize the world as we know it. IoE brings together people, processes, data/information/wisdom, systems, and things (devices, mechanisms, sensors, vehicles, buildings, etc.) to make networked connections more relevant and valuable than ever before by turning information into actions that create new capabilities, richer experiences, and unprecedented economic opportunity for businesses, individuals, and countries. Eventually, very little will exist outside the IoE (such as, the extreme loners, the paranoid schizophrenics, and criminals that want to exist outside the grid).

The significance, value, impact and power that the IoE provides to society and civilization is not fully understood or appreciated by any government yet, including the US government (as it is wonderfully explained in **The Seventh Sense** book, by Joshua **Cooper Ramo**). IoE represents a revolution, but very few people can comprehend yet its repercussions and implications. Our world is changing dramatically and it will alter both personal and business lives. Here are some quotes from the book (from an author that sees and understands the Big Picture:

- *"This book is the story of a new instinct, what I have called the Seventh Sense. ...the Seventh Sense is meant for our new age of constant connection."*
- *"**The Age of Network Power** — in which the Seventh Sense reveals a fundamental insight: Connection changes the nature of an object."*
- *"The Seventh Sense is defined first by this intuitive feeling for just how power is being re-geared."*
- *"The Seventh Sense demands grasping the nature of a connected age and seeing how it might be used to further, not erode, the things we care most about."*
- *"An entrepreneur with the Seventh Sense looks at a spare bedroom and sees the possibility of a network to unseat hotels. A financier looks at a currency and sees a way to make it algorithmically alive. A new and young discipline called "network science" will give us a framework for thinking about this because it shows how systems as different as the human brain and Facebook in fact follow similar patterns."*
- *"**Grand strategy** is a basic stance toward the world. If it works, it liberates the creativity and energy of a nation. It sets a clear direction. It protects against the steep price of surprise. Grand strategy holds, in a single concept, the nature of an age and our plans to use that nature for the aims—security, prosperity—that decide a nation's future. Like it or not, we all live under the umbrella raised by grand strategic choices."*

The Business Implications of IoE

IoE will connect enterprises of all sizes in ways that were not possible before. It will actually reduce costs as enterprises will be able to share information in real time through shared systems. Enterprises will have shared (and/or interconnected) ERP and SCM systems that will allow them to perfectly synchronize operations, allowing the entire supply chain of a major corporation (like Boeing) to behave as one "machine" that has no gaps, no hiccups and no breaks.

Big corporations will behave as the driving force (or big gear) in every supply chain. Moreover, enterprises of all sizes will be able to be part of multiple supply chains and value chains, sharing resources and information at will --- and benefiting everyone. At that point one will no longer be looking at supply chains and value chains, but rather looking at complex and intermingling business ecosystems that are global and ever-growing.

It is very possible that eventually, all business are interconnected, thus making the concept of **six degrees of separation** applicable to the business world. Everyone and everything becomes a node in a global network. This scares some people and enterprises, but the truth is that it is inescapable. So, the smart people and companies are already figuring out as to how to leverage such an immense business and technical infrastructure in order to gain a competitive advantage.

Business ecosystems in a way they will integrate both business and technical infrastructures into one. At some point in the future, technology will be an integral part of the business infrastructure and one will not have to worry about planning, designing, implementing and aligning a technical infrastructure to support the business infrastructure. At that point, processes and systems will be one and the same thing.

Furthermore, the IoE will integrate with Big Data and Sensor Technologies and make them an integral part of the infrastructure. A good part of the data will exist in The Cloud and be shared with all of those people and companies that are authorized to access it. Today, all of that is creepy and dangerous, but new technologies will take away both the fears and the risks. The networks will be intelligent enough to defend themselves. The current networks were not designed with security in mind. Security is an added layer, which has limitations due to the add-on features. The next generation networks will be designed with security in mind that will make it extremely difficult for hackers to penetrate.

As one can see the **IoE opens up the door to an infinite amount of innovations**. IoE will enable several emerging industries to emerge, such as Driverless Ground Transportation, Pilotless Aviation, Augmented Reality, Virtual Computing, Virtual Networking, Next Generation Drones, Next Generation Telecommuting, Telemedicine, Telemanufacturing, Telefarming, Telemining, Telediagnostics, Telerepair … Teleanything! In other words, **the sky is the limit for innovations.** This is truly the new era of life and civilization transforming innovations that will make the Industrial Revolution look like only baby steps in our evolution. Here are 4 takeaways from **The Seventh Sense** book re: Connectivity/Connections:

1. They are the power sources of tomorrow.
2. They will make everything more dangerous.
3. They will make everything better. They will accelerate, and enhance every kind of knowledge. They will bring us closer to Oneness --- one **Global Village**

The Biggest Problem Of All

The big question is what society will do with all the people that will be affected by all the emerging and impending innovations because the new technologies will replace huge numbers of people in most professions and industries, including the medical, legal, manufacturing, mining, farming, finance, and other professional services.

Very soon humanity will face a problem that has never faced before. **Society will be split into two camps.** In one camp we will have the people that are educated, skillful and capable to innovate and utilize the latest technologies, and in the other camp we will have the ones that are uneducated, inept and unable to contribute to innovation … or even being able to utilize the latest technologies and stay in lockstep mode with the rapid progress of civilization. Very few people realize today that our **speed of progress is accelerating at an exponential rate**. This speed of progress will leave many people behind just because they will not have the education and even the willingness to keep up.

Personal Anecdote: I have several relatives and friends that are technophobes. They feel that technology is taking over their world, losing their privacies and peace of mind, and a truckload of other theories, excuses and paranoias. And although some of their excuses and fears are justified, they do not realize that they are becoming the latest version of **Luddites** (a.k.a. Neo-Luddites). Civilization is moving forward without them, and pretty soon they will be viewed as dinosaurs. But it is not just some old people that feel that way. We see several young people behaving as technophobes. People like that will be left behind and suffer the severe consequences of their bad decision.

Thus, **education will become the number one problem in our societies** --- that will be even bigger than terrorism, wars, famines or anything else because it will accentuate the gap between the haves and have-nots. When that gap gets to be huge, people always try to change their fortunes through rebellions and revolutions (similar to the Bolshevik Revolution). And although we had those before, we did not have one based on the gap in education and abilities. So, the world is headed into uncharted waters, and unlike other localized revolutions, this next one may affect the whole planet.

Business Ecosystem Components

The business ecosystem at its core is the same as the value chain. It includes:

- Tier 1 (Symbiotic) Partners and their Partners
- Tier2 (Strategic) Partners and their Partners
- Tier 3 (Tactical) Partners and their Partners
- Suppliers and other 3rd Parties
- Own Employees
- Unions
- Vendors
- Transportation/Logistics Companies
- Distributors/Distribution Channels
- Wholesalers
- Retailers
- Customers
- Clients
- Customers' Customers
- Clients' Clients

However, the business ecosystem also includes:

- Financial Institutions
- Investors and Stockholders
- Board Of Directors
- Board Of Advisors
- Government Agencies and Regulatory Bodies
- Other Government Branches/Departments
- Standards Bodies
- Think Tanks and Research Institutes
- Academia
- Public Bodies and Social Institutions
- NGOs and NPOs
- Trade Associations
- Direct Competitors Willing To Cooperate
- Hostile Competitors; Indirect Competitors
- Other Complementors
- Other Stakeholders
- Other Influencers
- Startup Companies
- Public Opinion and "Voices"

Suggestion: Start seeing and treating nature's ecosystems and the planet as stakeholders. They have a voice too! You are that voice! So, speak up!

The business ecosystem is heavily influenced by forces such as economic, social, technical and environmental (including nature and natural disasters). Each one of these constituents has a voice. Listening, making sense of the voices, prioritizing them correctly and then responding accordingly is a monumental task. This is one of the reasons why SMEs keep failing at alarming rates. They do not have the people, means, or budgets to grab and manage all those voices.

Business Ecosystems need to have these following ingredients in order to thrive and produce positive results:

- A solid **"Master Plan"** (part of a Strategic Plan) for moving forward and knowing what to do with all the inputs and ideas that emerge from it.
- A great (and sustainable) **Business Model** that converts the collected ideas and feedback into business improvements, improved products and services, and even new products and services.
- An appropriate **Budget** to support all that. Business ecosystems are not entities that one must know be aware of. They are "partners" in making the enterprise work as a truly viable and sustainable entity. Partners require relationships, and relationships require money in order to thrive and prosper. Relationships cannot advance and be leveraged if they remain at the "Nice Knowing You" level.
- An **"Architect"** (sort of a Program Manager) that can orchestrate all of the relationships and the emergent activities. Big corporations typically have a **Chief Alliance Officer** in that role. SMEs cannot afford to add more overhead on their lean organizations and this is one of the reasons why their partnerships, relationships and approaches in leveraging the business ecosystem the right way do not pan out. It is not unusual that CEOs of SMEs assume that role without fully understanding what that role is or how to turn it into a meaningful "tool" for the company.
- A **Team** to support the Architect or CAO --- because relationship management, event management, workshop management and all the rest require people for executing the plan.
- The right **programs and initiatives** to involve the right people at the right time that will make the proposed improvements, changes, inventions and innovations

Turning The Business Ecosystem Into An Innovation Ecosystem

The above bullets offer several hints as to how to convert the Business Ecosystem into an Innovation Ecosystem. It all start with the willingness to "listen" (really listen) what all those people and nodes on the ecosystem are saying and incorporate them in a good and positive way into one's own business system. Thus, the Business and Innovation Ecosystem become one and the same, only if one has the ability to listen to the voices that are emerging from the ecosystem. Each node in the ecosystem has a voice. Can the ecosystem capture it? Can the ecosystem translate it the right way? Can the ecosystem leverage it?

If the answers to the above questions are "Yes", then the ecosystem can be one of the most strategic assets of an enterprise. The problem today that most companies have (even the biggest and most successful ones) is that they cannot collect all the voices because there are no such tools). However, we know of companies and entrepreneurs that are working on such mechanisms that will capture the "voices" on the WWW and translate them for the benefit of those that want to "listen". These new "mechanisms" represent the next generation of social media. As long as the node is on the WWW then the voice will be heard (after it clears the proper filters).

However, there is a major problem with this new generation of social media. There are some nodes that are not tied to the WWW. Mother Nature and its ecosystems are one of those nodes that have no means to "sign in". In those cases we have to depend for people and organizations to be the advocates and voices for them. The good news is that such people and organizations already exist today, but many of them still do not know on how to participate in the business ecosystems the right way. Most of them are still "voices in the desert".

Moreover, the voices on the WWW or IoE must be protected from the eyes and ears of others because if one puts a great idea on it then anyone and everyone can access it and jump on it, thus taking away the sender's competitive edge. There has to be a way to "privatize" voices and also reward them according to some formula that makes people excited and eager to participate and contribute. In the decades ahead such systems will be developed that will enable innovation ecosystems act and behave the right way. Society is not there yet.

However, the biggest problem we are having today is not technological. It is cultural. Inventing the right technologies to make the innovation ecosystem work is the easy part. The difficulty is our culture and mental models that prevent us from making progress in this area. The top three factors that impair and prejudice our culture are a) trust, b) commitment, and c) shared rewards. Yes, it is no different than marriage. If those three things are not present, relationships fail and the partnership is nothing more than a worthless piece of paper.

It should be noted that word culture refers to a) Sociopolitical Culture (i.e.: Democracy), b) Socioeconomic Culture (i.e.: Capitalism), c) Business Culture, and d) Personal Culture. All of these cultures need to be transformed and aligned in order for make progress the right way. One cannot afford to change one culture and leave the rest of them intact.

What Matters In An Innovation Ecosystem

The Innovation Ecosystem for startup companies is slightly different from the ecosystem of mature companies because much of their emphasis is on survival instead of expanding their influence and strengthening their position. This is no different than what we see in nature. The needs of an infant or toddler are different from an adult. However, after careful analysis, it is apparent that although the emphasis may be different between startup and mature companies, they all need the **same ingredients in order to thrive**.

The ingredients can also be viewed as stages in the process of turning an idea into a reality. The main ingredients, interestingly enough, all start with the letter "I". **The Nine I's are**:

1. **Initiation** --- making the decision to get started and moving ahead in solving a problem, tackling a challenge, creating something better …. It takes guts, backbone and strong passion to move ahead. If one does not have the mental and psychological strength to move ahead, then s/he is doomed from the start.

o Other words that describe this stage: Framing, Facilitating, Defining, Hunting, Searching, Researching.

2. **Information/Insights/Imagination/Ideation** --- gathering pertinent information, knowledge, and wisdom in order to improve one's insights and imagination. This is where all versions of brainstorming can play an important role. This is the stage where ideas, concepts and designs start to being formed and take shape. This is where the decision is made to whether or not it is worth to move forward with idea or dream. Where most individuals and companies struggle is how to translate the collected data and information into meaningful insights, or how to interpret dreams and imagination into reality. The typical process that happens inside people's brain is:

Data ➜ Context + Analysis ➜ **Information** ➜ Meaning + Synthesis ➜ **Knowledge** ➜ Insights + Profound Understandings ➜ **Wisdom / Deep Knowing**

When wisdom is coupled with imagination, then creativity flourishes. Creativity in reality is one's imagination at work.

o For large companies this stage is part of the Research stage.

Important Notes:

- This is by far the most difficult and challenging stage.
- It is not only about brainstorming. It is also about storming the brain.
- Insights can be derived from multiple sources. Outside knowledge, imagination, illumination and enlightenment can create super valuable insights. Listening to one's inner voices, paying attention to one's bliss and reaching higher levels of consciousness, can definitely trigger new ideas for improving life and even changing the world.
- Imagination is the ultimate competitive edge --- and it exists in other people heads, besides the R&D Department.
- True imagination has no boundaries and no limits. Limitations only live in people's minds.

3. **Innovation/Invention** --- turning the ideas and imagination into something concrete that the individual or company can take forward and make it real. The initial drawings and designs are produced that give "shape" to the idea or dream. This is also where the synthesis of ideas takes place and critical thinking evaluates as to what else is missing to make the offering even better.
   o For mature companies the Invention stage is part of the Research and Experimentation stage where different ideas, designs and concepts are explored and analyzed.
   o Other words that describe this stage: Exploring, Investigating, Debating, Testing, Validating.

4. **Incubation/Immersion** --- designing in detail what the new offering is going to look like. This is the stage where the "bugs" and showstoppers are identifies and resolved. This also the stage that the preliminary management team is formed and roles are identified. The initial foundations of forming a company and behaving as a company are set. This is also the stage that the critical choices of what technologies and equipment are needed to employ, what additional skills are required for execution, etc. are made.

- For mature companies the Incubation stage is the Development stage where the original research and experimentation is turned over into real products that can eventually be turned over to manufacturing for mass production.
- Other words that describe this stage: Committing, Proposing, Influencing, Deciding, Provisioning.

5. **Investment** --- finding the funds to proceed. When the individual is happy with the results achieved in the incubation stage, then it is time to look for serious investment to move forward. Without proper funding the greatest inventions will die in the lab. This is exactly what happened to **Philo Farnsworth** (inventor of first TV), and **Antonio Meucci** (inventor of first phone). Seeking and applying investment occurs throughout the life of the enterprise. Like all the other Nine I's, investment is an ongoing process that applies in all stages.

   - For mature companies the funding is available through pre-approved budgets. Occasionally, even big companies have to borrow money to fund new ideas and ventures.

6. **Implementation** --- being able to create the finished product and to prove the concept with tangible results (including customer acceptance, revenue streams, operational readiness, etc. This is the main role of Accelerators helping startup companies and the role of Product and Business Development organizations in corporations. This is where the company and its offering are more or less validated as viable entities ready to join the business world. In this stage the company must perform Proof Of Concept, Pilot the initial production, and demonstrate the ability to scale up. If the company (incl. strategy, structure and infrastructure) and offering do not pass the muster (or mustard) at this stage, then "the game" is over.

   - For mature companies the Implementation stage is the Pilot Program stage where preproduction and final debugging occurs.
   - Other words that describe this phase: Realizing, Delivering, Protecting.

7. **International Collaboration** --- seeking the assistance and synergy of others. This can be viewed as the trigger for creating the business and innovation ecosystems. The days of "going it alone" are over. Smart people and companies know that it is smarter to move forward with the help of others. It may originally be the help of outsourcing companies (for HR, Payroll, and Benefits Administration), and then later on adding the Strategic and Tactical Partners that strengthen one's value chain. This too is a never-ending process because Creative Disruption is always looking for ways to alter or invent new value chains.

   - Other words that describe this phase: Teaming, Coordinating, Synergizing and Synching.

8. **Improvement** --- seeking perfection and excellence in a continuous mode. Continuous Improvement is native and innate in all good brains. One does not need to make a special point about it, make it part of the company's culture, or even offer special seminars and workshops on this topic. It is a given: good people will always seek to improve their creation. They are never happy with what they've created.

   - For mature companies continuous improvement programs need to be formalized and institutionalized as large organizations suffer from certain forms of amnesia as to what made them great.
   - Other words that describe this phase: Optimizing, Assessing, Amplifying, Learning, Advancing.

9. **Intrapreneurism** --- continuously innovating and inventing. Unlike improvement, this

is not native or innate (at least in most people) need. Most people need to be motivated, prompted and cajoled to come up with more innovations and inventions. Inventing and innovating is not for everyone, and not everyone is capable of doing it. It takes certain traits and personalities that excel in this arena. Here are some of the **traits of creative people**:

- Great imagination
- Great curiosity
- Seeing the opportunities; seeing problems as opportunities
- Accepting and craving for challenges
- Optimism
- Ability to suspend judgment
- Being discontent in a constructive way
- Perseverance; courage; willingness to try and fail
- Ability to think outside-the-box; ability to see things from a different angle
- Willingness to turn ideas into business ventures
  o Other words that describe this stage: Institutionalizing innovation & progressing

Collectively the 9-I's create better people, stronger enterprises, and sturdier long-lasting ecosystems. It is imperative that the architects and managers of ecosystems pay attention to the 9-I's as it is them that will make or break an ecosystem, not only for startup companies, but for also for major well-established corporations. The 9-I's can be viewed also as stages or phases startup companies have to go through in order to reach maturity and permanence.

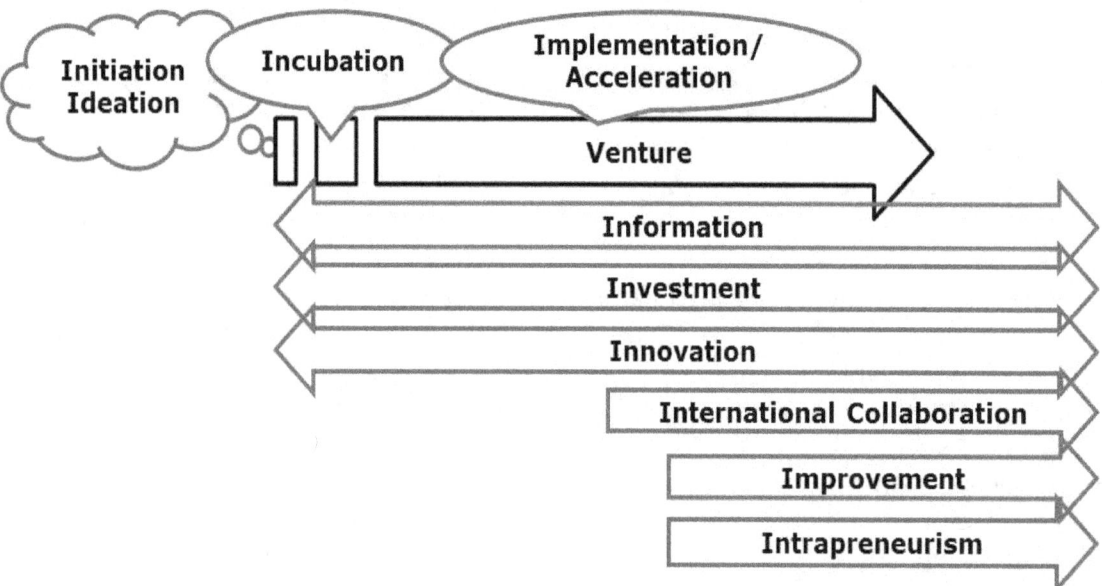

The Sub-Ecosystems

The interesting thing is that most large enterprises realize that they are not dealing with one huge business ecosystem, but rather several sub-ecosystems, such as:

- Cultural and Socioeconomic Ecosystems
- Technological/Technical Ecosystems

- Customer/Client Ecosystems
- Governmental Ecosystems
- Intellectual/Knowledge Ecosystems
- Supplier and Vendor Ecosystems
- Informal Ecosystems (consisting of Social Media, Websites, Blogs ...)
- Philanthropic and other Ecosystems

... And then there are sub-ecosystems within the sub-ecosystems. Each sub-ecosystem has its own nuances, needs and desires. It is impossible to merge all the ecosystems into one and cater to all of them the same way. And needless to say, those ecosystems are competing for attention, "love", money, and power/influence because everyone wants to think and believe that they are the most important "player" in the world. This is exactly what makes the management of ecosystems difficult, but not impossible.

Here are some suggestions in espousing the best companies as **Tier 1 nodes** in one's ecosystem:

- The nodes (= partners) are willing to make the commitments and investments to be part of a winning ecosystem.
- They want the ecosystem to gain momentum and expand its reach --- become more "powerful" and influential.
- They love synergy, collaboration and cooperation. They are willing to participate in teamwork and share the glory ... and fiascos.
- They are willing to forgive their partners for honest mistakes.
- They are willing to be held accountable for sub-standard results --- and do something to fix the problems. They have no problem establishing joint goals, objectives, and expectations, and putting them in writing.
- They set aside egos and parochial attitudes. They understand that "we in this one together".
- They are dependable and respectful of each other. They keep their word and honor their journey together as partners.
- They never judge or criticize their partners. They take their issues directly to the source. They don't talk behind others' backs.
- They help others solve their problems and critical tasks --- especially those that affect several nodes in the ecosystem.
- They are results oriented
- They are always looking for ways to improve the ecosystem by promoting win-win scenarios.
- They are willing to create joint customer impact and share the revenue (according to predetermined formulas) and "glory".
- They are willing to seize together opportunities.
- They are willing to advance relationships with customers and with each other. They realize that it is about selling value, not price.
- They have no issue with transparency.
- There are no hidden agendas.
- They are willing to take chances and share the risk.
- They love strategic thinking and long-term views.

Important Reminders:

1. The partnerships start at the top.
2. Partnerships are "living entities" --- one must treat them with respect and reverence
3. There is more value outside one's own value chain. However, one must be very careful in trying to tap into it.
4. *"If your business partners aren't working as hard as you, it's a sinking ship"* --- **Julian Hall**
5. *"Our success has really been based on partnerships from the very beginning"* --- **Bill Gates**
6. When one becomes an international company, then the role and importance of partnerships and relationships become very apparent. Companies with websites are automatically international, whether they planned it that way or not.

Suggestion: Attend seminars workshops re: Partner Management, Relationship Management, and Ecosystem Management. They all offer valuable nuggets of wisdom as to how to view the partners and work with them.

Conclusion

Innovation Ecosystems are not a business fad. They are here to stay forever because they reflect the natural tendency of people, businesses and societies to aggregate and collaborate. They are part of the New Renaissance. The challenge is managing the emerging ecosystems the right way because they have another natural tendency to form ad-hoc and stay informal. For most companies the choices are either create their own business/innovation ecosystem, or be part of one. The only other choice is to do business as usual, which usually leads to the stagnation and death of the enterprise. Smart business owners and execs recognize that ecosystems can benefit all those that are members of larger ecosystems, such as the ones formed by **Ford, Toyota, GM, Apple and Microsoft**.

The key to success is to develop and cultivate a fluid, adaptive and agile innovation ecosystem – internally and externally – that is flexible enough to deal with the task, project or program at hand. Finding the right partners for the ecosystem is as critical as finding the right employees and management team for the enterprise.

9 THE RIGHT STRATEGY, BUSINESS MODEL, AND BUSINESS PRACTICES FOR INNOVATION

Phillip Andrews

Introduction

Innovation starts right in the Business or Strategic Plan of the enterprise. If the Strategy is wrong then innovation is DOA. Having been in the consulting profession for over two decades, and seen plenty of Strategic Plans, it always left me speechless because I only saw a handful of plans (all from major corporations) that addressed innovation. There was not one SME that addressed innovation in their Strategic Plans or Business Models.

They simply took it for granted that their engineering departments will do their "thing", and produce new and/or improved products as their job descriptions outlined. By the way, none of them even had a Business Model. Business Models obviously do not mean anything to them. But that is a different story. It is not a secret that most SMEs do not have any strategists in their midst and care less to see a business model. They prefer to shoot from the hip as it offers them (in their own minds) the ultimate flexibility and adaptability.

It is very difficult to change those mentalities and beliefs, but if one is truly serious about innovation, then one needs to rethink all that. Innovation is all about thinking about the future. What is the future all about? What will it look like? What will people want and need? What will be different from today? What is doable? What are we missing in order to achieve our dreams? And so on. Most SMEs are so focused on today's operations that it is very difficult for them to think about the future. They are stuck in the survival mode and cannot look up to see what is coming down the pike.

It is smart for companies to develop their strategies and shape their business practices around innovation because innovation is what keeps companies afloat. They don't have to be extensive, and they don't have even to be complete because "completeness" comes over time as the company becomes smarter and better. Some companies only offer services and believe that innovation does not apply to them. But it does. Innovation is critical for all types of companies, even if one only has a candy store or a boutique. So, here are some suggestions aimed at SMEs to help them get started down the road of innovation.

Strategic Plan For Innovation

Strategic Plans address (among other things) the Vision, Mission, Business Model, Offering, Competition, Markets (incl. Market Position), Customers (incl. needs and wants), and Value Proposition. All of these aspects of the Plan require addressing innovation.

- **Vision**: Inspires fuels and drives innovation. If the vision is dull and is full of blah-blah, then innovation has no chance of thriving or even showing up.
- **Mission:** Explains the purpose (who we are and what we are doing to achieve the vision of the enterprise). The purpose must also inspire innovation because the company's mission will not be achieved by old, worn-out and BAU solutions.
- **Business Model**: (Is addressed in the next segment).
- **Offering**: Most companies are content to describe only their current offering because they believe that investors and stockholders are only interested in what the company offers today. However, it is smart to briefly discuss what are the other offerings in the pipeline (or innovation funnel), as it is that which makes one's company truly valuable and viable. We must not forget that employees should be aware of the company's plans as well. One cannot keep them secret and expect that employees will contribute their own innovative ideas. This implies that the company follows the "open book" management approach and promotes transparency (as a best practice).
- **Competition**: Competitors represent one of the most important triggers for innovation and change. Being fully aware of what competitors are doing or planning to do is critical to innovation. The SWOT Analysis is useless if it does not address Strengths, Weaknesses, Opportunities and Threats with competitors in mind. It is not about establishing differentiation alone. It is about setting a course for the future --- explaining how the company's products and services will stay ahead or leapfrog ahead of those offered by competitors.
- **Markets**: There are current markets and future markets. There are also tapped markets and untapped markets. It behooves companies to map their offering against all of those buckets/categories (along with their competitors' offerings) and reinforce the strategy by explaining how one's offering is in better position than anyone else to capture market share, along with the hearts and minds of customers and/or consumers.
- **Customers**: In a similar fashion with the markets discussion, there are current customers and there are future customers. There are identified customer needs, and unidentified ones. The company's offering must address all those categories and show where, why and how one's offering is best suited to meet customer demands, expectations and trends. Innovation plays a major role in offering planning and development.
- **Value Proposition**: The value proposition is one of the most important elements of the Strategic Plan and Business Model because it makes the key point that the company's offering has either unique value or better value than competition and therefore it will open the markets, entice the buyers to purchase the offering and create the needed revenue streams that will generate wealth and prosperity for the company.

If the Value Proposition is weak or unprovable, then the company not only does not have a good offering, but it does not have a leg to stand on. **The definition of value is:**

- o Something considered being important or beneficial; having a high opinion of.
- o Something that deserves the attention, adoration, importance, worth, love … and price of owning it.
- o Something that is useful, helpful, advantageous, beneficial, handy, convenient … and worthwhile.
- o Something that improves well-being, life, society and the human race.
- o Something that improves people's self-esteem, self-worth, abilities, skills and performance.
- o Something that pleases the senses and creates euphoric feelings.

Innovation plays a major role in meeting the above criteria. Value along with differentiation opens the doors to success. This is an old proven formula!

Moreover, strategy must be deeply steeped in the following thinking:

- The **Innovation mentality, approach and process**
- The **Blue Ocean mentality** --- because it promotes outside-the-box thinking and encourages bold moves aimed at making the competition irrelevant.
- **Breakthrough and Discontinuous Innovations are a must-have and a must-do** (on top of Serendipitous, Ad-Hoc and Sustainable Innovations --- as they are needed too)
- Focused on **significant** (orders of magnitude) **value**
- The selected **Strategic Enablers** should deeply influence the innovation process and offerings

  For Example: **Going Green** mandates that the products will be green; will promote the Reduce-Recycle-Reuse approach; and will safeguard the environment

  For Example: **Total Sustainability Management** mandates that the company itself will have a sustainable business model that promotes the 4BL (quadruple bottom line); the products will introduce new methods and techniques to support 4BL or be made with 4BL in mind

- The selected **Key/Strategic and Disruptive Technologies should be leveraged as strategic weapons** to both revolutionize the offering and the method of operation. Key technologies should not be viewed as mere tools and enablers. They represent another major trigger for innovation and creative disruption. Continuous scanning and evaluation of the latest technologies is crucial for the survival of the business. The key technologies must be captured in the Strategic Plan document and properly explained to employees in terms of their value and applications. This is where education & training play an important role.
- Attending technical society meetings (like IEEE meetings) is not enough for employees to stay abreast of the latest technologies. Companies must make a concerted effort in selecting the key technologies and then identifying the in-house champions and "gurus" that will be responsible for leveraging them the right way. The champions must offer the workshops and training sessions that explain how those technologies could change business and manufacturing processes, relationships, services, offering features and capabilities and even introduce new offerings.

> **Personal Anecdote:** I was never invited to such a workshop inside the major corporations that I've worked for. Never was offered the opportunity to learn the latest and greatest technologies and how to use them. It was always left up to me to ask permission to attend outside workshops, shows and conferences in order to learn what was new and "hot". This reflected the employers' mentality, which implied that it was the engineer's responsibility to learn on her/his own what is going on in the industry and business world. This attitude is one of the many ones that have to change.

Some Sad Realizations Pertaining To Strategic Planning

- Most enterprises (especially SMEs) have outsourced strategic planning to consulting firms. They hire consultants only occasionally to "improve" their awful strategies. **Outsourcing Strategic Planning is one of the most fatal strategic mistakes** --- and it cripples innovation.

- Most SMEs treat **Strategic Planning** as an event, not as a **continuous process.** They make the same mistake with innovation. Most enterprises have no clue that **innovation is a continuous process,** and also one of the most important ones. Most startups cannot go past their original offering. They think that adding more bells and whistles is adequate enough to thrive and create growth. They do not realize that (in most cases) after a while the additional bells and whistles are nothing more than "lipstick on a pig". Example: the biggest threat for GM is not Ford or Chrysler. It is the startup automotive companies in Silicon Valley. Detroit is facing the possibility of losing the crown as being the automotive capital of USA. **Tesla** Motors has opened their eyes to a new way of making vehicles and the same thing is happening in phones, computers, TVs, universities, taxis, hotels, retail stores, and so on. The automotive industry's new competitors are **Apple, Google, Tesla** and another 20+ companies all residing away from Detroit.

- Most companies isolate their strategic planners (if they have any) in corporate headquarters or head offices, thus isolating them from the real action and contact with the "doers", believing that it is smart to keep them apart. They tend to isolate those people physically and organizationally as if they are the only ones that understand the innovation and invention game. Of course, for major corporations like **IBM and HP** the main reason for isolating their R&D folks is the fear of losing their corporate secrets and patents. So, at this point in time it is still very difficult to totally open the doors to the business ecosystem partners (both internal and external). One could see the problem of this mentality in the old **IBM**. The isolation of their geniuses has led them to believe that the only thing that really mattered was main frame computers and nothing else. They forgot that they are in the business of Business Machines (yes, it is part of the IBM name).

The Business Model

The original Business Model Canvas was created several years ago, and represents the old capitalistic thinking that businesses are in business strictly for profits. Thus, the business model canvas does not reflect the 4BL mentality or the other important factors, including Strategic and Creative Innovation. In reality the Business Model does not reflect other important aspects, such as:

- Strategic Assets
- Cores Competencies/Core Capabilities
- Structure
- Technical Infrastructure
- Strategic (or Key) and Disruptive Technologies (beyond the ones adopted for the Technical Infrastructure). There are technologies that affect the offering, lead generation, channels and even PR Campaigns
- Culture

So, if one sticks to the traditional Business Model design and captured information, one not only will end up with an incomplete model, but also with a failed model for the enterprise. The idea of the Business Model is to describe the total "powertrain" of the enterprise, not just the engine or transmission. This is not any different than trying to describe what powers a car. One cannot simply explain the engine block and transmission and ignore the spark plugs (or COP ignition system), fuel injection system, fuel pump, water pump, electrical and computer systems, radiator, tires, fans, etc.

Thus, from Strategic and Creative Innovation point of view, as well as Creative Disruption point of view, one must go well beyond the current Business Model Canvas and look forward to designing something that makes sense according to one's beliefs and business goals.

If one were to fully develop a Business Model Canvas according to the 4BL body of theory or knowledge, one would have to add the following canvases (layers) to the **Profit-focused Canvas**:

1. **The Environmental Canvas** (addressing the Ecological aspects and Planet itself)
2. **The Social Canvas** (addressing the Societal and all People aspects)
3. **The Cultural Canvas** (addressing the Cultural and even Spiritual aspects)

The above aspects should be captured in the Business Model and fully explained in the Strategic Plan so that everyone in the enterprise understands what the company is trying to do and where it is trying to go. Without this knowledge and direction, the company appears to employees and other stakeholders as a floundering entity.

Strategic Goals

No Strategic Plan is complete without outlining the Goals of the enterprise. Drawing from the consulting experience, it appears that there is confusion in this area as well because most companies only pay "lip service" to the goals. They post traditional goals that offer no excitement, not true motivation and no energy. If the enthusiasm and inspiration is not implied in the goals, the employees translate them as BAU --- doing the bare minimum to survive another year. Here are some of the **traditional goals**:

- Increase revenue
- Improve productivity
- Improve quality
- Improve customer satisfaction
- Improve operations and logistics
- Improve processes, layouts, and flows

- Improve inventory
- Reduce labor costs
- Reduce environmental damage
- Conform to regulations

These are the same goals that drove the Industrial Revolution for over 200 years. However the **new era** promotes additional **goals**, such as:

- Foster a strong collaborative culture
- Support the community
- Be an exemplary corporate citizen

Total Sustainability Management offers additional suggestions for goals, such as:

- Create Shared Value (CSV)
- Demonstrate with actions Corporate Social Responsibility (CSR)
- Introduce totally green products
- Pursue all practical aspects of: Green Economy, Circular Economy, Shared Economy, Digital Economy

These types of goals then influence the operating plans and actions that each business function or organization has to design, develop and put into action in order for the enterprise goals to materialize. The new era is promoting **Superordinate Goals** that supersede the typical business goals. Here are some examples:

Johnson & Johnson (Citizenship and Sustainability 2020 Goals)

- **People:** We'll help people be healthier by providing better access and care in more places.
- **Places:** We'll make the places we live, work and play healthier by using fewer and smarter resources.
- **Practices:** We'll team up with partners and employees to create a culture of health and well-being.

Dow (2025 Goals)

- Leading the Blueprint (for a sustainable world)
- Delivering Breakthrough Innovation
- Advancing a Circular Economy
- Valuing Nature
- Increasing confidence in Chemical Technology
- Engaging Employees for Impact
- World-leading Operations Performance

Here are some other goals that other companies put in place:

- Address head on Climate Change
- Improve Energy Efficiency and Conservation

- Promote Breakthrough Solutions to World Challenges
- Contribute to Community Success
- Aid Local Protection of Human Health and the Environment
- Stimulate Sustainable Innovation
- Lead Product Safety
- Work for a Safer and Healthier Society
- Advance the company to the next level of excellence

These types of **Superordinate Goals** capture what the new era is all about and the role of Strategic and Creative Innovation. The message should be clear: **BAU (Business As Usual) is dead! Simple Models and Canvases are dead!** The Superordinate Goals set the tone for the company's direction, behaviors, attitudes, culture, style of management, product development, innovation, employee treatment, brand image, and company's standing, reputation and relationships with local communities.

Additional Input re: Goals Of Strategic and Creative Innovation

The Superordinate Goals need to be augmented with lower level goals and objectives, so that leaders and organizations have a crisper understanding of what they need to work on (both short-term and long-term). For example, one may "translate" the Superordinate Goal of **"Advance the company to the next level of excellence"** into these types of actionable goals and/or objectives:

- Become an international company (**Note:** Websites make all companies international, but only if they want to "play" there)
- Pursue new ventures, partnerships and alliances
- Expand the business and innovation ecosystems; integrate the two into one ecosystem
- Enrich the product and service portfolios (with new products and services) (**Note:** it is very smart to wrap every product with one or more services)
- Open up business in new markets and geographies
- Reduce or substitute current raw materials
- Drastically change the org structure or company formation
- Significantly improve customer service
- Introduce a **BHAG** (Big Hairy Audacious Goal) that "stretches" the organization

Innovation is behind every one of these goals or objectives. The only challenge and question is how creative one wants to be with each one of them. This is exactly what differentiates the industry leaders and superstar startups from the rest of the pack.

Additional Input re: The Key Ingredients For Strategic Innovation

These ingredients are necessary to support Strategic Innovation, aimed at driving growth, stimulating a "wake-up call" for the organization and advancing the company's name, reputation and brand. The ingredients are:

- **Industry and Business Foresight** – Understanding emerging trends (incl. micro and macro or megatrends), undercurrents and other factors of change
- **Consumer/Customer Insights** – Understanding articulated and unarticulated needs
- **A Stimulating Innovation Process** – Allowing non-traditional and traditional approaches and techniques to bring forth the best ideas. Prioritizing those ideas and funding them the right is key to bringing ideas to fruition
- **Core Technologies and Competencies** – Leveraging and extending corporate assets
- **Organizational Readiness** – The ability to take action
- **Disciplined Implementation** – Managing the path from inspiration to business impact
- **Strategic Alignment** – Rapid decisions, effective implementations

The differences and value of Strategic Innovation is captured in this table:

	Traditional Innovation Approaches	Strategic Innovation Approaches
Main Technique	Extrapolation --- from present (as the starting point) to future (as the end point)	Imagination --- starting with the end in mind and/or letting the mind soar with no limits or starting points. Bridging back to the present can be a challenge
Mentality	Usually cautionary --- afraid of breaking any of the existing "eggs". Usually follows the rules of the game Willing to accept established business boundaries and/or product categories	Revolutionary --- not afraid to "break some eggs to make an omelette". Looking to create unique competitive space(s) and change the rules of the game or even invent a new game Unafraid of boundaries and explore new frontiers
Posture	The innovator or inventor assumes a follower posture -- simply extrapolating	The innovator or inventor assumes a leader (rule-breaker) posture
Focus	Incremental innovations (a.k.a. sustaining innovations)	Breakthrough, disruptive innovations
Process	Following traditional linear processes	What process? All it matters is imagining and creating Parallel and circular processes are acceptable
Sources	Seek input from obvious, traditional sources	Seeks inspiration from unconventional sources
Customer	They matter; must know	They don't really matter

Needs	articulated consumer needs	because most people don't know what they really need or want until they see it
Willingness To Stay With Company	High level of willingness to stay because they like the security blanket of established organizations	Low level of willingness to stay. Prone to quit to start own company. Willing to gamble it all. Wanting to experiment with entrepreneurial "new venture"
Results	Average to exciting	Exciting to thrilling
Rewards	Average to great	Great to phenomenal

The right-hand column will produce better results and practically guarantee the sustainability of an enterprise.

Summary

Here is a simple formula that captures the discussion from this and previous chapters:

Strategic Innovation = Radical Innovations + Disruptive/Creative Innovations + Sustainable Innovations

Strategic Planning not only needs to be forward thinking that integrates vision(s), aspirations, dreams, hopes, targets, and goals, but also reflect the overall philosophy and higher purpose of the enterprise. Enterprises that have no philosophy (or ideology) and no higher purpose lack the most important ingredient of the enterprise: its soul.

Soulless Enterprises are doomed to failure from their very inception. The reason is very simple. They lack the inspiration and motivation to excel, reach higher levels of achievement, excellence and … existence. Enterprises that are focused exclusively on profits and making the stockholders happy fail every time.

Higher Purpose provides the extra needed ingredient that drives people to invent and innovate in order to achieve that purpose … that Holy Grail. And most good and gifted people knowingly or unknowingly are always in a pursuit of a Holy Grail. Good enterprises help people find their Holy Grails, by giving people's lives meaning and purpose. They tie the personal Holy Grails to the Business Holy Grail. How one does it makes all the difference in the world. The Apples and Googles of the world know the trick and they apply it very successfully.

The Higher Purpose needs to be imbedded in the Strategic Plan, just like the Vision and Mission Statements, and the plan then must reflect that. The best way to achieve the Higher Purpose is to focus the Strategic Plan on innovation/invention because those are the very vehicles that will bring the enterprise closer to it. **The Higher Purpose demands people to be bold, courageous, risk takers and innovative.** One cannot get to the Higher Purpose (and Holy Grail) by being afraid, timid, and reticent.

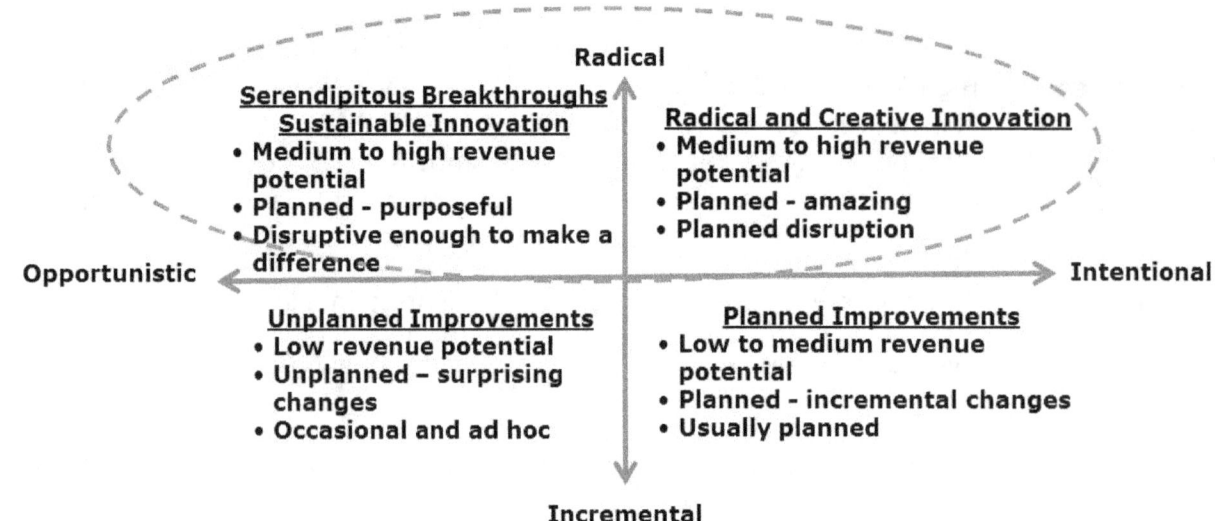

The best strategic plans are focused on the upper (circled) quadrants.

10 THE RIGHT ORGANIZATION STRUCTURE, CULTURE AND STYLE OF MANAGEMENT FOR INNOVATION

Phillip Andrews

Introduction

In order for innovations to thrive in enterprises of all sizes, one must pay attention to all the elements that influence the organizational creativity and innovation. Those elements are:
In this chapter we are only addressing the structure, culture, and leadership styles as they are the ones that play the most strategic role in establishing innovation the right way in startup companies and SMEs. Skills, climate and to some degree techniques are discussed in parts of this book.

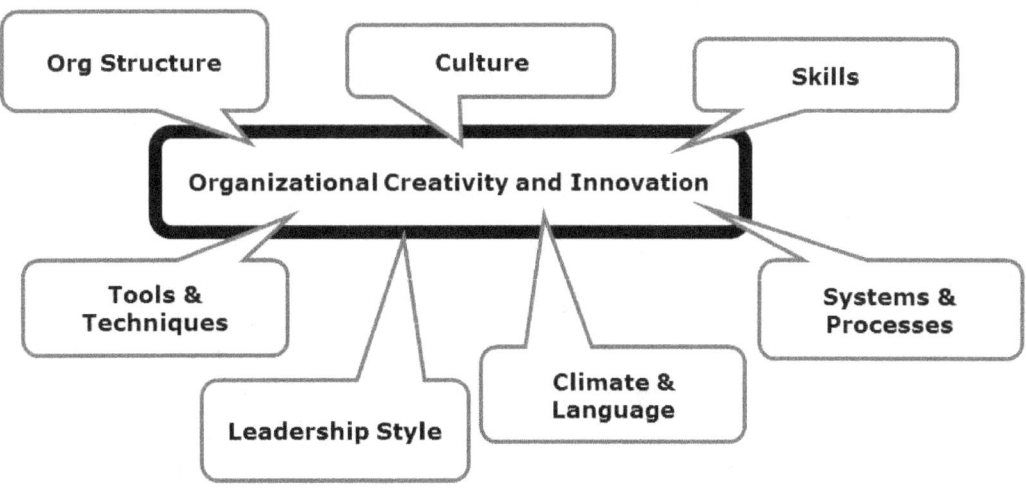

Organization Formation and Structure

The goal is: Innovate by leveraging the organizational structure!

Key Realization: There is no one formation that fits all situations in all industries and all

types of enterprises. There is no one magical formation that creates the best results because the culture style of leadership and other factors carry a lot of weight and influence as well. For some companies in certain industries, the centralized formation is the best, while in others the decentralized formation is the best, and in others yet a hybrid formation is the best. However, it is safe to say that decentralized organizations that have true autonomy and say-so, seem to do better with innovation. Centralized organizations seem to stifle innovation as they tend to hoard decision making and control functions too tightly. And although control and centralized decision making are important for managing the bottom line and reducing overhead costs, on the other hand, they penalize free-thinking, self-rule and self-determination, flexibility, speed and closeness to customers, which in return become obstacles to risk taking and originality. Centralized organization employees, usually feel disempowered by just following orders.

However, the actual **organizational structure** underneath the big umbrella of centralized, decentralized, and hybrid formations it does make a difference. Here are some suggestions that are proven to help organizations of all sizes. They are:

- **Eliminate the silo mentality**; consider the **networked type organization**
- Eliminate the deep hierarchies and bureaucracies that stifle innovation --- having **flat and networked organizations** improves collaboration, synergy, communications, speed and idea generation
- Establish **cross-functional and self-sustaining teams**; authorize them to drive or map out their own innovation path. Allow teams to execute freely, bypassing organizational dependencies and politics.
- Develop core processes that run horizontally across several functions --- the so-called **Horizontal Organization** is a great idea, but very few companies know how to implement it the right way or make work for them. Establishing Core Process Managers that have equal or more authority than the functional managers helps manage the Horizontal Organization the right way
    Example Of Core Processes: The most typical core processes are: a) Idea-To-Production, b) Customer Contact-To-Enthusiasm, c) Production-To-Delivery, and c) Order-To-Cash
- **Empower the employees** that are driving innovation; adopt the project management mentality --- allow them to behave as Project Managers or Team Leaders

Moreover consider these:

- Allow emerging businesses to establish their own organization --- do not force them to fit within existing organizations. This is the concept of having **Ambidextrous Organizations** (accommodating both existing and emerging businesses or offerings)
- Spin-off and establish a **subsidiary** to operate the new venture
- Some companies go as far as implementing a new structure called **Holocracy**. It's best suited for certain professional organizations that have great staff that can manage themselves without managers. The online retailer **Zappos.com** is one of those organizations
    - **Holocracy.org**, the website of the organization that administers the Holocracy trademark and offers training courses, describes Holocracy as:

"Unlike conventional top-down or progressive bottom-up approaches, it (Holocracy) integrates the benefits of both without relying on parental heroic leaders. Everyone becomes a leader of their roles and a follower of others', processing tensions with real authority and real responsibility, through dynamic governance and transparent operations."

Holocracy combines autonomy with accountability, but is not based on consensus management. It is based on being focused on actions and results. Everyone working in such an environment understands that her/his actions affect others and the performance of the entire organization. One's failure becomes everyone's failure. Peer pressure and personal accountability are keys to success. Employees in those environments know (and learn) not to depend on others to fix their problems. They have to fix them on their own. Needless to say one must have the right employees to be able to expect that out of them.

In a way, **Holocracy** combines the structure, culture and style of management into one "package", rather than three --- and hence the name Holocracy which manifests the holistic approach.

Culture

Over and above Values and Beliefs one must take the following actions in order to create the right Culture of Innovation. Here are some of the top actions (some of them were mentioned previously):

1. Have **vision** and **mission statements** that are inspiring and exciting.
   Reminder: In order for employees to be inspired about innovation the leader has to be inspired. The enterprise or leader must have the passion and make her/his passion contagious/infectious. Here are two examples pertaining to mission statements:
   a. **Coca Cola's Mission Statement** reads: *"To refresh the world, inspire moments of optimism and happiness, create value and make a difference".*
   b. Avoid meaningless statements, such as *"We offer the best product in the world"* or *"We provide the best customer service".*
2. Have a crisp and clear **strategy for moving forward** --- where you want your offering and company to be way down the road, not just tomorrow.
3. Integrate your **Business Strategy with your Innovation Strategy.**
4. Allow time for employees to innovate --- by putting it in their job descriptions, like **3M** does (or did at one time) (allotting 15% of employees' time to innovation). **Google** offers its tech community "20% time to follow their passions" (every week --- that's one day per week!).
5. **Foster a culture of ideas.** This includes a culture of collaboration, teamwork, mentoring, coaching, and constant encouragement. Smart people are sensitive people.
6. **Recognize employees' innovation contributions**. The best rewards are monetary (incl. company stock). Secondarily, trophies and other rewards that recognize an employee's contribution are important, along with special ceremonies and rituals. Better yet, recognize entire teams, not just individuals. The idea behind it is to avoid jealousy and antagonism. Team awards and rewards stimulate collaboration and synergy. Others have tried other rewards systems, including donating money to NPOs/charities under an employee's name or offering non-monetary awards, such as fully paid vacations, cars and even condos.
7. **Permit failure / create the space for experimentation.** It is critical for employees to

feel safe in failing. If they are penalized, chastised, criticized and their chances for raises and bonuses are taken away, then employees will eventually shun away from taking chances and trying to invent new things. They would rather stick with incremental improvements, rather than take the big brave steps into the unknown and uncharted waters. This why mentoring and coaching are needed. People need encouragement and prompting to stick to their dreams, aspirations … and convictions. Sometimes people need to be reminded that **courage matters**.

8. **Promote learning**. Leadership and organizational learning are critical to the innovation effort. The **Learning Organization** culture is one of the best cultures for those that are eager to innovate-innovate-innovate. **Be a polymath** (learn from all disciplines) --- cross-fertilization of knowledge and skills is a form of Enlightenment. Learning from arts & crafts disciplines is not only smart, it is a mind booster for the creative juices. The more one learns the more of the big picture one can see and appreciate. It is then that the brain can start connecting the dots.

Some authors and consultants have recommended other approaches as well, such as returning to the past (paying attention to the company's legacy and heritage), and putting more emphasis on the culture than the current business trends, and so on. Some of those suggestions are applicable for some companies (like **John Deere**), but for companies they need to stay on top of the latest advancements in technology and sociotechnical trends as they do change the culture.

Cultures are not static. They are dynamic. Cultures benefit greatly by paying attention to the latest megatrends and adjusting themselves accordingly. For example, one of the biggest megatrends today is sustainability (incl. **Going green**). If the business strategy and culture do not accommodate that, then the company will be erased from the map.

The list of companies that ignored the current trends and paid severe price is endless --- from **RIM (Blackberry)** to **Sony, Nokia**, and **Dell**. Cultures, just like strategies, are not static or engraved in stone. They need to be modified on a constant basis. We all know that certain companies like **Coca Cola** and **Kraft** made strategic product mistakes with **New Coke** and **Carbwells**. But that is product decision mistakes, not misreading trends. The trends that they were trying to accommodate were fine, but it was the decisions as to how to satisfy those trends that were wrong. So, one should not pass judgement about adapting latest trends based on the failures of some big corporations.

There are two other topics that always come up when one discusses the right culture for innovation. The first topic has to do with internal competition, and the second one has to do with considering teaming up with competitors. So, let's briefly discuss both of those topics:

1. **Internal competition.** Some companies and people encourage this concept and even thrive under it, while others totally despise it. So, it is more of a personal preference, rather than a preferred choice based on solid criteria or proven results. Some people thrive when they compete against others, including their own colleagues, as they feel energized by the adrenaline that is flowing in their veins. They need the adrenaline to "put it in high gear". This is more of an emotional and psychological trigger than a proven managerial method/approach. Others are totally turned off by competition as it fills them up with negative feelings to the point of blocking the mind and free expression. Competition brings out fear and intimidation that are not pleasant in most (normal) brains. If one is

determined to pursue internal competition, one should at least lay the groundwork for channelling rivalry in a positive way, by challenging the team leaders to develop their formal and informal networks, and compete at the intellectual level (as opposed to personal level).

> **Personal Anecdote:** I had the opportunity to work for **Apple Computer** in the mid '80s, as the VP of Manufacturing. I was invited for an interview and everything was going great, until the interviewer asked me how I felt about internal competition. I did express my strong antipathy for it and I explained that this is not my style or preference. I thought the interviewer would give me a big brownie point for promoting collaboration and synergy. To my surprise the interviewer went out his way to convince me that internal competition was a good thing and he wanted me to endorse that approach. When he realized that my attitude was unchanged, my interview came to a sudden halt. At the time apple was struggling for survival and Ii did not feel that I made a mistake. But now that I look back, Ii realize that maybe that was one of my biggest mistakes in my career --- but I still have not changed my mind about how I feel about internal competition.

2. **External competition**. Unlike internal competition, external competition not only makes sense, it is a natural phenomenon that cannot be denied or ignored. However, even in this arena, it is important today to realize that the old style of cutthroat and callous competition (emulating Sarnoff's, Rockefeller's and Carnegie's styles) is dead. Today's concept revolves around **coopetition**, which emphasizes the cooperative type competition. The original basic principles of coopetition have been described in game theory and the work of **John Forbes Nash** on non-cooperative games. It must be noted that coopetition occurs at inter-organizational or intra-organizational levels.

   A. At **inter-organizational level**[24], coopetition occurs when companies interact with partial congruence of interests and objectives. They cooperate with each other to reach a higher value creation (as compared to the value created without interaction and struggle to achieve the desired competitive advantage).

      Often coopetition takes place when companies are in the same market. They are interested in sharing the R&D costs, but then introduce different products based on their understanding of the R&D findings. This was exactly the arrangement between **PSA Peugeot Ccitroën** and **toyota** (aimed at introducing a new city car). Thus, the **Peugeot 107, Citroën C1,** and the **Toyota Aygo** were introduced out of that collaborative effort. In other cases the collaboration is aimed at sharing production methods, and overhead costs, while remaining fiercely competitive in other areas (as was the case of the Toyota and GM collaboration, called **Nummi** --- 1984 to 2009). Several advantages can be materialized from such collaborations, such as cost reductions, knowledge and technology transfer. Some difficulties also arise pertaining to control, decision making, risk taking, direction, priorities ... and trust.

   B. At the **intra-organizational level**[25], coopetition occurs between individuals or functional units within the same organization. Based on game theory and social interdependence theories, it is possible to have simultaneously cooperation and competition among functional units.

[24] According to Wikipedia.

[25] According to Wikipedia.

Key Reminder: Culture becomes the company's DNA. Good DNA will produce great future generations, while incomplete, bad or damaged DNA will produce incomplete, bad or damaged future generations. Translation: good DNA ➔ great offerings, great future, sustainable organizations. Bad DNA ➔ bad offerings, bleak future, crippled organizations. Companies that have great DNA include: **Ford, GE, Johnson & Johnson, Berkshire Hathaway,** and **Wells Fargo**.

Preferred Culture for Creative Disruption

Most people and companies usually describe their culture in terms of brief statements of Values and/or Beliefs, such as: **Excellence, Respect, Integrity, Collaboration, Trust, Teamwork, Collaboration, Synergy, Quality, Creativity, Innovation, Customer Focus, Responsiveness, Pride, Enthusiasm,** and the like. Those are fine and they do offer great value (if they mean anything at all), but in most cases they are empty words that only make great posters in the halls of corporations. Very few companies even discuss them with their employees during onboarding sessions, and even fewer of them even bother to explain them the right way or the consequences of not practicing the implied culture behind those words, and practically none of them offer in-house workshops on how to fuel creativity and innovation. Thus, employees do not pay any attention to them --- further reinforcing the prevalent and sarcastic attitude of *"This too shall pass!"*

Creative Disruption companies add the words like **Risk Taking, Outside-The-Box Thinking, Imagination, Responsibility, Growth,** and **Resourcefulness.** Those are words are equally undefined and unexplained because (God forbid) most of them require strategies behind them, which companies, not only do not have, they don't even know what they mean or do. Yes, there should be a **Risk Management Strategy**, and an **Innovation Strategy**, and a **Corporate Social Responsibility (CSR) Strategy**, and a **Growth Strategy**. Heck, most companies do not even have a **Talent Management Strategy**, much less worry about all the rest. It is easy to see, why after all these years of Capitalism, we still have so many companies failing at an alarming rate or find themselves on "the wrong track". In reality they never were on the right track because they never saw the value of doing the right things.

Here are some key points that affect the creation of a solid, beneficial and productive culture:

- It is difficult to excel on strategy when there are **no strategic planners** inside the enterprise

  Reminder:
  No Strategy ➔ Usually means No Culture
  No Culture ➔ Usually means that the Strategy is BS

- It is impossible to be good with innovation when there are **no innovators, thought leaders and master minds** inside the enterprise
- It is impossible for employees to think-outside-the-box or be creative when there are **no workshops or training classes**
- It is impossible for employees to be creative when there are **no tools, techniques or examples** of how to use them
- It is impossible for managers/leaders take risks when the **system penalizes them for failing**, and only rewards those that "make the numbers"

- It is impossible for managers/leaders to thinks about innovation when the whip is constantly cracking over their heads. Example: **Wells Fargo** and the major fiasco of creating over two million bogus accounts to pretend that they are a prosperous and growing company. **John Stumpf** (Wells Fargo CEO) was another empty suit he joined other infamous CEOs, incl. Moody's **Raymond W. McDaniel Jr.,** Compaq's **Eckard Pfeiffer**, and Eastman Kodak's **Kay R. Whitmore** (all of them on the CEO Hall Of Shame).

With all of that in mind, the suggestion is that the **right innovation culture is actually a mixture of all these ... and more**:

1. **Audacious Innovation Culture**
2. **Going Green Culture**
3. **Creating Social Value (CSV) Culture**
4. **Corporate Social Responsibility (CSR) Culture**
5. **High Performance Culture** (based on HPO)
6. **Conscious Culture** (based on Conscious Capitalism Culture)
7. **Lean And Agile or Lean 6-Sigma (LSS) Culture** (incl. promoting **Lean Startups**)
8. **Learning Organization Culture**
9. **Collaborative (and/or Relationship Management) Culture**
10. **Other pertinent cultures** (based on the company's strategy and direction)

It is crucial for enterprises to create their own "cocktail of culture" based on their choices of **Vision, Mission, Values, Strategic Enablers** (= espoused Bodies Of Knowledge), and **Core Competencies**.

Most of the above cultures are well-defined in numerous books and workshops, but the **Audacious Innovation Culture** is a relatively new. It is based on the aforementioned principles/tenets plus these practices:

1. **Unrelenting innovation** --- never stopping for a moment. Going to bed thinking about innovation, waking up thinking about innovation
   - Treating everything as a trigger for innovation
   - Treating innovative ideas as projects
   - Constantly scouring, harvesting and leveraging the business ecosystem for fresh new ideas; turning the innovation ecosystem into an **ecosystem of disruption**
   - Integrating the business and innovation ecosystem
2. Espousing **flexible processes** for product research, development, and engineering
3. Increasing **organizational agility** (fluidity instead of rigidity) --- self-directed, self-managed (SDSM) teams. Promoting the principles of **The Autonomous Workforce**
4. Taking **concurrent product development** to the next level because speed and synergy matter
   - Increasing collisions of ideas between distributed departments and people
   - Eliminating the silos and silo mentality
   - Encouraging experimentation
5. Willingness to **grow both organically and inorganically**

Style Of Management

Just like structure, and to some extend culture, there is no one style of management or leadership that produces the best results. We have seen leaders that were dictators and tyrants that had their organizations humming with great innovations, and then at the other end, we have seen totally hands-off leaders with touchy-feely style produce equally well great innovations.

There are several leadership styles, including:

- Authoritative (Dictatorial)
- Controlling / Directing
- Advising / Coordinating / Guiding
- Collaborating
- Delegating / Empowering
- Participating (or Participative)

Others prefer these styles (per Goleman):

- Commanding
- Visionary
- Affiliative
- Democratic
- Pacesetting
- Coaching

Others have other labels to assign to the different styles of management. The actual labels do not really matter. Having experienced all of them through my long career, it is easy for me to conclude from my own experience and perspective, that the leaders that are focused on **supporting, coaching, mentoring, pacesetting, empowering and motivating** others are the best --- based on my personality and character as an employee.

Here are the **qualities that employees admire in their leaders**:

- Authenticity
- Trust
- Appropriate Control (for the right situation --- ranging from tight control to touchy-feely)
- Visionary, but also a Doer (thinking far and thinking short or near)
- Patience coupled with Perseverance
- Resilience and Flexibility
- Vulnerability

These qualities foster an invisible bond between the leader and her/his team, which is important in feeling comfortable, not to just follow, but to also climb outside-one's-box. So, it appears, once again, that it is the personal preferences that play a major role for both the leader and her/his team members (= employees). I always had a strong antipathy for dictators and slave drivers, and that was the major trigger in my decision where I wanted to work and belong. My contributions were always greater when my leader totally trusted me, and gave me full freedom to do my thing (whatever it was). However, I've seen others that like the crack of the whip and being told what to do. It is more than being self-driven, self-motivated and self-relied that makes some people crave independence, while others are inspired and enthused by external triggers and stimuli. Personal character traits, upbringing, education and a variety of other factors play a role in the way people get energized and stirred.

As a reference point, here is **Elon Musk's pacesetting style of management**:

- **Strengths:**
  - Mentality: True visionaries can revolutionize an industry and cater to future untapped markets
  - Approach: Lead by example and empower people with their own deep-seated values
  - Attitude: Stay at least two steps ahead of competitors
- **Weaknesses:**
  - Staff can easily burnout by trying to keep up pace with a maniacal pursuit of a lofty goal
  - Can be outdone by other change agents (incl. people and technologies)

Leadership Best Practices (That Promote Innovation)

1. **Robust communications 360^0, all the time.** Continuous feedback. Keep reminding others what the organization's goal is all about and what is the end result of a particular endeavor. Constantly obtaining feedback and offering ideas about the challenges to be able to innovate on relevant areas.
2. **Redefine metrics and incentives.** Measured progress by the number of "experiments", not by the number of successful experiments, in order to continue moving ahead.

   One of the biggest mistakes that companies make is to hold new ventures under the same metrics that are used to evaluate business activities that have been in existence for a long time. As a result the new ventures struggle to prove their value and potential to the decision makers, who predictively become very nervous very quickly and label the new venture as a bad experiment.

   Thus, it is smart to change the performance metrics to reflect realistic expectations based on the challenges that new ventures face. Accordingly incentives and compensation packages need to be designed to reflect the importance of innovation --- encouraging more innovation, not less.

3. **Assign a high ranking executive as the sponsor (as well as a mentor) of one or more innovation teams.** Ensure that the sponsor has both solid hard and soft skills. Having one or the other is not enough. The innovators need both the soft skills in order to harmonize and "sing together", but they also need the hard skills that will tell them whether or not they are on the right track. The truth is that everyone needs a coach and a mentor, even at the age of sixty five. Extremely few people do not need a coach and a mentor.

One the roles of the sponsor is to push back against the "bouncers". The bouncers are the usually the middle managers that their role by definition is to work on the business processes and activities assigned to them. **Middle managers** (in most cases) **do not:**

- Care about innovation because it jeopardizes their roles and performance measures. They view innovation as a disruptive force that creates confusion and disorder, which goes contrary to their thinking and behavior. Their goal is to achieve optimum performance, not deal with turmoil. After all their performance measures are structured that way. Their rewards depend on maximum results, smooth operation and minimal trial and error. Innovation blows up all that.
- Have the capacity, education, or skills to deal with creative disruption and chaos. Those skills and techniques are not offered to them.
- Have the time to deal with extemporaneous errands and chores.
- Have the processes, tools and methodologies to deal with innovation.

Thus, it is not a surprise that middle management is one of the biggest obstacles to innovations. The problem is created by the enterprise itself by the way they structure the company, assign roles and responsibilities, design performance measures, and way they prepare employees both mentally and psychologically.

Sponsors should:

- Assist middle managers with the above points, and help them achieve quick results, wins and praises for introducing innovation in their organizations.
- Make the necessary changes in the job descriptions, performance measures and reward systems.
- Improve the courses and training offered through their leadership and organizational learning programs.
- Show middle managers how to be good coaches and mentors themselves to their own employees.
- Provide the "safe space" for people to test their new ideas and even fail. They should use failures as lessons learned. Thus, the goal (and focus) of the organization shifts away from running smoothly (and behaving like machine), to running smartly and becoming the best that it can be.

4. **Add an Innovation Council** (if one can afford a council of senior advisors). The advisors represent an additional check point and an additional set of mentors and coaches. The members on the Council should be veterans that have the battle scars or previous ventures and endeavors. The Council should have minimal participation and governance because it is easy for them to want to get all the credit of what the innovation teams are producing (dealing with human nature, again).

5. **Make the inner workings of the enterprise transparent.** The tendency is for enterprises to keep their business models and strategies secret from their own employees, based on the notion that they don't need to know. So, how does one expect employees to improve and innovate the company when they know so little about the company? It appears that outside the Strategic Planning Department no one else knows the enterprise's business model or even roadmap to the future. Enterprises forget that innovation does not apply only to products and customer-facing dealings. Innovation applies to profit models, processes, policies, procedures, roles, equipment, layouts,

flows, and whatever else affects the business, both directly and indirectly. It is important to make it everyone's job to improve the company through innovative ideas. Several companies (e.g.: **Microsoft**) now actively encourage employees to get involved with offerings, business models and policies.

Conclusion

Structure, culture and style of management greatly influence the innovation effort inside a company. Smart companies are very careful in selecting the right structure, right culture and right leaders as they are the ones that will "spell out" from the start whether or not a company will promote, stimulate and encourage innovation or thwart it and impede it.

The best structures, cultures and styles of management are the ones that promote harmony, synergy, great collaboration and teamwork. Unfortunately, telecommuting, and teleconferencing are not great substitutes (at the present time) for achieving those key ingredients. Thus, it is not a surprise that **IBM** in the Spring of 2017 urged its employees to avoid telecommuting and get back to the office (http://money.cnn.com/2017/05/19/technology/ibm-work-at-home/) for the main purpose of synergizing and collaborating the right way. However, it is expected that **virtual reality, virtual computing and virtual networking** will dramatically improve the current telecommuting problem. It should be noted that telecommuting is not going away. It is a necessity.

It is a fact that certain types of people will invent and innovate under the worst conditions and environments, but that should not imply that management teams should care less about the environment and climate they create around them.

11 MIND OF THE INNOVATOR

Lynn Scarborough

Introduction (Exploring the Roadmap of Innovation)

This and the next chapter are dedicated to evaluating the attributes, principles and patterns of Innovation and the dynamics of team innovation. The focus of **The Mind of the Innovator** section is to provide entrepreneurs, business owners, corporate executives, project managers, investors, educators, mentors and students a better understanding of the creative/innovative process and then how to replicate and support it. This understanding will hopefully contribute to stronger products, more invention, technological advancements and great economic growth for companies and communities.

This section address the mind and thought process of innovation. It is divided into two chapters;

1. **Mind of the Innovator** –
   This chapter will address the principles of innovation and the attributes of the greatest genius and innovator of all time Leonardo da Vinci. Leonardo identified seven areas of intelligence which have been foundational to understanding the multidimensional nature of genius and the creative process.

2. **The Innovation Thought Map** –
   When we peal back the layers of thought processes that make an invention it exposes the patterns and cognitive processes of innovation. These patterns give a type of blueprint or structure that contribute to innovation.

   This chapter explores the universal pattern of innovation through a five-stage model of Conception, Visualization, Adaptation, Evaluation, and Incubation.

   The first four stages of the innovation thought map is explained using the popular **DiSC behavior assessment model** to help identify the four distinct thought categories. The fifth stage is the Incubation stage which identifies the thoughts and mindset that contributes to creating a productive culture which supports and allows innovation to grow.

There are many who have described the complexities of the innovative process from the academic, psychological or scientific perspectives. These are valid and important writings. However, this analysis was developed for teaching and immediate application to help people in the trenches understand the Innovative creative process and become successful. As a veteran TV coach, media expert and corporate trainer, I have helped thousands of individuals to be more successful and effective. The "Strategic Business Communications Training has helped teams to be productive, cooperative and creative. It is the hope that exploring the 'Mind of Innovation" will help every business owner, student, entrepreneur, manager and dream to reach their greater potential in business and life.

How does an Innovator Think and Process?

What makes the mind of an innovator different? Is it genius, creativity, personality, IQ, experience, observations, education, gut response, heart, passion, logic or all the above? And what is the genius of an innovation? Is it need, survival instincts, inspiration from the muses, higher wisdom or base desires. How does the innovative thought process work? Is it methodical, predictable, practiced, spiritual, or random like a pinball machine? Or could it be more like a multi-layered puzzle with a special combination of forces, forever changing and unique as a genome?

It starts with a spark

In the beginning, there is a flash of light. A tiny spark, caused by a neurological impulse in a microscopic portion of the brain, flashes in the darkness to signal the birth of an idea. This spark travels faster than 250 miles an hour. This impulse connects with other nerves and ignites more and more bursts of microscopic energy. Like lightening from a distant storm the impulse grows and runs swiftly along nerve endings until it becomes a conscious thought. A thought that in turn sparks dozens and uncountable impressions of memories stored in the remarkable data storage within each brain. Every day over 70,000 thoughts are produced by every brain. Layers of thoughts become ideas, impressions and mental pictures which make the unseen visible. And, if my chance the thought is strong or important enough then what was once a simple impression advances into the cognitive area of the brain to be evaluated, filed or verbalized.

The brain is mysterious and remarkable organ. The brain is the birthplace of innovation and the vehicle which carries us to the stars and helps us unlock the code of DNA. Each brain, weighting only three pounds is unique and manages more data than a thousand computers. Every day a single brain generates more electrical impulses than all the phones in the world.

All innovation begins with a single thought created by a microscopic electronical impulse in the brain. But still science can't explain the why and how of a thought's beginning. Much of what we know about the brain and how it functions has only been revealed in the last 70 years. The scientific understanding and research about how brains function, grow, age, learn is rapidly expanding. The understanding of the brain is growing exponentially, as new discoveries unfold every week.

For all the knowledge that we have about the brain and human psychology, it would be expected that we would have a better understanding of how we create and think. However, when it comes to understanding the creative process and cultivating innovation, our knowledge is still evolving. Creativity is not always celebrated in our educational and business cultures. Creatives can be difficult and take too much time.

The Challenge with Talented and Gifted

Educators have long lamented that there is never support for the talented and gifted students. In our school system, there is often a reverse discrimination against the more intelligent and creative children. It's often a result of resources. Creatives are often forced to perform at a lower level which can cause the spark of genius to be suppressed. Educators are over burden and the multiple-choice testing system rewards conformity rather than development thought. There are great educators who work to develop their student's capabilities however the system and culture are challenged.

Unfortunately, this type of culture is often repeated in business and corporations. Like the over worked educators, too many businesses, work places and corporations don't understand the dynamics of creativity which is the foundation of innovation. Too many corporations, business, foundations, educational institutions and governments are ill equipped to recognize the creative genius in their job pool and if they do they don't know how to support them or cultivate the innovative ideas that can lead to success. To make it even more complicated, in corporations the process of innovation has shifted from a one or two-person process to team collaboration.

Is There A Road Map Of The Innovation Thought Process?

This leads to the question: **Is there a way to map the innovative thought process so it can be repeated and extrapolated for further study?** And if so, what can we learn from the "Innovative Thought process"? Are there principles that act like directives on the road map of innovation? Could there be key indicators that could help guide the way to improve the innovation process? Would it be possible to learn from these to help cultivate the innovators of the future and make innovative-friendly cultures?

The market need for innovative products and processes has never been greater. The emerging markets, lower costs abroad, international competition and internet access to training is leaving America behind. The fast-paced technology, rising cost of testing, compliances, research and rate of advancements require that companies use teams to develop innovative products. The era of the individual innovator creating products has been replaced in corporations with high powered teams who often collaborate globally.

What Does Innovation Mean To My Business?

This pressure is impacting businesses. With all the growing competition, companies need to recognize the potential of innovation and how to embrace it. Entrepreneurs, business leaders, managers and investors, must consider these questions:

- How do I recognize a person with potential and what may be an important innovation or invention for my company?
- How do I help build a strong creative team or help them get work together more effectively?
- Why does one innovation make it to market and others die after the first round of funding?
- What allows companies to creative innovative products year after year and other companies to dry up after a great market run?
- Is there a way to strategically identify keys to healthy ramp-up and ensure market acceptance?

Survival and Success

All success depends upon change and all survival depends upon adaptation to unanticipated change. Innovation is the critical thinking skill that helps people to survive, overcome and succeed regardless of problems and obstacles. Innovation is the single most important life skill foundational for the survival of a company, community, industry, institution or nation.

The "Innovation Process" has universal principles which are foundational and applicable of any technology, process, application or industry. Yet with as important as creative and innovation process is for every business, institution, service or product, there is a lack of definitive information and education about innovation in the general marketplace. Businesses and managers are focused on the bottom line and taking time to encourage, build, stimulate, cultivate and guide the actual process of innovation is a mystery and not a priority. Experts in innovation can be found in Business Schools and large corporations. Research about the cultivation of the innovative process is well known to industry leaders like **Apple, Google, Samsung, and Facebook**, but these are protected trade secrets and not available to the average business person.

In presenting the concept of Holistic Innovation it is our goal to provide education, inspiration, analysis and practical suggestions that can help any person, company or organization, or investment group press on to stronger and higher levels of success. Here are some questions that we have head from business owners, corporate executives, investors or project managers involved with innovative products:

- How can I help guide my teams to success?
- Are there ways to help guide the developmental process to improve productivity?
- What are the key indicators that indicate progress?
- How does one manage a team of talented and gifted individuals that are diverse, independent, visionary and even stubborn?
- When the process seems to be stuck, or cycling through the same issues, how does one kick start the process.
- When do you bail on idea that isn't working?
- How do I help my team communicate effectively and avoid turf wars?

Innovation in Real Time

Innovation is everywhere. It is more than technology, biochemical, engineering, nanotech or artistic expression. Another area of innovation is in the world of television programming. The basic innovative process is demonstrated relentlessly through participants in many "Reality Shows",

Reality television has been the fastest growing genre of television programing since the late 1990s and early 2000. Some of the first Reality Shows, like Queen for a Day, Candid Camera or Truth or Consequences, began in the 1940s-1950s and build an immediate and loyal following. Most began as comedy shows however the expansion of the cable industry and dozens of new networks in late 90's spawned dozens of new shows some good, some bad but always interesting. [26]

~~The basic Reality show invol~~ves an everyday person involved in a conflict, talent competition, game

[26] Wickipedia, Reality Television.

show, special life situation, survival scenario, hoax or similar unscripted situation. Alongside of the America's Got Talent and Biggest Looser, a new genre evolved that is called "Edutainment", meaning that people are educated while being entertained. The popularity of Reality shows has swept the globe with at least ten franchises have had over 30 international adaptations each. (Reality television, from Wikipedia[27]).

The Price is Right!

The major advantage of the Reality shows is they are less expensive to produce than sit-coms, movies or dramas because they don't need elaborate sets, scripts and crews. Combined with the advent of cheaper equipment, smaller cameras, laptop editing, and digital technology, it didn't take long for networks to believe that the price was right. If the shows delivered the "eyeballs" then the advertisers were happy and ordered more shows. The reality genre has grown into over a dozen subgenres and hundreds of shows worldwide. The reason for the worldwide popularity is because of the principles of story, conflict and problem solving[28].

What's Your Line?

From Shark Tank to Myth busters or Fixer Upper to Supernanny many these shows have a common formula. They feature a person with an issue that needs help to discover or activate a solution. There is conflict, drama, emotion and interesting people.

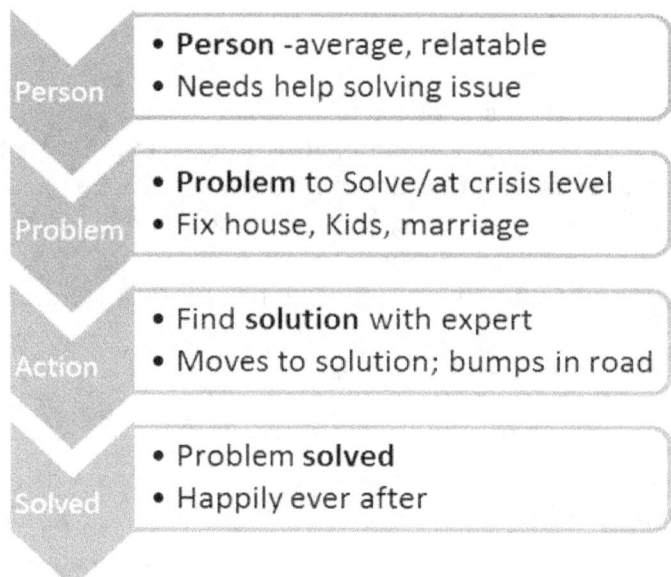

Many reality shows are about creative problem solving (innovation). In a matter of minutes, we get to experience the challenges of others and see if we can think faster or have better solutions to their enhanced problems. We live vicariously through the contestant's struggles.

The Apprentice winner must be able to create, develop, collaborate and execute a concept. The <u>successes of Entrepreneurs</u> on Shark Tank depend upon four things: marketing an idea,

27 Wickipedia, Reality Television.

28 *Levin, Gary (May 8, 2007). "'Simple economics': More reality TV". USA Today.*

presentation pitch, business skill set, and ability to do the deal. In Top Chef, the cooks compete with a limited number of ingredients to make the most memorable dish in a limited time frame. Fixer-upper takes the house with possibilities, brainstorms about preferences and then turns a dream design concept into a reality with a big reveal.

What makes these shows interesting is that we are seeing problem solving and basic innovation in real time. (Psychologist might define the problem solving as more of an adaptation instead of true innovation.) In a few minutes, as the audience we are given the opportunity to walk in the shoes of the participant. We are giving an opportunity to experience their thought process, share the conflict and the tension, wonder how they are going to adapt to each crisis (real and simulated) and judge their decision against our own choices.

Finally, as the ride comes to an end, we see how the person is successful at solving the problem, able to win the rose, or sign the deal. These shows engage by pulling us into the puzzle and give us a glimpse into the mind of the person. We are engaged because we are either cheering someone on, watching them fail or measuring our ability to solve the problem or make a better choice than the contestant.

The innovation process demonstrated in reality shows is about problem solving and life skills rather than the creation of world changing money making products. However, the dozens of reality programs on every network demonstrate that people love watching others be creative, especially the younger generations. There is a new generation of pre-teens and children who are learning from Reality shows how to cook, launch businesses, blow things up, and talk to millionaires.

The Erosion of Innovation in America

With as many reality shows that are on the air, American businesses would be thriving. America has been a leader of innovation in dozens of industries including technology, software, retail, industry, medical, arts, music, film, entertainment and more. But in less than a few decades American has fallen behind in high-tech exports, oil production, manufacturing, many commodities and other industries. Without a doubt innovation is the single most critical factor integral to the survival of any nation, company, or community. As explained in previous chapters, innovation is more than a simple idea it takes a complex organic business ecosystem to grow. It takes capital and valuable resources to incubate a startup company. It also takes time for a company to birth the seed of an idea for a new technology or product. From the seed stage, it is time to feed the idea until it becomes a prototype. This is followed by time and testing and redesigning. And if a company makes it this far the issue of capital and deeper pockets are necessary for a proper market launch.

Like the elephant in the room the questions remains, so how do businesses, investors, and communities support today's innovators and build the innovators of the future? How do we launch centers for innovation that are thriving, successful, sustainable and replicable when even corporation's leaders like Apple, are struggling to create the next big consumer "WOW?" Even the Madison Avenue advertising giants are losing their grip to smaller agencies filled with tech savvy millennials who tap dance through social media, breaking and changing the long-established marketing rules. Meanwhile America faces international completion in the field of innovation, as India, China, and 3rd world companies, with lower cost to market, are pounding the world markets with technology and new products.

Today's world has an unprecedented rate of change and technological advancements. This has redefined the rules that business, corporations and entrepreneurs have depended upon for decades. Different times require different thoughts and radical times require radical paradigm and systematic changes. It is critical that we think differently about innovation, inventors, creatives and how we approach innovation within the culture and companies. The breakneck rate of change means that Agile, the management systems used to improve IT team productivity, should be more than a method, it is a life style. Agility, adaptability, resilience and future casting are character attributes of thriving businesses, boards and companies. Before one can be agile there is a basic issue which need to be addressed, the seed of the idea and where it came from.

Find The Genius In The Room

In the movie, **Hidden Figures**, Kevin Costner's character reproves his manager for oppressing the administrative assistant, Katherine Johnson, who was black, female and an outstanding mathematician. He redirects the manager with these words, "Your job is to find the genius in the room … (and let them work)." This is an important management skill for any leader to remember.

Innovator – Heretic or Hero

Innovator was not always a celebrated position or word. Prior to the 14th century, to be an "Innovator" was an insult and could lead to excommunication for heresy. The reason was that the Catholic Church held the control of the beliefs and scientific advancements. They believed that the Earth was the center of the solar system, the earth was flat and that scientific discovery would cause conflict with faith. Leonardo Da Vince was one of the first to observe that sun did not move.

In the 17th century **Galileo Galilei**, whose breakthroughs ushered in a scientific revolution, presented research supporting the existence of a solar system. Yet, despite being one of the most celebrated scientific minds of his time, he was excommunicated and lived under house arrest for the remainder of his days.

Approximately a century later, Newton was knighted and celebrated for his scientific discovery of gravity. At this point in history the church, unable to stop the emerging scientific discoveries, had reached a truce with the field of science and allowed them to operate outside the role of faith and spiritual explanations[29].

Change and accepting new ideas takes time and paradigms introduced by visionary creatives are often never celebrated until they are dead or long after introduced. One of the major poetic voices of the 60's cultural rebellion, Bob Dillan, the "Unwashed phenomenon"; now fifty years later, was given the Noble Peace prize for literary writing. This is a great reminder of how the prophetic voice of the innovator is rarely understood, embraced or celebrated until decades afterwards. Sadly, Vincent Van Gogh only sold one picture in his lifetime. Today, a Van Gogh painting will be the star attraction of auctions and sell for millions.

Innovation = Change

True innovation is synonymous with change. Like pebbles dropped into a pond the impact of innovation has a rippling affect that expands out. When innovation is adopted it disrupts systems, rocks the status quo, threatens the security, and even more alarming affects financial of existing

---

[29] Scott Peck, *Further Along the Road Less Traveled*, A Touchstone Book, Published by Simon & Schuster, 1993

systems. Change is never comfortable and technology is forcing us all to move faster and learn more and more each day. Automation is replacing workers in service industries and lights out factories. The Internet of Things is merging all our personal computers and devices into one handheld control. Some individuals are threatened by innovation and find the geeks and creative genius too difficult to deal or work with; but, the wise and evolutionary savvy individuals learn to embrace it.

Consider the Innovator

Every year articles and lists are published that identify the greatest influencers in business, technology, government, medical, media, arts, social entrepreneurial efforts, etc. These lists and profiles are interesting to read but, in the last decade, they have expanded exponentially with the emerging markets and technological advancements.

The lists of the top innovators of all history are very familiar[30]. The lists usually contain:

Thomas Edison	Steve Jobs
Nikola Tesla	Wright Brothers
Benjamin Franklin	Alexander Graham Bell
Marie Curie	Louis Pasteur
Galileo Galilei	George Washington Carver
And, Leonardo Da Vinci.	

Who is the greatest, is often debated? If innovation is measured by finished projects then Edison, Carver, and Bell would be tied for accomplishment. If innovation is measured by sales, then Jobs and Gates would win. If innovation is measured by the discovery then Galileo, Tesla and Curie are the choice. But, when innovation is measured by the depth of experience, mastery of technique, classic impact and breadth of vision, then Leonardo da Vinci is undoubtable the greatest genius and master innovator we know.

Leonardo's World

Leonardo was an artist, sculpture, doctor, engineer, musician, architect, city planner, military scientist, mathematician, costume and stage designer, inventor, writer, humorist, and more. He was brilliant in all that he did, even if many projects never were completed due to funding, resources, time and distraction. Leonardo was disciplined and driven by a fire that is unknown to most men but desired by many. His story has simple beginnings but his ending achievements were extraordinary.

Leonardo Da Vinci was born April 15, 1452 in Vinci, Italy the illegitimate son of a prosperous accountant and notary for the city of Florence. He was taken from his mother at the age of five and raised by his paternal grandfather, who was also a notary. Only children born in wedlock were qualified for membership in the Guild of Notaries so he was sent as an apprentice to the master sculpture and artist **Andrea Del Verrocchio**[31].

As a young man, he was known for his talent, good looks, grace, storytelling ability and charm. While under the tutelage of Verrocchio, Leonardo's talent attracted the attention of his prime

---

[30] *Vezzosi, Alessandro (1997). Leonardo da Vinci: Renaissance Man.*
[31] *Ryan Allis, The 12 Greatest Innovators of All Time. The Startup Guide.com.*

patron, Lorenzo de 'Medici. This opened the door to vast community of artists, philosophers, mathematicians and scientists employed and supported by the de' Medici family.

Leonardo was fortunate to have lived in Florence Italy during this extraordinary time of art, discovery and talent. During the 1400's, Florence is considered one to be one of the richest culture and supportive environments for artists of all history. It was in these decades that a series of inventions, including the printing press, compass, clock and long-range cannon and rush for consumer goods fueled exploration and inventions. Renaissance means rebirth and under the patronage of the de Medici's art, philosophy, science and culture flourished.

Cross Cultural Interaction

There were several aspects of the culture and practices of the ruling families that made Florence successful. There was a practice of socializing and dining together regardless of wealth, rank, discipline or culture. The nobles were known to dine with the artists. And the master artists interacted with the craftsmen of different guilds such as stone masons, engineering. This revolutionary culture helped to stimulate ideas, fuel discussion, share techniques and accelerate discoveries.

Additionally, there was a great sense of freedom and protection from religious oppression in Florence. During the late 1400s the inquisitor movement was starting to grow in parts of Europe. When one Catholic priest arrived in Florence with the focus to discover potential heretics, he was thrown out and banished from the city by the rulers at the time. This allowed protection for innovators at a time when others like Galileo were being imprisoned and persecuted.

Leonardo Master of Many

One of the greatest gifts that Leonardo left is his journals and sketch books. In his writings, we can hear his thoughts and questions that lead him in inventions. His drawings were more than images they were meditations that capture the life and form of a flower or wonder of human body. One of the most profound comments about himself and what he considered his talents to be was,

"All our knowledge has its origins in our perceptions"
-- Leonardo da Vinci

Leonardo believed that his greatest contribution and gift was that of observation. He considered his ability to see and observe was what his most important talent. Observation was foundational to the development and growth of Leonardo's multiple areas of expertise.

As an apprentice, he learned; as a master, he taught others. In every field, he brilliantly studied and disciplined himself into level of mastery. Leonardo identified the capabilities that allowed him to excel into the Seven Intelligences.

These were the aptitudes that Leonardo attributed to his diversity of talent. **Leonardo's Seven Intelligences are:**

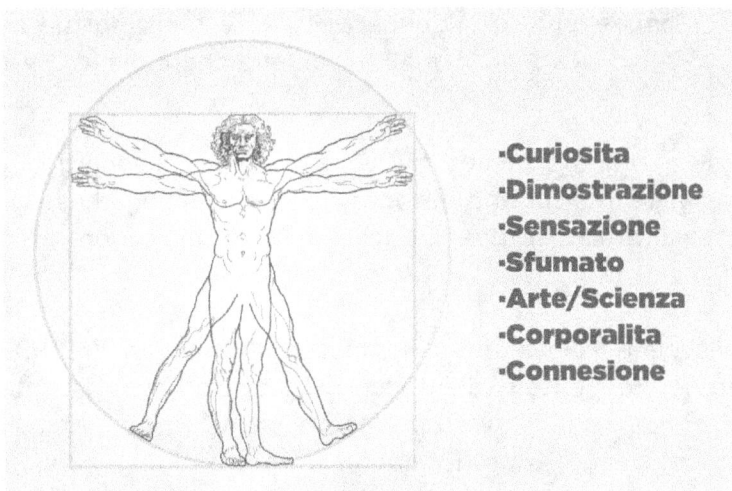

In his bestselling book, **How to Think Like Leonardo da Vinci**, **Michael Gelb** translates these terms into practical terms. Gelb explains these principles with exercises that help individuals learn to think and develop these skills. Here are the Seven Intelligences and the meaning, based on Gelb's interpretation[32]:

Meaning	**Seven Intelligences**	**Definition (M. Gelb)**
Curious Observant	Curiosita	Insatiably curious approach to life. Power of observation, Quest for lifelong learning
Independent Thinking	Dimostrazione	Independent thinking. Test knowledge through experience, persistence
Sensory Awareness	Sensazione	Senses. Awareness of the five senses, especially sight and enliven the experience
Embrace Paradox	Sfumato ("Going up in Smoke"	Embrace ambiguity, paradox, uncertainty. Holding conflicting truths at same time. Literally means going up in Smoke.
Whole Brain Thinking	Arte/Scienza	Balance between art and science. Whole-brain thinking
Balance control	Corporalita	Physical grace, poise, fitness, dexterity. Balance mentally, physically and artistically.

---

[32] *Michael J. Gelb, How to Think like Leonardo da Vinci, 1998, Bantam Dell, Random House, Inc. New York.*

7 Steps to Think like Leonardo da Vinci: The Guide to Everyday Genius, Andrea Balt, April 4, 2014 Creative Rehab blog @ andreabalt.com

Connections and Connessione Systems	Connectivity – recognizing the interconnectivity of all things and phenomena. Systems Thinking

Like his anatomical drawings and sketches of flying machines, Leonardo's perceptions about the way the mind functions were radical and visionary. In explaining these areas, Gelb has helped millions to recognize their own capabilities and learn how to think more a genius, if only for a few moments.

Leonardo's areas of holistic intelligence are still impacting our world. In 1983, they were used as a model by Howard Gardner to develop the modern theory of multiple intelligences. Gardner, a development psychologist work and Harvard professor, identified nine areas of intelligence. These nine intelligences represent a more "Holistic" approach to evaluating individuals. It recognizes the multiple dimensions of a person's capabilities from physical, sensory, emotional, logical, and experiential. Gardner's multiple intelligences model created a paradigm shift in education that challenged the more restrictive definition of IQ. Gardner's nine intelligences are still being researched, and many believe that there are more than nine[33]. A new model from **Gallup, Clifton StrengthsFinders** identifies 34 different talent themes.

Gardner's Nine Intelligences

Naturalist	Nature smart	**Logical-Mathematical**	Number/reasoning smart
Musical	Sound smart	**Existential**	Life smart
Linguistic	Word smart	**Bodily-kinesthetic**	Body smart
Spatial	Picture smart	**Intra-personal**	Self-smart
Inter-personal	People smart		

Genius, Intelligence and Innovation

So, does this mean that successful innovation depends upon intelligence or a high IQ? According to experts, the answer is no. An innovator may be a genius but a genius may not be an innovator. The person with the highest IQ ever recorded, **Marilyn vos Savant** (IQ 228) is a question-and-answer columnist for Parade Magazine. **Psychologist J. P. Gilford**, conducted an extensive study in the 60's and concluded that creativity is not the same as intelligence. Meaning that a personal can be far more creative than they are intelligent, or more intelligent than they are innovative[34].

A high IQ will contribute to the innovation process, but the innovation does not depend solely on intelligence. Innovators have a combination of intellect with passion, will, emotions, spirit, skills and adaptability. Innovators have discipline to see a job through and regardless of the time and sacrifice make it happen. But they may need help to stat and support to help push them through to

[33] Gardner, Howard (1983), *Frames of Mind: The Theory of Multiple Intelligences*, Basic Books.

[34] Michael Michaiko, How Genius Think, April 28, 2012 Creativitypost.com/how geniuses think.

the completion.

"Innovation" is a separate area of intelligence that needs to be measured and studied. I would suggest perhaps, "Innovation Intelligence" may need to be added to the nine intelligences in Gardner's model. But the question remains, how can we measure a person's innovation quotient? Is innovation in the genes that one is born with? Or is innovation a behavior or skill that can be trained and cultivated?

A Profile of an Innovator

My grandfather, **Edward "Burke" Wilford 2nd** was an electrical engineer, inventor, early aircraft design engineer, visionary and humanitarian. One of his early inventions was motorizing a dental chair (something that I whisper a thank you for every time I'm at the dentist.) He had a wide range of interests which were focused on how to improve the world. In the 1930's, he identified the preventive need for annual checkups. He wrote and self-published a pamphlet which he took in person to meetings with heads of major Insurance companies. Those that he couldn't meet with he mailed a copy with letters encouraging them to change the policies and make the Annual Check-up a standard preventive practice.

Like all inventors, my grandfather loved a challenge in a new field. **The Franklin Institute** gave him an award in 1939 for his invention that controlled the speed of small motors. (This was the first multispeed mixer and became known as "Mix master".) Harold Vanderbilt owes one of his America's cup victories to Burke Wilford's innovations. He used his expertise in aeronautical design to redesign the rig system for The Ranger yacht in 1937. My grandfather would tell us that he was very sleep deprived when they worked on this because Vanderbilt wanted him to play cards (bridge) all night.

Of all of the areas that my grandfather worked in, he was passionate about and dedicated to the field of Aircraft development. He was an aircraft pioneer who designed and built the first gyrocopter for the Navy in 1931 and contributed to development of the rotary system for helicopters. In his office, there were always blueprints, drawings and models of aircraft, motors, sail boats and engine parts. When visiting his office, all of the grandchildren would be required to hear him explain how the different designs worked and why they were important to the future. Burke Wilford 2nd had a very generous spirit and, much to my grandmother's surprise, he helped other aircraft pioneers with financial support.

Decades after his passing, while watching the science fiction movie **Avatar**, I felt like my grandfather was with me. It was at the beginning of the battle scene on the alien planet; when the fleet of aircraft was headed into destroy the natives' energy source. As I watched the futuristic aircraft, that were part plane part helicopter, that I could hear my Grandfathers words. These aircraft were giant tilt wing air craft that functioned like fighter jets but could hover at slow speeds like helicopters. The giant tilt wing propellers could move (tilt up) from front to top position and give maximum mobility and speed. They are called VTOL aircraft (Vertical takeoff and landing). These were not futuristic aircraft to me, but familiar because we had seen pictures like these on the walls of my grandfather's office. This was normal to us as he loved to describe how they worked and why they were so important to the future of the military and safety of lives.

As I watched the remainder of the Avatar Movie I was both sad and inspired. Sad that my grandfather never got to see how much the technology he loved is being integrated today. At the same time, I was grateful that my life had been blessed with a person who was an inventor and visionary with a huge heart of generosity.

He was pioneer that was passionate about helping improve the lives of others and wanted desperately to help our nation. To his credit many of his children, grandchildren and great grandchildren are carrying on the legacy of creativity, innovation, compassion and love of family.

The Passion of the Innovator

So why does an Inventor invent, artist create or a designer build? From the true innovators and inventors, I have had the privilege to know, some build and sold great companies with financial reward and fame but underneath the success there is a force from within that is core. For many it is an internal drive that seeks out the challenge and once it is solved, they lose interest and go to the next challenge.

There is a passion and drive to create, design, build, test and launch that is as basic as breathing. There is a commitment that makes their head like flint that gives them the strength to blow through the hardest wall. There is a joy and satisfaction of building something new. There is a gift of seeing that is as far reaching as an eagle.

On another level, the innovator has an intuitive or gut level sense of why an invention is important. Most innovators share a desire to make the world a better place and contribute to the greater good. Some call this faith other call it ego. For many, and not to minimize the need for profits and market success, innovation is about the world. Many innovators want to create something that will make a difference, such as a better product, better system, medical discovery, consumer product and more. There is a passion, love, drive, desire, dream, curiosity, analysis and research all wrapped and twisted together.

Summary

The Mind of the Innovator is complex and unique. There are different types of Intelligences from which different colors, flavors and types of Innovation evolve. The process of innovation is a basic need and drive but can be illusive as a unicorn.

An innovator may be a genius but you don't have to be a genius to be an innovator. Not all geniuses are good innovators. Innovators have a combination of intellect with passion, will, emotions, spirit, skills and adaptability. Innovators have discipline to see a job through and regardless of the time and sacrifice make it happen. But they may need help to stat and support to help push them through to the completion.

Companies know that innovation can be nurtured and developed in teams and individuals. The process of business building through project management has established successful protocols and methods. However, the innovators of the future and innovative teams need to be understood, supported and cultivated. One way to approach is by analyzing the dynamics of the thought process of innovation.

The focus of these chapters is not to be the final word, but; to be a glimpse and overview of the creative process, which is both wondrous and mysterious at the same time. Everyone and every team has the capability to create. The challenge is how to encourage potential innovators, teach and develop new innovators, breath hope into discouraged innovators and instruct managers and investors so that they can cultivate innovation in their spheres of influence. The human mind and capability of humans to create and adapt is remarkable. Creativity is the first action that was taken by the Almighty and, if indeed we were made in His image, then creativity is a gift that we must explore.

In the next chapter, **The Innovation Thought Matrix,** will examine the process, principles and patterns of the Innovative process. The chapter will identify the five-step thought process and the contributions that individuals make to the team. This insight will give understanding about the ingredients of innovation and how they blend and build toward success.

12 THE INNOVATION THOUGHT MATRIX

Lynn Scarborough

Introduction

Every innovation begins with a single thought that is invisible. That invisible thought is like a seed, pregnant with opportunity, waiting to grow, longing to flourish, and hoping to be made real. So how does that seed of a thought grow? Does it grow like a tree with roots and branches or is it like a vine that produces more fruit only when pruned?

As an idea grows, are there universal patterns of thought that a successful innovator follows? Like an invisible migratory pattern, is there a "true north" or invisible gravitation force that pulls the innovative process into completion? And when we study those patterns can we discover principles that can be mapped and replicated?

In a world of team innovation, what makes a creative team successful? Is the pattern different or like that of a successful entrepreneur? What are the dynamics at play for dynamic collaboration? How do their minds and thoughts engage? How do they connect, challenge, push and strengthen the innovative process?

For business owners, corporate executives, investors or project managers involved with innovative products, how can you help guide your teams to success? Are there ways to help a team remember the budget and bottom line? What are the key indicators that indicate progress? How does one manage a team which is diverse, intelligent, creative, independent, visionary and even stubborn?

Exploring the Roadmap of Innovative Thought

As we learned from the previous chapter, the mind of the innovator is a multi-dimensional, complex and fascinating; although it is still virtually uncharted territory. For teams of innovators the potential expands exponentially. When the capabilities of innovators and innovative teams are supported and directed it can lead to spectacular inventions and remarkable advancements.

This chapter will address the journey of the innovative mind and identify the dynamics through the

Innovative Thought Matrix. The Innovation Thought Matrix is a holistic model that groups the phases and cognitive questions (or thought zones) that are universal to the innovative process. These phases are a "whole-brain" approach inclusive of all portions of the brain. The exploration of these concepts will help innovators, managers, entrepreneurs and businesses understand, encourage and integrate innovative-friendly practices in addition to trouble shooting and guiding groups when needed.

The five phases of innovative thought include:

- **Conceptualization**
- **Visualization**
- **Application (Utilization)**
- **Evaluation**
- **Incubation**

Why Innovative Thought Matrix

Quantifying and qualifying the process of innovation is not an easy challenge. The name Innovative Thought Matrix was derived for several reasons.

1. A "Thought Matrix" gives a 3-D image of the holistic process. The process of development is unique to each person, team and innovation. A developmental process can be linear, circular, networking, multilayered or a combination of these and more.
2. A Matrix is like a brain - in structure (neurological connectivity), function and the ability to process in a thousand directions simultaneously. A "Thought Matrix" has multiple layers of connectivity, functionality and process.
3. Matrix means origin, mold and "mother". The word 'matrix comes from 14th Century English word, **matris** which derived from the Latin matrix, which was a female animal kept for breeding purposes. Matrix is also a derivative of the word mater or mother.

Dictionary Definition[35] of *Matrix*

1.   something within or from which something else originates, develops, or takes form
2a: a mold from which a relief; die: an engraved or inscribed die or stamp.

Matrix is also a symbolic allegory. When most people hear the word "matrix" they usually think of the sci-fi **movie** series **Matrix**. In this popular series with cutting edge special effects, the normal world is only an illusion because the human race is enslaved by aliens in a giant industrial web.

The challenge of the hero is can he develop the mental control, break free from the Matrix web and crush the evil net into submission and free the world? Of course, he does but, only after his pain gives him the strength to build an alternative reality and use the matrix's energy against itself. Matrix illustrates how complex, resilient, resourceful and determined that the brain is when forced to survive.

---

[35] Merriam-Webster.

In examining the process of Innovative the Matrix helps define the process because like innovation a matrix is:

- Unique in form
- Created and like the structure of the brain
- Innovation is a birthing process and matrix derives from the word mother.
- And finally, a matrix is a symbolic analogy of the challenge that each person must conquer to discover their destiny and save the world.

Before addressing each of these areas, it is important to identify some of attributes contributing the road to innovation.

Mining for Innovation

Like diamond mining, great innovation and ideas are rarely on the surface. It takes time and hard labor to dig to reach the gems. Once found diamonds must be shaped and cut with care to extract their true beauty. In a company, a manager may not have to dig for ideas but it is necessary to create an environment where creative ideas and solution can come to the surface. Additionally, a diamond needs work and skill to reach its true potential, likewise, ideas will pass through a developmental process that helps them grow into innovators.

Innovation Requires TOT – "Time on Task"

The advantage of a media flooded world is that people have incredible access to instant information. The disadvantage is that the conception of time, effort and "time on task" is distorted so that people think that their experience will be like the "Celebrity Inventor" and immediately snatch the golden ring and deal in ten minutes.

An innovative process that is summarized in 60 seconds is not fully conveying the amount of time, sweat and energy that went into its development. Television, news and information compress the time demand of a project. Shows like Shark Tank help inventors by giving them funding to start but it is important for future inventors to remember that the process is not as easy as it looks and for everyone that succeed, there's hours of projects that have failed.

Great innovation takes time. While having a "Kick starter" success or creator of disruptive technology may seem glamourous, but it is not as easy as sounds. The innovative process is not a "microwave process". The invention or product may take decades to get to the market and for every one that becomes a hit, there are 100s and even thousands that never see the camera lights. Innovation is a layered process that takes hundreds if not thousands of hours.

Five Phases of the Innovative Thought Matrix

The five phases of the innovation turn the unseen into a visible reality. Understanding the attributes of the Mind of Innovation will help to increase awareness and promote stronger and more advanced and innovative thinking and inventions. The mental creative process is similar with layers of thoughts, evaluation, testing and discussion required to bring it to life.

The growth Innovative Thought Matrix process is unique to everyone or team; however, there are five distinct phases which contribute to the success of the concept, invention or project. The

Innovative Thought Matrix is a way of analyzing the phases of thought that contributes to a successful innovation. The concept and launch of all products flow through each of these phases multiple times and grows from the questions and answer that a person or team addresses.

The five phases are:

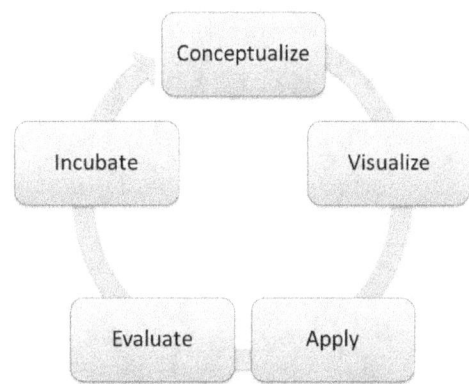

Every Process is Unique

Every mind is unique and so is the creative process. The five phases are listed in a circle sequence which is a logical order of development but is not necessarily correct for all innovations. Creative thinking and problem solving are individual and holistic processes which incorporate all parts of the person and the team. Great problem solving engages the "Whole Brain and the "Whole Person". It calls upon the mind – cognitive, memories, conscious, subconscious, experiences, emotions, passions, spirit, and physical state.

Holistic Innovation is not about a specific map that if followed will lead to great innovation but instead it provides the tools that you can use to chart your own journey. The Innovation Thought Matrix provides a list of questions, thoughts, and questions that are found in the journey of innovation but the way, sequence and how they are processed are unique to everyone and person.

How Does This Differ From Design Or Project Management Cycles?

Please note that in other design process they use the terms Concept, Design, Application, Testing and Funding. The concept of the terms is approximately the same, but the terms of the Innovative Thought Matrix are based on the cognitive thought process not the outcomes of each stage. In project management for IT, military and corporate manufacturing there are six stages of project management. The purpose of project management is to help guide and execute a contract project not develop new inventions. The focus is delivery of specific goods and services based on a contractual arrangement. Project Management utilizes the phases of the Innovative Thought Matrix, but the focus is on performance not development. The six phases of Project Management are: Initiation, Definition, Design, Development, Implementation, and Follow-up.

Five Phases Origins

The five phases are based upon an industrial management testing model and the corporate training model used by Empower.com for media and "Strategic Business Communication training". The first four phases address the types of thought processes and the fifth is the culture which contributes to the completion of an innovative project.

The aspects of first four phases are based upon the contributions and strengths of the four personality styles developed by the **DiSC behavioral Assessment Tool** which was pioneered by William Moulton in 1928 and then later adapted for businesses by **Walter V. Clarke**, an industrial psychologist. (3)

The **DiSC** is used by over a million people every year and helps improve teamwork, productivity, leadership, communication and for job screening by employers. The letters DiSC stand for the four major behavior areas of:

- **D   Dominate**
- **I   Influencer**
- **S   Steady/Stabilizer**
- **C   Concise**

Each of the DISC areas have various strengths and thought processes that they use to thrive, function and adapt. The following chart gives a summary of the traits of each of the DISC behavior traits.

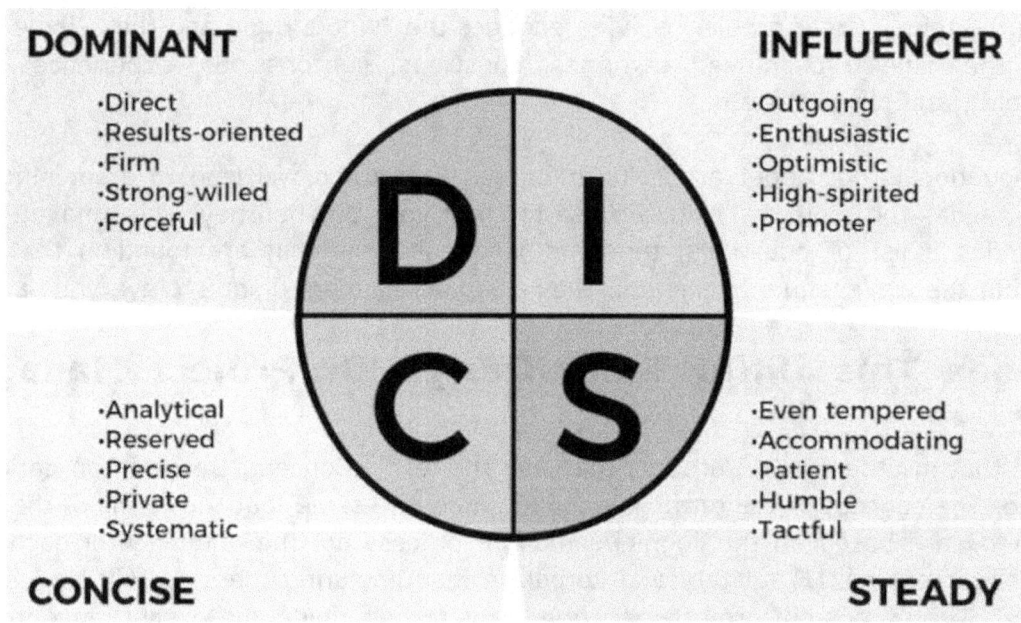

Each of the DiSC profiles has strengths which support work and person success.

Research has shown that most people will have dominance in two areas, even though they use all the areas in different situations.

It is easy to see how people with **"D"** or dominant behavior trends will be needed in leadership positions or jobs that require immediate results like sales or construction. Individuals with a strong **"I"** profile make great promoters, advertisers and cheerleaders. The **"S"** or steady person can excel as a counselor, teacher and manager. The **"C"** is ideal for research, investigative and work that requires detail and testing.

Each of the behavior styles contribute valuable imputes and service to the innovative process which need to be utilized by the project manager or supervisor. When a project needs direction then the **"D"** will provide focus or the **"C"** will have research to provide guidelines. If a project is stuck, then the **"I"** individual can see opportunities or the **"S"** will remind a team about the core customer's needs.

Communication conflicts and disconnects often happen because of differing perspectives of individuals. For example, if a supervisor with a strong **"D"** or direct leader role asks for a summary of a project, what they usually expect is a short concise answer of how close to the goal they are.

However, if a team member with a dominant **"S"** or Steady behavior gives a long explanation of how everyone is doing instead of addressing the specific goals and accomplishments, then the **"D"** supervisor will not think that the **"S"** person is professional enough and may cut them off in a meeting to save time.

When the **"S"** is cut off they may shut down because they think the "D" leader is rude and disrespectful.

DiSC a Model for Holistic Innovation

The four parts of the DISC profile is a very concise and easily understood model that identifies the strengths of each personality style. Along with thousands of other corporations, I have used this testing method to build managers, increase skill levels, identify strengths, build teams, facilitate projects, construct strategic plans, support media training, reduce conflict, and kick start a "dead in the water" project. When I began to try to chart the cognitive process of innovation, it became obvious that the principles of the DiSC model had value.

The foundation of the Innovation Thought Matrix is based on the DiSC model because this provides a way to succinctly capture all the contributions that a holistic process provides. The strengths and contributions of each of the four DiSC behavior patterns - Dominant, Inspiration, Steady, Concise – align with the innovative process. The fifth phase is the Incubation which is the culture or environment, which insures or stimulates the growth and success of any invention or team.

Phase One – Concept stage. The **"D"** personality traits can provide the driving force that has the strength to identify the need for a product and the fortitude to drive a project to the finish line. The "D" team member may not be the originator of an idea but they are often the champion when they believe in the value. The "D" behaviors are aligned with the Concept or the birth of a project because when they will see an opportunity, they will back it, sound the trumpet, assign tasks, push forward and identify deadlines for a project.

Phase Two – Visualize stage. Consider the Visual-I-zer. The **"I"** personality can dream, promote and visualize a project for others so that a design structure can be realized. This is the time when teams "fall in love" with an idea. The "I" tends to see bigger, higher and farther into the future than others which can be both inspiring and overwhelming to managers. The "I" personality has a network of contacts they can draw into a project. The "I" has a strong sense of play and right brain function that makes the innovative process fun, unites the team and prevents burnout.

Phase Three – Application stage. The **"S"** personality is stable, grounded in details and sensitive to the community around them. The "S" has the need to understand why and how projects will impact the group, customer and team. The "S" personality can put a face on the customer, has the heart to care about customers' needs and the ability to build community. Knowing who the customer is and the market application of an invention is the core of success and the value that the "S" profile provides.

Phase Four – Evaluation stage. The "**C**" profile stands for concise and correct which is why the "C" is identified with the Evaluation or Testing phase. This personality tends to have strong skills in researching, teaching, developing, and analysis. The conscientious C will provide critical analysis, tireless testing and boldness to ask tough questions even at the risk of angering others and missing deadlines. In a well-balanced team the "C' will drive the questions deeper, challenge the status quo and improve quality control.

Phase Five – Incubation stage. The Fifth phase in the Innovation Thought process is Incubation. The Incubation phase provides the time and support that an invention, technology, or innovation needs to grow. Without support, guidance, resources, time and appropriate incubation, ideas will never be brought into reality. It is as simple as an artist needs time to paint and a startup company needs the right environment and resources to get to market.

In the corporate and startup worlds, support and the culture is the responsibility of the managers, business owners and entrepreneurs. Incubation is critical to innovative growth and has a variety of names. In the business world, these are called Incubators. Corporations call it, Research and Development. In the theater world, it is called "Off-Broadway." Artists call it patrons and mentors. Most major cities are developing Business Incubators but the success rate depends upon the understanding and commitment to the innovators and the process.

Dissecting the Layers of Innovation

When we dissect the layers of thought that comprise an invention, like the anatomical sketches of Leonardo, it helps us to see the muscles and bone structure of the body.

When we look closely at each of the five phases we discover that each phase makes different contributions to the innovative process. Each phase has specific key indicators or questions that are attributed to that phase. In the same way, the five phases of ITM are like the structure or skeleton of an invention and the key indicator questions are like the muscles that give the body strength and form.

For managers and team leaders, understanding these phases and the key indicator questions will give support to the process of innovation and recognize when the process gets stuck or in a rut. The Innovative Thought Matrix is a holistic approach that helps to understand the Innovative process from 360" and 3-D view point. Here are the diagram of **The Five Phases of the Innovation Thought Matrix** and the key attributes produced by each of the phases:

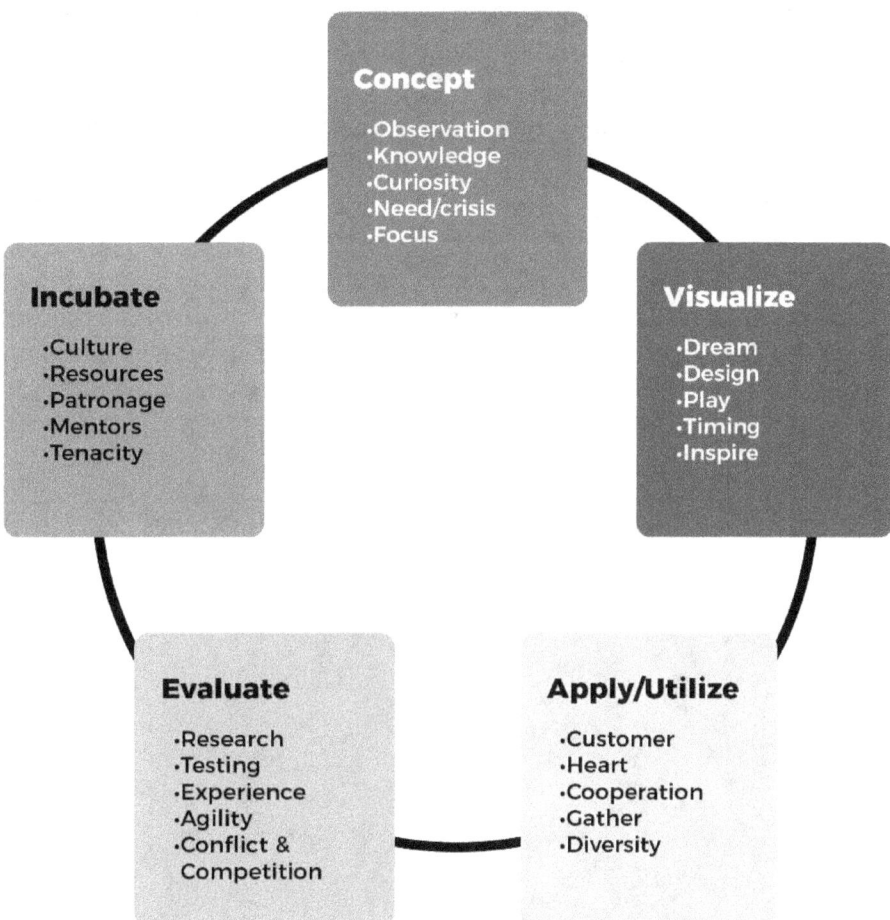

These five phases are universal concepts of the design process. The information can flow from back and forth from any of the phases as it progresses. The questions for each area will spark more discussion. As questions are asked repeatedly, layers are added to the concept. Then it is shaped, designed, tested, evaluated, analyzed, questioned, tested, redesigned, over and over until it is ready to be launched.

This process is fluid, spontaneous and cycles like a spiral in all directions. The energy will drive the project forward and hopefully in the right direction. The cycle is expansive and ideally grows in multiple ways at same time.

a. Goes deeper into research
b. Goes higher to expand for scaling up into the market
c. Goes wider/larger with inclusion of more entities and phases
d. Goes broader with diversity of application into additional industries

Summary

Journey to Innovation: Each innovation process is a unique journey. Genius may combine with intelligence to birth an invention; but, training, education, environment, mentoring, visual, experience and testing also contribute to the foundation.

There are many ways to define the innovative journey but the like a compass there are critical stages and questions that every innovator or development team must ask, answer, test, analyze, adjust, test and retest. For innovative teams, it is important to maximize the strengths and contributions of each member of the team and minimize weaknesses and reduce conflict.

Even though the process of innovation is different for individuals or teams, there are universal thought phases that together create a matrix that holds success. The five phases of the Innovative Thought Matrix are: Concept, Visualize, Apply, Analyze and Incubate. Identifying these phases can help guide, accelerate and increase the chances of success for an innovation or invention. The phases of the Innovative Thought Matrix can be used for questioning and project development by creatives, inventors, designers and project managers. When questions for each area are presented it will spark discussion, deepen analytical function, address roadblocks, enhance creativity and build stronger business and marketing plans.

13 THE ROLE OF SPIRITUALITY IN INNOVATION

Phillip Andrews

Introduction

Spirituality is one of these words that are difficult to define because it means so many different things to different people based on their religions, ethnic backgrounds, methods of prayer, accepted symbols and ceremonies, education level, IQ, EQ, SQ and other factors. One thing we know for sure about spiritual people is that their temporal lobe is busier than other folks' brains. One definition that works pretty well (according to **Todd Murphy**) for spirituality is *"being prone to altered states of consciousness"*. Murphy explains that *"It doesn't matter whether a person is drawn to union with God, 'oneness with the universe', the state of total 'emptiness' of Zen, the experience of channeling the spirits as a medium, or to heal others through prayer or 'energy'."* What matters is that each person is capable (has the ability) to reach higher levels of consciousness and awareness that allow that person to see the world, situations and issues under a "different light".

Furthermore, spirituality is one of the most maligned words in our culture (just like the words "Holistic" and "Sustainability". It has been attacked by religious leaders, political leaders, scientists, intellectuals, philosophers, activists, atheists, brain-dead people, and everyone else that works and lives at the low levels of human needs and/or suffers from insufficient brain and spiritual powers and "gifts" from God or nature. Those that don't believe in spirituality this chapter is a waste of their time as it is not written in order to convince them that spirituality is real and it has value. It is written for those people that already believe in it and want to leverage it the right way.

It is interesting that even great authors that have written books about spirituality in business avoid using the term. They would rather call managers and businesses "conscious", "mindful", "humane", "virtuous", "righteous", and "awakened". The only aspect that businesses are willing to adapt is the ethical part that is reflected in their **Codes Of Conduct**, employee contracts, and the typical values and beliefs (such as Integrity, Honesty and Cooperation). It is apparent that most people have been brainwashed to believe that spirituality does not belong in the business world, and by believing that that they end up suffering a mental block of how it fits. This is one of the biggest myths in business because certain styles of management, organizational designs, cultures and even product designs are soaked and marinated in spirituality. It is very hard for one to be a loving, caring, thoughtful and compassionate person and not be a spiritual person[36].

Spirituality affects every aspect of the business, including the business model, higher purpose, strategic intent, product design, service design, organization structure, style of leadership, relationships and partnerships and everything else ... everything that craves innovation and creativity! And yet most people are brainwashed to avoid this discussion (about spirituality) as if it will damage the reputation of the enterprise! Very few people realize that spirituality plays a major role in innovation and that it could be a major tool and technique for innovation.

Personal Anecdote: In one **Spirituality In Business** Workshop, one attendee went as far as to ask the presenter if he was a member of a cult. The presenter very politely responded *"No"* and continued his lecture, which was great and I personally agreed with everything he had to say. However, he made one comment that bothered me pertaining to spirituality. In order to remove any negative thoughts or feelings towards spirituality, he said that *"words do not matter ... they are nothing"*. Well, they do matter and they do make a huge difference in the attitude of the people of how they see and translate things in their own brains. Words affect thoughts, and thoughts affect feelings / emotions, attitudes, and behaviors. Some doctors go as far as to say that they affect a person's physiology as well. Did you notice that spiritual people have calmer and gentler faces? Their very physical appearance exudes confidence, trust and hope --- all key ingredients for innovation.

Lessons Learned: Be careful of the words that you use. Don't be afraid to use the word spirituality --- be proud of it because it is a good label to have on your forehead --- it declares who you are!

By the way, here are the **main points** of that workshop:

- Spirituality In Business revolves around "seeing, experiencing and practicing the spirit"
- Spirituality without action is useless and pointless
- Spirituality has positive impact on productivity and profits
- Spirituality starts with having a higher purpose, a shared vision and a common agenda
- Spirituality must be maintained and "fed" continuously by:
  - Reinforcing the spiritual culture --- (... and exiting those that are toxic employees; ensuring that agreements and promises are kept; applying shared measurements ... and sharing the gains)
  - Pursuing mutually reinforcing activities
  - Communicating continuously 360^0
  - Making everyone around you better ... every day
- Spirituality is you. Foster an environment of integrity, trust, optimism, cooperation, open communications, and community (of brothers and sisters). Offer continuous encouragement, support and guidance
  - Be the "light"

---

[36] For a person to be spiritual at home and anti-spiritual (or totally void of spirituality) at work implies compartmentalization of the brain that leads to all kinds of psychological and mental problems. Most people do not realize that they are doing that to themselves. This is why we have so many executives (and employees) that suffer mental illnesses, mental breakdowns and burnouts (according to The Center for Association Leadership and other institutions and researchers). **Professor Campbell** proclaimed that some people even fall in their own personal "abyss", when their careers (and associated behaviors) take them away from their bliss and true character.

o Be the teacher and Zen Master. Show people how to reach higher levels of achievement, excellence, awareness and consciousness; enlighten people
o Be the "glue"
o Be the "positive energy"
o Be the cheerleader; be the backbone of continuous support
o Support personal growth
o Lead by example

Spirituality's Influences

Spirituality of course influences everything in life and offers a rich array of stimuli to people that are in tune with it. Thus, smart people espouse and welcome spirituality as it opens their minds and eyes to possibilities that are invisible to others. Spirituality affects all aspects of the business (incl. strategy, org structure, style of management, culture, processes, relationships, and ecosystems), but here we only address (very briefly) a handful of areas, such as the ones listed below:

a) **Inspiration** affects:
   i. **Product Designs** by following certain spiritual design rules (see segment below).
   ii. **Processes** by pursuing green and sustainable principles (including new processes to create those products, and the know-how to take them from raw materials to finished products --- and place them in the hands of eager customers and consumers).
   iii. **Services** by exciting, thrilling and enthusing customers (turning them into repeat clients). We have seen countless Customer Service scenarios out there that their only purpose is to get rid of customers and defend the company at all costs. They have installed impersonal computerized answering systems and useless websites with FAQs that not only do not help the customer, but add to the irritation of having to deal with them. **Microsoft** is one of the worst offenders as one cannot get answers to what they need. If Microsoft did not have such a lock on the market due to its established product, it would have been blown out of the marketplace as an unfeeling, uncaring and unsympathetic company.

b) (Personal and collective) **Physical, Emotional and Spiritual Health** --- by supporting and maintaining good health one is able to obtain an all-around perspective of what is needed in a holistic solution. In other words:

Holistic Health ←→ Holistic Thinking → Holistic View → Holistic Solution

It is difficult for one to come up with holistic solutions when her/his total health is ailing. The question arises, how was Steven Jobs able to come up with so many great ideas while he was suffering from cancer? The answer is that most of his ideas were circulating in his head for years. Some geniuses need a gestation period prior to unveiling their ideas. Moreover, **Jobs** was smart enough to surround himself with great people that could turn his vision and dreams into reality.

c) **Awareness / Insight** --- spiritual people have sort of a 6th and 7th sense that makes them very keen of other people's feelings, unspoken words or requirements, tacit or inferred desires, wants or wishes, delicate situations, and uneasy state of affairs

Spirituality's Influence On Product Design

Let's continue with the **Microsoft Company** as their products are characteristic of what anti-spiritual designs are all about. They are focused on functionality and ease of use, but not what people want to see and how to use their products. It is almost certain that their brainstorming sessions consist of requirements gathering pertaining to new "bells and whistles". No one bothered to ask clients what bothers them and irritates them. No one bothered to ask what the customers want to see. No one bothered to ask how customers use their products. They have taken the approach of *"We know better because we are the technical gurus"*. This exactly why **Apple** and others took so much market share away from them, and the trend will continue until Microsoft wakes up to the fact that customers and their habits matter.

Being in tune with customers' true needs and wants and market trends in general is a spiritual exercise. Avoiding irritations and negative feelings is part of it, and so is avoiding losing customers. Smart and spiritual companies try all they can to maintain their customer base and turn everyone into clients. Most major companies have instituted programs that collect the voice of the customer (VOC) and encourage customer loyalty, but then turn them into meaningless and mindless processes pretending to be responsive to customers. In many cases Customer Service is a joke and a façade.

Automating customer-facing processes is an anti-spiritual practice. Making things impersonal, in general, is anti-spiritual. The minute people talk to machines instead of people, the spiritual bond/connection is broken.

Companies are treated by law as human beings that have all kinds or rights, protections and privileges. Unfortunately, most corporations have forgotten that wholesome human beings have three dimensions: **Body** (physical) – **Mind** (intellectual and psychological) – **Soul** (spiritual).

Companies like individuals that ignore the Soul aspects of our existence miss all the important points in life, and live superficial lives, without meaning, without purpose, without real value, and without substance. In other words, they are inconsequential in more ways than one. They live lives for the mere purpose of existence and making a living. But this is not life, or what life is all about.

So, **how does all that affect product design?** Very simply one must follow certain principles, such as the ones shown here:

- Offer a product that:
  - Represents an **inspired design** (this is where art matters)
    - Is based on holistic thinking (exciting Body-Mind-Soul)
    - Utilizes **sacred geometry** (like the golden ration, balance, symmetry and anchored geometry)
    - Makes technology transparent and "unobtrusive" to the user
      - Offers seamless interfaces between man and machine
        - Makes technology and machines an extension of people's abilities, skills, and senses
        - Diffuses technology-based tools and techniques
    - Leverages human factors engineering and ergonomics

- Offers real value to society and human race
- Shares knowledge and wisdom --- improves understanding
  - Helps people become better people
  - Helps people reach higher levels of existence
  - Advances the abilities and competencies of people
- Makes life better and better
- Is responsive to customer needs (incl. seasonality and flexibility)
  o Encourages **social innovation and transformation**
    - Provides new lifestyle choices
    - Enables and utilizes "good" technologies
    - Engages the community --- delivers more linkages/connections
    - Promotes social and emotional well-being
  o Obeys the **Green and Sustainability** rules
    - Does not harm the planet or beings
    - Eliminating all types of pollution
    - Mitigates packaging materials
    - Reduces energy requirements
    - Reduces use of fresh resources
    - Utilizes the right (green) materials)
      - Supports the Circular Economy (w/closed loop value chains)
    - Reduces ecological footprint, etc.
  o Invigorates/stimulates the **economy** and promotes **economic vitality**
    - Offers a financially viable product
    - Creates jobs locally
    - Enriches the community (beyond jobs and taxes)
    - Uses local products and services to help the local community

One can write an entire book on this subject alone, but our purpose here is simply to illustrate that spirituality plays a major role in inventing the next generation of products and services. People and enterprises that ignore the spiritual aspects of our existence are zombies or walking dead[37].

Spirituality-Based Techniques For Innovation

There are techniques aimed to help individuals and there are techniques to help teams/groups with inspiration, imagination and insights. Both sets of techniques are valuable to everyone. It is impossible to address all of them in this chapter, thus we will focus our attention to two of them, without discussing the specifics or how-tos.

a. Channeling

In **Ancient Greece** people immediately assigned spiritual traits and gifts to creative people, such as poets, artists / sculptors and even architects. One could not possibly build great temples (like The Parthenon) and great statues of Zeus, Athena, and other Gods without being spiritual. The same mentality was prevalent in other cultures and civilizations. It is very difficult to imagine great pieces of work and not associate them with some kind of divine inspiration.

---

[37] For more information pertaining to the role of love, mindfulness and empathy please visit this great website: http://www.businessballs.com/love.htm and read this article: **"Love And Spirituality In Management And Business"**.

Today, we tend to believe that all great works of art or architecture tend to be the mere product of creative geniuses that simply have learned and acquired good skills in school. But it is not so! We see architects that come out of the same schools with the same degrees, skills and knowledge and yet they produce "average-looking" buildings, while others produce masterpieces. So, what is the difference?

The difference is very simple. Some people "got it" and others do not. What have they got? **Inspiration! Imagination! Intuition** (= Insight, Perception, Awareness, Acuity, Sensitivity, Instinct)! Where do all these things come from? There are several theories, but the most valid one is the one that puts forward the "**Channeling**" view. The proof is out there, if only people want to see it. We see it with very young song writers[38] (like **The Beetles** and **Michael Jackson**) that knew nothing about life (while they were young), but yet they wrote very profound songs that had the depth and wisdom of 60 year olds. We see young movie directors (like **Steven Spielberg**) that were green behind the ears, but yet they produced masterpieces. They cannot even explain themselves where those inspirations came from because it is not strictly a matter of IQ or training. "Something else" has influenced their works of art, or whatever else they have created. The questions are a) what is the *something else*, and b) how does one go tapping into it?

Without getting too deep into it, the answer to the first question is **"Spirituality"** (is the influence), and the answer to the second question is **"Channeling"**. The most fascinating thing is that some of those inspired artisans and inventors when asked about their inspirations they claim that they don't believe in spirituality or channeling. No one can fully explain this phenomenon, but yet it is a safe assumption that those who "channel" possess the right ingredients for channeling. Ideas, inspirations and insights naturally are finding their way to the right channel; no different than water finding the right beds to roll downhill. Unfortunately, it is impossible to properly and fully address these topics in this short chapter, but we encourage people to learn more about these topics from other sources as they are super valuable.

It is interesting that well-respected business publications are finally starting to publish articles and white papers on this subject (e.g.: **HBR** Nov. 2014 issue: **"Where To Look For Insight"** (https://hbr.org/2014/11/where-to-look-for-insight) ---it identifies 7 channels for insight, but fails to mention the most important one: **Cosmic Consciousness**).

Caution: Many New Age and religion-based books and workshops offer distorted views on these subjects. Some New Age self-proclaimed gurus will even suggest drugs for altered states of consciousness, while some religious pundits proclaim that there is no such thing as Cosmic Consciousness, just God. It is not worth elaborating any further.

Most people know when they are channeling because "things" are flowing through and out of them so effortlessly and naturally, without having to think or contemplate what they mean or ponder *Where did this idea come from?* So, what are the right

---

[38] Some song writers refer to channeling as "**automatic writing**" or being under "the spell" of some past or present personality or other entity.

ingredients in a person to become a channel? We don't really know, but the main assumption is that personality traits and dispositions along with values and beliefs play a major role. There may be other factors, such as destiny and upbringing, but they are difficult to address. Here is sample of:

Personality Traits and Dispositions Of Spiritual People
Being:

- Open
- Sociable; "Networker" / "Connector"
- Gentle / Considerate / Thoughtful
- Vulnerable (a sense of vulnerability coupled with being cool)
- Sensitive / Emotional
- Bright / Intellectual
- Deep / Philosophical
- Perceptive / Insightful
- Artistic
- Creative / Innovative / Imaginative
- Introspective / Intuitive
- Curious

Having:

- A strong desire to excel and be somebody --- an accentuated need for self-actualization
- A passion for life
- Fascination with Spirituality
- A positive outlook about everything --- w/o the Pollyannaish attitude
- "Big Heart" /Loving / Caring
- A (burning) desire to create and improve
- Ability to get totally absorbed and/or immersed in one's area of interest and stay focused
- An obsession with reaching higher levels of knowing and awareness
- The desire to channel. **Pablo Picasso** said: *"I do not care who it is that has or does influence me as long as it is not myself."*

As a reference point here are the main traits of **Steve Jobs personality**:

- Polymath (thirsty for knowledge)
- Predatory Mentality (grab whatever idea would make him look good and smart)
- Unbelievable imagination
- Perfectionist; Obsessive
- High Energy
- Extremely Passionate
- Spiritual
- Great Motivator
- Great Communicator
- Unwilling to be defined by "normal life" and acceptable lifestyles

Reminder: Steve Jobs was the a unique individual that excelled extremely well both as an entrepreneur and as a professional manager.

> **Personal Anecdote:** When I was working at **IBM** we were getting rumor mill reports about **Steve Jobs.** The rumors were very nasty against Jobs, including drug-fueled parties and several other misbehaviors and indiscretions --- later on, many of those rumors proved to be true. The general feeling was that this guy will eventually crash and burn ... *"He is no threat to us".* Little did we know back then what a legend this guy would eventually become. Very few people fully understood back then (or even now) his personality, his drives, his motivations and inspirations. He fooled everyone!
>
> **Lesson Learned:** One cannot draw conclusions about one's ability to be innovative by just looking at a person's appearance, lifestyle, IQ, degrees, or anything else that people use to judge others.

Moreover **personal Values & Beliefs** play a role in innovation.

- Virtuousness (believing that virtues such as honesty, integrity, courage and curiosity matter)
- Wanting /Visioning a better world
- Wanting to leave behind a better world and make a difference
- Wanting to leave a legacy and a long-lasting reputation
- Wanting to reach new levels of excellence
- Willing to challenge and break the rules (a rebel attitude). **Pablo Picasso** said: *"Learn the rules like a pro, so you can break them like an artist."*

One of **Steve Jobs'** best quotes is: *"Being the richest man in the cemetery does not matter to me ... Going to bed at night saying 'We've done something wonderful' ... That's what matters to me".* This captures perfectly the essence of having strong beliefs about one's purpose in life.

b. Meditation and Mindfulness

Meditation and mindfulness are great tools to invoke and/or initiate channeling. But they are also used for relaxing the mind, getting rid of negative thoughts and energies, and obtaining a sense of euphoria[39] that is conducive to channeling.

A study by cognitive psychologist **Lorenza Colzato** (published April 19, 2013) in **"Frontiers in Cognition"** magazine confirmed something that many of us believed for a long time that certain meditation techniques can promote creative thinking. The findings support the belief that meditation influences human cognition, including how we think, how we experience events and how we translate inputs in our heads. There are several meditation techniques (ranging from **traditional meditation** and **Transcendental Meditation** to **Yoga**) and they all produce different results and have different effects on people. Some of them are more effective than others. One may want to experiment

---

[39] Euphoria is another Greek word that implies achieving a state of elation, bliss, ecstasy, expiration and rapture.

with different types of medication until one finds the right one for her/himself. Surprisingly, meditation helps both of those that utilize Convergent Thinking and Divergent Thinking.

It is proven that some people prefer to mediate alone, while others prefer to meditate in groups. All meditation techniques require the emptying of the mind, which has become very difficult task in our extremely busy and complex world. Some people have reached the point of not being able to leave their smart phone behind. The minute there are divorced from their phones and laptops many people start getting anxiety/panic attacks, and don't even know what to do with their empty hands and unburdened minds.

Steven Johnson, author of several books (including **"Where Good Ideas Come From"**), explains what companies need to do to foster an **innovative culture**. He suggests that people that want to meditate need to stay away from meeting and conference rooms, in order to find a quiet place suitable for meditation. A quiet room does not have to be an isolated room free of noise, or dark room that promotes a hypnotic state. It can be the cafeteria, the lawn garden, or even the hallway.

Personal Anecdote: When I was working at **IBM** I met a couple of colleagues that their job was to follow around Fellow level geniuses and record their ideas as they were roaming the hallways of IBM buildings because they would not record their own ideas and they would tend to forget them after long pacing. Thus, we had note takers following them around to record the ideas that the geniuses came up while they were walking and talking (mostly to themselves).

Lesson Learned: There are many ways to capture ideas. One needs to be innovative for idea capturing … and dissemination … and storage!

Some major corporations have made great strides the last ten years with **Knowledge Management**, and now they are shifting their efforts to **Idea Management**. This is the next big thing in the technology arena (incl. integrating the two into one system, along with integrating **Strategic Collaboration** and **Social Media**).

Inspiration can "hit" anyone at any place. I saw innovators get great ideas at Starbucks while drinking their lattes. I heard from others that got a great idea while in the shower, forced to run out naked to write their idea down before it was lost --- reminding me of the *"Eureka"* moment that **Archimedes** had in his bathtub. However, there are several people that believe that *"silence is the mother of all creativity"*.

Companies that have utilized different meditation techniques include, **Disney, Shell, Goggle, Apple, Prentice Hall Publishing, Nike, AOL, Time Warner, P&G, Procter & Gamble, Yahoo!, McKinsey, General Mills, Green Mountain Coffee, Aetna and HBO**. There were several famous people that have utilized meditation techniques, including **Einstein, Steve Jobs, Oprah, John Lennon, Sting, Martin Scorsese and Rupert Murdock**.

The Value Of Spiritual Quotient (SQ)

Businesses typically talk about IQ and EQ, but very, very rarely refer to SQ. The main reason is that they do not understand its value and significance. Here is a quick summary of IQ, ED and SQ that capture their value in the business world:

- **IQ** ➔ Measures a person's intelligence and capabilities. Can the person analyze, synthesize and otherwise make the right decisions in the business world? This is typically a measurement of the left brain's ability to decide, solve and leverage resources.
- **EQ** ➔ Measures a person's emotional stability and maturity to deal with an array of feelings and emotions, as well the ability to leverage those emotions in creative and inspired ways that produce all the great works of art that we see around us. EQ also offers the motivation to accomplish and succeed. This is the value of the right brain.
- **SQ** ➔ Measures a person's spiritual abilities in terms of sensing the value of all life forms of life in the planet, the planet itself, and its ecosystems. "Sensing" is not seeing and liking animals and flowers. "Sensing" is used in the sense of feeling the beauty and magnificence of all, "seeing" and appreciating the inter-connectedness of all, and more importantly "feeling" The Oneness. SQ is the conscience of IQ and EQ because it provides the meaning and (higher) purpose that intelligent beings need. IQ and EQ are not enough to guide a human being through life. SQ is key to synchronize left and right brains. In other words, SQ is about leveraging the whole brain (which is key to Holistic Thinking and Holistic Innovation). Thus:

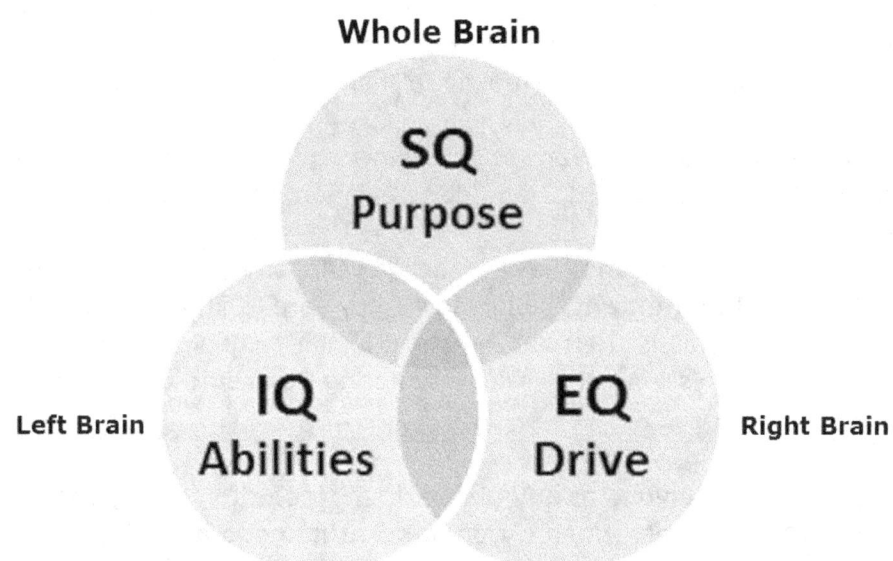

Unfortunately, enterprises, just like schools, only recognize IQ as the only important measurement of a person's value in the business world because they still have to wrong mentality that people that pursue careers only need intelligence in order to survive and thrive. This mentality is another bad remnant for The Industrial Age. Today's professionals need all three quotients ... and in balance. In reality, they always needed them and always used them. They just did not highlight them like we do today.

Summary

As people and companies learn the value of meditation, they start applying it more and more inside their business practices[40]. This does not imply having long sessions chanting **AUM or Ohm**, but rather spending the time to think outside-the-box, take a different view and perspective on a pressing matter or issue and clear the mind of pre-conceived notions, concepts and ideas. The meditation technique is extremely valuable and should be cherished instead of ridiculed by people that think only scientific thinking and analytical minds have all the answers.

It is worth mentioning that there is a paradox involving innovation. On one hand, people are told to stay super-focused and breathe, eat and live innovation, and on the other hand, they are told to relax and empty their minds in order for new **provocative ideas** to enter their "system". Super busy minds eventually suffer saturation and inundation that overwhelm one's brain and psyche. Thus, knowing how to **balance "focusing" and "relaxing"** is part of the value of good meditation techniques.

Meditation is now becoming a powerful technique for CEOs (and actually for all executives in all roles), as the **HBR article** published December 14, 2015 indicates.

The main point with IQ, EQ and SQ is that collectively they help a human being in becoming a holistic or complete being/total person. This is important because:

Holistic Being → Holistic Thinking → Holistic Views → Holistic Innovation

This also explains why the polymath mentality and continuous learning are so important in the development of a Total Person.

---

[40] **Fast Company** magazine published an article about how **Shell** is fostering innovation with meditation. In the Shell example, a chemical engineer named **Mandar Apte** created a program within company to teach yoga and breathing techniques as a way to inspire creativity. Here is an excerpt from **Fast Company's** article regarding **Apte's program**:

"But it's not his own practice that made him a winner of the League of Entrepreneurs. It's the grassroots, employee-driven initiative that he co-created at Shell called Empower. The initiative encourages employees to bring their authentic self to work, helps participants unleash their leadership potential, and enables them to identify and overcome the blockers to creativity and innovation. Embedded in the nine-hour training program are practical yet profound instructions on breathing and meditation techniques along with interactive processes to master the skills for boosting creativity and cultivating the mindset for innovation. At the heart of his innovation learning program is the belief that silence is the mother of all creativity, and each employee can play a role in the innovation process."

At last count well over 2,000 **Shell Oil** company employees have gone through the **Empower Program** with great reports of acceptance and success. The fascinating thing about breathing is that although we all breathe in order to stay alive we become oblivious to it. We all have to learn that meditative breathing can be used to relax, to think deep thoughts, to slow down, and to make space (in our brains, hearts and souls) to create. This is the main "trick" of successful entrepreneurs and thinkers. As **Fast Company's** article points out *"It's hard to discount the merits of conscious breathing, no matter how skeptical you might be."*

14 STEVE JOBS AND THE PROCESS OF INNOVATION

Douglas M. Berman

Introduction

> *"All the work that I've done in my life will be obsolete by the time I'm fifty ..."*

This chapter does not cover the life and achievements of Steve Jobs. That subject has been covered exhaustively in such books as **"Steve Jobs"** by **Walter Isaacson** and **"Becoming Steve Jobs"** by **Brent Schlender and Rick Tetzeli**.

> *"This is a field where one does not write a "Principia" which holds up for 200 years. This is not a field where one paints a painting that will be looked at for centuries. Or builds a church that will be admired and looked at in astonishment for centuries ..."*

The purpose of this chapter is to examine Jobs' process of innovation and the influences that pushed Jobs to create one of the most innovative companies in a generation.

> *"So, it's sort of like sediment of rocks. I mean you're building up a mountain and you get to contribute your little layer of sedimentary rock to make the mountain that much higher. But, no one on the surface will, unless they have X-ray vision, will see your sediment. They'll stand on it. It'll be appreciated by that rare geologist..."*

In reviewing Jobs' approach that results in innovation, we are able to see approaches that focus on small details and elements that focus on the bigger picture. When we look at the small, exacting details, we see:

- A design-driven approach that forces innovation in order to produce incredibly complex products for the masses that are simple and intuitive to use; and

- A focus on the essence of a product that innovates by stripping away unnecessary elements to achieve elegance and simplicity.

The bigger picture is equally important as Jobs was famous for his spiritual side and for his outsized ambitions for his products. The bigger picture shows attention to:

- A grand vision and higher purpose that inspires others to work to meet and proselytize the vision;
- Creating a culture of innovation that permits creativity to advance;
- The use of meditation to stimulate mental processes and promote creativity; and
- The power of association connecting disparate concepts in innovative ways.

"But, no, it's not like the Renaissance at all. It's very different. Very different."
– Steve Jobs[41]

Vision and the Higher Purpose

"The greatest people are self-managing. They don't need to be managed. . . . What leadership is, is having a vision, being able to articulate that so that people around you can understand it and getting a consensus on a common vision." – Steve Jobs[42]

It is not an exaggeration to say a cult of personality developed around Steve Jobs and the products he created.[43] Great products do not command this level of loyalty and adoration. There have been plenty of good computers, portable music plays and cellphones. But how many people get tattoos of a CEO of Sony or Nokia?

Why does Steve Jobs command this level of respect when other CEOs are condemned to treatment as mere mortals? More importantly, what is the relation to Jobs' thought process and how this relates to innovation?

Inspiration
Most people do not think of mass produced commodity products as particularly inspiring. Yet, Jobs vision was to take a tool and turn it into something accessible and available to the masses.[44]

Steve Jobs did not view Apple merely as a company that sold boxes of silicon chips. Jobs viewed

[41] "Steve Jobs on his legacy (1994) (https://youtu.be/zut2NLMVL_k)

[42] "Steve Jobs in a documentary about Apple (1985) (https://www.youtube.com/watch?v=ldpfl5SgMi8&feature=youtu.be)

[43] David Pierini, "Steve Jobs left an imprint on tech and the skin of some devoted fans." Cult of Mac, May 11, 2016 (http://www.cultofmac.com/426643/steve-jobs-left-an-imprint-on-tech-and-the-skin-of-some-devoted-fans/); Whitney Mallett, "How Steve Jobs Drew on Myth to Build the Cult of Apple," Vice—Motherboard, September 2, 2015 (http://motherboard.vice.com/read/how-steve-jobs-drew-on-myth-to-build-the-cult-of-apple); Alex Godfrey, "Aaron Sorkin on the cult of Steve Jobs: 'I hadn't seen anything like it since John Lennon was killed'" The Guardian, November 11, 2015 (https://www.theguardian.com/film/2015/nov/11/aaron-sorkin-steve-jobs-michael-fassbender)

[44] David Sheff, "Playboy Interview: Steve Jobs," February 1, 2985, reproduced at Genius.com (http://genius.com/David-sheff-playboy-interview-steve-jobs-annotated)

Apple as a company that would change the world. It would change how people worked, learned and played.[45] This was the bigger picture. This bigger picture drove the innovation that drove Apple. A vision, a higher purpose, yields advances and inspires people to meet your vision and preach it to others.

Jobs started Apple with Steve Wozniak. Wozniak was interested in figuring out engineering problems, but Jobs wanted to change the world. Both men are revered and admired and considered influential in their respective fields, but Jobs became the cultural icon.[46]

Leadership

Jobs was not necessarily the person in the lab coat producing patentable technology. He had to communicate his vision to people capable of implementing it. He understood that creativity is at the heart of innovation. Innovation is about the new, different and better. A lack of passion can kill creativity and leave an organization stagnant.

"There needs to be someone who is sort of the keeper and reiterator of the vision." –
Steve Jobs[47]

A vision must be communicated before it can be implemented. It is a leader's job to communicate this vision and how the employees' work brings meaning and advances the vision. In addition, a leader must support his or her employees' ability to achieve their goals.[48]

Jobs understood that communicating a bold vision with a higher purpose can inspire people to innovate to meet that vision. Rather than weigh people down with bureaucracy, Jobs hired creative, talented people and unleashed them to meet his vision. This is how Macintosh was created, as opposed to just another IBM-compatible box, a risky strategy at the time.[49] Apple's employees were creative and passionate people inspired to innovate.[50] And something new had to be created to get this tool to the masses and to improve their lives.

Jobs showed that when people are inspired by a vision, they will work harder and be more productive. In addition, that productivity can be harnessed to innovate to meet the leader's vision and higher purpose.[51] Instead of stamping out a production unit, Jobs inspired Apple to reach for a higher purpose and to put a dent in the universe.[52]

---

[45] Carmine Gallo, "The Innovation Secrets of Steve Jobs," page 47

[46] Ibid

[47] "Steve Jobs brainstorms with the NeXT team" (http://everystevejobsvideo.com/steve-jobs-brainstorms-with-the-next-team-1985/)

[48] Teresa Amabile and Steve Kramer, "To Give Your Employees Meaning, Start with Mission," Harvard Business Review, December 19, 2012 (https://hbr.org/2012/12/to-give-your-employees-meaning)

[49] Sheff

[50] Sheff

[51] Gallo, page 54

[52] Jason Snell, "Steve Jobs: Making a dent in the universe," Macworld.com, October 6, 2011 (http://www.macworld.com/article/1162827/macs/steve-jobs-making-a-dent-in-the-universe.html)

Radical Innovation and the Power of Thinking Big

*"I saw these third and fourth graders growing up completely different than I grew up because of this machine." – **Steve Jobs**[53]*

When people think of "innovation," they tend to think about the big picture and radical changes to what currently exists. Innovation becomes a world changing product.[54] Thoughts turn to the ideas that become fundamental building blocks of society and progress, such as the printing press, nuclear power, the integrated circuit, and the internet.[55] Even thinking to earlier periods and breakthroughs that we take for granted, large-scale innovations encompass such things such as paper, cement, the sailboat and the abacus.[56]

Innovation can come in all shapes and sizes. An idea and the manifestation of that idea do not necessarily have to change the course of human civilization to count as innovation. In fact, large, civilization-altering innovations are few in number, which is why they can be listed. Most innovation occurs on a much smaller scale. In addition, smaller, incremental innovation constitutes the building blocks of larger-scale innovation.[57]

Small-scale innovation provides plenty of opportunity for the innovator and the business person. This can, and often does, take the form of advancing things that already exist. This is not just opportunity, but for many businesses, this is necessary.[58] This can come in the form of "everything the same, but nicer" with improvements to existing products and services or other advances that branch from or overlap with existing products or services.[59]

Like any products that feature technology in area that develops quickly, Apple products often exhibited incremental innovation. However, the thinking of Steve Jobs exhibited Radical Innovation.

"What we're about isn't making boxes for people to get their jobs done, although we do that well. . . . We believe that people with passion can change the world for the

---

[53] "Steve Jobs brainstorms with the NeXT team" (http://everystevejobsvideo.com/steve-jobs-brainstorms-with-the-next-team-1985/)

[54] James Fallows, "The 50 Greatest Breakthroughs Since the Wheel." *The Atlantic*, November 2013. (http://www.theatlantic.com/magazine/archive/2013/11/innovations-list/309536/).

[55] Ibid

[56] Ibid

[57] The Innovation Policy Platform, "Radical and Incremental Innovation." Organisation for Economic Cooperation and Development (OECD) and the World Bank. (https://www.innovationpolicyplatform.org/content/radical-and-incremental-innovation)

[58] Karen Harris, Austin Kim and Andrew Schwedel, "The Great Eight: Trillion-Dollar Growth Trends to 2020." *Business Insights*, September 9, 2011, Bain & Company (http://www.bain.com/publications/articles/eight-great-trillion-dollar-growth-trends-to-2020.aspx)

[59] Ibid

*better. That's what we believe." – **Steve Jobs**[60]*

Vision vs. Scope

Radical innovation and thinking big are related to concept of vision, but they are a separate category. Like innovation, vision can relate to the small or to the large. For example, in the section of this chapter entitled "Beauty and Innovation Through Simplicity," Jobs had a vision of how products should be designed and how users would interact with them. Fonts and white space may seem small when thinking in terms of "vision," but Jobs absolutely had a vision for these concepts that changed an industry's entire philosophy of user interface design.

Thinking Big

*"We should be augmenting the libraries we have with links to the Library of Congress. Then, to put the Library of Congress in even the smallest town, all we have to do is run a network spigot into that town and hook it up to the computers, and we will have the entire Library of Congress at our fingertips." – **Steve Jobs** Anticipating the Internet in 1990[61]*

Jobs exhibited large-scale thinking for Apple and its place in the world. When looking to approach a concept like Steve Jobs did, think big.

When Jobs was recruiting **John Sculley** to run Apple, Sculley was already running **PepsiCo.** Thinking big was not a matter of chasing a powerful executive of a global powerhouse to run an upstart computer company. Thinking big was in the packaging of the offer. Jobs famously asked Sculley whether he would want to sell sugar water for the rest of his life or whether he would want to change the world.[62]

At the time Jobs was recruiting Sculley, computers were either big hardware for business or game machines. Sculley later said that Jobs was thinking about computers on another level.[63] The computer was more than a game machine. The computer would be available to everyone and would provide people with capabilities that they could not imagine.[64]

Similarly, when Jobs saw the potential of **LucasFilm**, Jobs was not content with creating cool things with new technologies for computer animation. His vision was for **Pixar** to become a brand on par with **Disney**.[65]

~~Jobs was thinking about ch~~anging the world. This was a bold vision for a radical re-imagining of a

[60] Apple Confidential - Steve Jobs on "Think Different" - Internal Meeting Sept. 23, 1997 (https://www.youtube.com/watch?v=9GMQhOm-Dqo)

[61] "Steve Jobs talks about the Library of Congress (1990)" (http://everystevejobsvideo.com/steve-jobs-talks-about-the-library-of-congress-1990/)

[62] Leander Kahney, "Inside Steve's Brain," page 152

[63] Leander Kahney, "John Sculley: The Secrets of Steve Jobs' Success [Exclusive Interview]." *CultofMac.com*, October 14, 2010. (http://www.cultofmac.com/21572/john-sculley-the-secrets-of-steve-jobs-success-exclusive-interview/)

[64] Ibid

[65] Gallo, page 55

tool. This is Thinking Big.

"That's maybe the most important thing is to shake off this erroneous notion that life is there and you're just gonna live in it versus embrace it, change it, improve it, make your mark upon it . . . . Once you learn that, you'll never be the same again."
– Steve Jobs[66]

Design-Driven Innovation

When thinking about innovation, it is natural to consider the science and complexity "under the hood." It is not easy to advance technology, whether that means computer science, robotics, pharmaceuticals, space travel or manufacturing. It is easy to picture the laboratories, exposed electronics and blinking lights and whirring components.

Science for the sake of science is a worthy pursuit. But, what if innovation results from the demand to make life better, easier and more productive? What good is innovation that is inaccessible? Steve Jobs' mind for innovation was directed to making products that were not just advanced, but that could be easily used by the masses.

Consumer Focus

Consider the iPhone. The hardware and software constitute amazing, cutting-edge technology with innovation at every turn. By the end of 2007 at the time of the iPhone launch, Nokia commanded about half of the smartphone market, but it entered a decline that landed with its acquisition by Microsoft in 2013.[67] Debates still rage over whether the iPhone's current rivals can keep up with its technology.[68][69]

Despite the incredible technological achievement of the iPhone and its competitors, the genius of Steve Jobs' approach to design produced a product that a baby could use.[70] Parents are introducing children to their smartphones, and those children are able to manipulate them in meaningful ways, even before their first birthday.[71] Does anyone believe this could have been done with anything Nokia made before the introduction of the iPhone?

More Than Looks

"He really approached it as a problem that had to be solved, not an artistic challenge for its own sake." **Steve Jobs** *on designer Paul Rand*[72]

---

[66] "Steve Jobs: Secrets of Life" (https://youtu.be/kYfNvmF0Bqw)

[67] Quy Huy, "Who Killed Nokia? Nokia Did," Knowledge.Insead.edu, September 22, 2015 (http://knowledge.insead.edu/strategy/who-killed-nokia-nokia-did-4268)

[68] Zack Epstein, "Have Apple's rivals finally stopped copying the iPhone," BGR.com, February 23, 2016 (http://bgr.com/2016/02/23/iphone-vs-android-samsung-lg-copycats/)

[69] Timothy B. Lee, "Yes, Google "Stole" From Apple, And That's A good Thing," Forbes.com, October 25, 2011 (http://www.forbes.com/sites/timothylee/2011/10/25/yes-google-stole-from-apple-and-thats-a-good-thing/#38aec07b8692)

[70] Karen Kaplan, "More than a third of infants are using smartphones, tablets, study says," LATimes.com, April 25, 2015 (http://www.latimes.com/science/sciencenow/la-sci-sn-babies-screen-time-iphone-ipad-20150424-story.html)

[71] Ibid

Apple products have enjoyed a legendary reputation for design.[73] However, aesthetics were only a part, even a minor part, of the story. Design had a purpose. Jobs wanted to make products that were easy to use and accessible to the masses.[74]

*"I think one of the things that really separates us from the high primates is that we're tool builders." – **Steve Jobs**[75]*

When Jobs and Steve Wozniak began working together, computers were expensive and technically inaccessible. They were toys for the experts, not tools for the masses.[76] From the beginning, Apple products were designed for use by everyone as mass market appliances.[77] This was a lesson he learned from exploring gizmos and electronic kits as a child. They become familiar as the mystery is removed from them.[78]

The Product Drives the Technology, Not the Other Way Around

*"We don't really talk about design around here a lot. We actually just talk about how things work." – **Steve Jobs**[79]*

To Jobs, design was not just a product looked, but about how the product worked. The user experience, and the industrial design with which the user interacted, were very important aspects of Jobs' Apple philosophy.[80]

Design was about how people interacted with it.[81] For example, many of the technological innovations that went into the Macintosh were derived from Jobs' insistence that the computer's footprint be no larger than a phonebook.[82] Why? Because people kept their telephones on a telephone directory on their desk. This was his size limit for a new desktop appliance.[83]

---

[72] "Steve Jobs interviewed about Paul Rand (1993)" (http://everystevejobsvideo.com/steve-jobs-interviewed-about-paul-rand-1993/)

[73] Cliff Kuang, "The 6 Pillars Of Steve Jobs's Design Philosophy," Fastcodesign.com, November 7, 2011 (http://www.fastcodesign.com/1665375/the-6-pillars-of-steve-jobss-design-philosophy)

[74] Kahney, page 7

[75] "Steve Jobs talks about the Library of Congress (1990)" (http://everystevejobsvideo.com/steve-jobs-talks-about-the-library-of-congress-1990/)

[76] Gallo, page 8

[77] Ibid, page 90

[78] Kahney, pages 5-6

[79] Steve Jobs on Design (2002) (https://www.youtube.com/watch?v=9GMQhOm-Dqo)

[80] Leander Kahney, "John Sculley On Steve Jobs, The Full Interview Transcript" Cultofmac.com, October 14, 2010 (http://www.cultofmac.com/63295/john-sculley-on-steve-jobs-the-full-interview-transcript/)

[81] Kahney, page 71

[82] Gallo, page 91

Beauty and Innovation Through Simplicity

"Focus is about saying 'No.' And the result of that focus is gonna be some really great products where the total is much greater than the sum of the parts."
– Steve Jobs[84]

In describing the creative process of the sculpture of David, Michelangelo is often[85] quoted as describing the process as chipping away parts of the stone that do not look like David.

In the previous section, we discussed the importance of design to Steve Jobs' innovation process. To achieve his objectives, design could drive the innovation process.

Jobs knew that he wanted Apple to create things that people would actually use en masse. To achieve this, the products had to be usable by the masses. In addition, the masses had to be comfortable using the products, even if they contained complex, cutting edge technology.

Jobs was not out to build technology for technology's sake. He was creating simple, comfortable and beautiful tools that would improve people's lives. This philosophy preaches paring the ideas and presentation to their core and avoiding function creep.

Know Your Customer and the Folly of Focus Group-Driven Design
There was an episode of The Simpsons where Homer's long-lost brother was an automobile executive named Herb. After getting frustrated with his designers, Herb asked Homer to design a call assuming this would reflect what everyday consumers really wanted. Homer did not understand cars or even what he wanted in a car. Homer took his cue from what he thought others wanted. The result was hardly innovative. It was a disaster.[86]

Jobs famously avoided focus group-driven product development.[87] Rather than respond to users, Jobs and Apple created innovative products that provided them with a new way of thinking about their tools.[88] It is a philosophy that gets you even closer to your customers by anticipating what they want before they know, and providing them new ways to approach their problems.[89] If those new ways of thinking and using tools are cumbersome, complex, convoluted and confusing, the customers will go elsewhere. As a result, Apple pursued innovation and aesthetics through simplicity.

---

[83] Ibid

[84] ""Focusing is about saying no" - Steve Jobs (WWDC'97)" (https://www.youtube.com/watch?v=H8eP99neOVs)

[85] This quote seems to be attributed to many authors. (http://quoteinvestigator.com/2014/06/22/chip-away/)

[86] The Simpsons, "Oh Brother, Where Art Thou?" (http://www.imdb.com/title/tt0701191/)

[87] Gregory Ciotti, "Why Steve Jobs Didn't Listen to His Customers," Help Scout Blog, March 6, 2013 (https://www.helpscout.net/blog/why-steve-jobs-never-listened-to-his-customers/)

[88] Gallo, page 113

[89] Ibid

Simplicity and the Essential Meaning

Many companies prefer to throw everything and the kitchen sink at a complex problem. Additionally, companies often stuff their products full of unnecessary features in order to project value. This often results in a complex solution. And this often results in loss of potential customers and forgotten products.

However, simplicity is not just striking things. It is about getting to the core meaning of a product. It is about doing away with the distractions and the unnecessary.[90] While this concept is seemingly simple, in terms of technology it can often require sophisticated innovation to achieve. Apple designers take a holistic approach to make sure all of the pieces, internal and external, apparent and hidden, come together in a beautiful, easy to use package.[91]

Jobs designed with the user in mind. Consequently, simplicity and human factors were key. While Apple's competitors were focused in improving individual technologies, Apple was focused on enriching the customer experience. When designing OS X, features often hidden in obscure menus were simplified and made more prominent, such as connection settings for the Internet.[92] Similarly, the iPod was a simple music player with a navigation wheel that was singularly focused on playing music.[93] The lack of unnecessary features and complications, and even its original neutral color, made it stand out against the hordes of less expensive digital music players busy cramming complexity into their products.[94]

Products First, Innovation Follows

When conjuring new products, it seems like innovation would be a natural result. Creating something new requires innovation, so it seems. However, creating something new that works well is more in the spirit of innovation – advances that can be implemented commercially. Apple Chief Design Officer **Jonny Ive** had said that Apple does not consciously think about being innovative, it thinks about making great products.[95] In other words, the idea of a new product or service comes first and is followed by the process of creating it. The innovation does not result from deliberately trying to create new things. The innovation results from the process of cutting the unnecessary and developing the technologies that permit it.[96]

Even the most complex problems can have simple and elegant solutions. The genius of Jobs and the Apple teams was stripping the problems down to their essence. From that point, they created solutions accessible to the masses.

---

[90] Rob Walker, "The Guts of a New Machine," New York Times, November 30, 2003 (http://www.nytimes.com/2003/11/30/magazine/30IPOD.html?pagewanted=all)

[91] Marcus, "Jonathan Ive," iconeye.com, July/August 2003 (http://www.iconeye.com/diary/item/2730-jonathan-ive-%7C-icon-004-%7C-july/august-2003)

[92] Kahney, pages 52-53

[93] Gallo, pages 142-143

[94] See Gallo, pages 143-144; Nicholas, "iPod and MP3 Players Compared – MP3 vs. iPod," BrightHub.com, July 1, 2011 (http://www.brighthub.com/electronics/mp3/articles/63535.aspx)

[95] Walker

[96] Ibid

Culture of Creativity and Innovation

"Life can be much broader once you discover one simple fact, and that is everything around you that you call life was made up by people that were no smarter than you. And you can change it. You can influence it. You can build your own things that other people can use." – **Steve Jobs**[97]

Steve Jobs famously took a trip to India in the early 1970's after dropping out of college. This trip sparked in Jobs an interest in Buddhism that manifested itself in identifiable ways, such as:

- Aesthetic choices with respect to Apple products;
- A demanding leadership style;
- Constant change and adaptation; and
- An interest in meditation.[98]

Jobs was also known to exhibit outward influences from the India trip. For example, he could be seen walking barefoot around the office.[99] He used the **Dalai Lama** in Apple's "Think Different" ad campaign.[100]

The interest in India and its culture may have inspired Jobs to institute a deeper culture of innovation at Apple and Pixar.

Culture influences and directs human behavior. The combination of the eastern spirituality and Silicon Valley technology influences on Jobs may have driven Jobs to institute a culture of creativity and innovation that allowed Apple to put world-changing products in the hands of the masses. It has been argued that:

- Cultures produce geniuses in the subjects valued by the culture; and
- Cultures produce specialized knowledge in subjects valued by the culture.[101]

These values direct behavior. For India, spirituality is such a valued subject matter.[102]

In this respect, Jobs maintained a culture conducive of innovation at Apple and Pixar. However, there were positive and negative aspects of this culture.

[97] "Steve Jobs: Secrets of Life" (https://youtu.be/kYfNvmF0Bqw)

[98] Brent Schlender and Rick Tetzeli, "How Steve Jobs found Buddhism," Lionsroar.com, November 3, 2015 http://creativecriminals.com/celebrities/apple/think-different (http://www.lionsroar.com/how-steve-jobs-found-buddhism/)

[99] Susan Donaldson James, "Steve Jobs' Mantra Rooted in Buddhism: Focus and Simplicity," ABCNews.go.com, October 6, 2011 (http://abcnews.go.com/Health/steve-jobs-buddhism-guided-life-mantra-focus-simplicity/story?id=14682458)

[100] Sander Janssen, "Apple: Think different," Creative Criminals, 6 October 2011 (http://creativecriminals.com/celebrities/apple/think-different)

[101] Dharm Bhawuk, "Culture's influence on creativity: The case of Indian spirituality," International Journal of Intercultural Relations, February 2003 (https://www.researchgate.net/publication/228585025_Culture's_influence_on_creativity_The_case_of_Indian_sprituality)

[102] Ibid

Jobs had described his relationship with eastern spirituality and meditation as allowing the mind to slow down and to see things more clearly.[103]   Many practitioners believe that this state permits focus and creativity, which can lead to innovation.

Jobs was also a notoriously demanding, and even combative, boss.   Meetings with Jobs could become antagonistic and aggressive intellectual slugfests, which Jobs found to lead to high level problem solving.[104]

Meditation and Innovation

Steve Jobs' fascination with India and Zen practices is legendary.   While the extent of his adherence may be debatable, the extent of its influence over Jobs and the culture of innovation at Apple and Pixar is not.   From rigorous simplicity to courage in the face of naysayers, Zen Buddhist philosophy and the practice of meditation had a profound influence on Jobs and quality and quantity of his innovation production.[105]

Meditation and Brain Activity

There are practitioners of meditation all over the world.   But, there are numerous studies that show that meditation positively impacts brain activity, including in ways that could produce the seeds of innovation in the practitioner.   For example, meditation may activate parts of the brain involved in higher functions.[106]   Even short-term meditation programs have demonstrated increased activity in left-side brain activity,[107] which influences such things as:

- Logic;
- Higher math; and
- Long-term memory.[108]

Even though crafting complex mathematical equations like *Good Will Hunting* are not necessary for innovation to take hold, it is easy to see how logic, higher math and memory are necessary. Complex mental processes and procedures are necessary to produce something new and useful even if the mathematical mechanics or the roadmap of firing neurons is hidden to the innovator.

The focus on logic, math and memory instills a cold, sterile and mechanical feeling that is at odds with the highly emotional portraits of Jobs.   In addition, Jobs did not describe his relationship with

---

[103] Drake Baer, "Here's How Zen Meditation Changed Steve Jobs' Life And Sparked A Design Revolution," Business Insider, January 9, 2015, (http://www.businessinsider.com/steve-jobs-zen-meditation-buddhism-2015-1)

[104] Kahney, page 124

[105] Baer

[107] Richard J. Davidson, et al, "Alterations in Brain and Immune Function Produced by Mindfulness Meditation," Psychosomatic Medisone 65:564-570 (2003)(http://centerhealthyminds.org/assets/files-publications/DavidsonAlterationsPsychosomaticMedicine.pdf)

[108] Remy Melina, "What's the Difference Between the Right Brain and Left Brain," LiveScience, January 12, 2011 (http://www.livescience.com/32935-whats-the-difference-between-the-right-brain-and-left-brain.html)

meditation in such a fashion.

Research has demonstrated evidence to show that various forms of meditation:

- Support creating thinking;
- Reduce reliance on known stimuli;
- Increase cognitive performance on complex problems;
- Support seeking of novel ideas;
- Promote cognitive flexibility;
- Promote awareness of subtlety;
- Promote motivation to go beyond limitations;
- Increase awareness generally; and
- Foster the sort of brain functioning that may be necessary for creativity.[109]

There is additional science to suggest that meditation favorably impacts creativity. Although there are different styles of meditation, they may enhance creativity by:

- Allowing the practitioner to generate new ideas for a problem where there may be more than one solution; and
- Allowing the practitioner to focus on a problem to generate a single solution.[110]

If those seem like opposites, that is correct. However, by clearing the mind and allowing focus, meditation can help the practitioner focus the mind to the bigger picture or the smaller element. Jobs' innovation process included both elements as we have discussed in the sections entitled "Vision and the Higher Purpose" and "Beauty and Innovation Through Simplicity."

The Power of Association

"You can look at [video games] as games and dismiss them. Or, you can look at them as very simple simulated learning environments." – **Steve Jobs**

We have spent the previous parts of this chapter dissecting various elements of Steve Jobs' relationship with innovation. We have seen how ...

- Vision
- Big picture thinking
- Design
- Simplicity
- Culture and
- Meditation

... have played a role in creating some of the most highly accessible and successful innovations of a

---

[109] Roy Horan, "The Neuropsychological Connection Between Creativity and Meditation," Creativity Research Journal, 01 May 2009 (http://www.docfoc.com/the-neuropsychological-connection-between-creativity-and-meditation)

[110] Lorenza S. Colzato, et al, "Meditate to create: the impact of focused-attention and open-monitoring training on convergent and divergent thinking," Front. Psychol., 18 April 2012 (http://journal.frontiersin.org/article/10.3389/fpsyg.2012.00116/full)

generation.

Association

Even with these powerful concepts, there is one last concept that may be the most effective in producing innovation: creating associations among a wide range of experiences.

Steve Jobs famously paraphrased Pablo Picasso by saying "good artists copy, great artists steal."[111] Jobs then said that Apple was "shameless" about taking the ideas of others.[112]

Jobs was not talking about infringement of intellectual property. He was making a broader point about what may be the key to his legacy of innovation. Specifically, bringing wide-ranging and seemingly unrelated ideas together to create something new.

In creating a culture of innovation, Jobs continued the quote by noting that the people he hired were musicians, poets, artists, zoologists and historians who also happened to be the best computer scientists around. The point Jobs was making was that these incredibly talented people could draw on their wide ranging knowledge and experiences to create something new. In the case of Jobs' quote, the Macintosh was the something new.[113]

This is not a matter of stealing. It is a matter of building on the developments of predecessors.[114] This is done is ways that are not intuitive. For example:

- Apple's **MagSafe** power connector was influenced by power cords on rice cookers and deep fryers;[115]
- Apple's fonts and user interfaces were influenced by a calligraphy class Jobs took in college;[116]
- Jobs' pondering of the role of the telephone on peoples' desks inspired many design changes, and the technical innovations needed to accommodate them, in the Macintosh.[117]

It is not limited to computer science or industrial design. For example, chef **Chris Young** has told the story of how renowned experimental chef **Heston Blumenthal** had him create an innovative tea drink based on a conversation Blumenthal had with a psychiatrist about how the mind interprets sensation of contrasting temperatures.[118]

[111] "Steve Jobs: Good artists copy great artists steal," YouTube.com (https://www.youtube.com/watch?v=CW0DUg63lqU&feature=youtu.be)

[112] Ibid

[113] Ibid

[114] Dan Farber, "What Steve Jobs really meant when he said 'Good artists copy; great artists steal,'" c|net, January 28, 2014 (http://www.cnet.com/news/what-steve-jobs-really-meant-when-he-said-good-artists-copy-great-artists-steal/)

[115] Jason D. O'Grady, "More on the mysterious MagSafe connector," ZDNet, March 21, 2006 (http://www.zdnet.com/article/more-on-the-mysterious-magsafe-connector/)

[116] Molly McHugh, "Steve Jobs: The Godfather of Fonts As We Know Them," Digital Trends, October 7, 2011 (http://www.digitaltrends.com/apple/steve-jobs-the-godfather-of-fonts-as-we-know-them/)

[117] Gallo, page 91

The Beginner's Mind

The 'Beginner's Mind' is a concept about sparking creativity by opening yourself up to new experiences. For example, traveling to a new place and engaging in new experiences can enhance creativity.[119] Your brain works in a new way that promotes creativity. This allows you to engage with a novel experience and incorporate it later into your other experiences and create something new.

This concept is central to **"Zen Mind, Beginner's Mind,"** by **Shunryu Suzuki**. Jobs had attended classes by **Suzuki** and was influenced by this book.[120] When approaching something new, the mind is open to all possibilities.[121] Before you are saddled with the baggage of an expert, anything is possible.[122] This permits connecting what others would never consider connecting.

Connecting the Dots

The ability to bring disparate experiences together in innovative ways is not necessarily an immediate process. **Jobs** had said that it is only looking back many years later that you can make these connections. He said, "If I had never dropped out, I would have never dropped in on this calligraphy class, and personal computers might not have the wonderful typography that they do. Of course it was impossible to connect the dots looking forward when I was in college. But it was very, very clear looking backward 10 years later."[123]

Having a diverse inventory of knowledge and the ability to connect pieces of the inventory in unusual ways can be the key to amazing innovation.

Summary

Not everyone can replicate Steve Jobs' achievements any more than one could read a book and replicate the life and achievements of Thomas Edison, Henry Ford or Nicola Tesla. However, we can look at his influences and processes to see how we can approach creating and problem solving. Maybe for some, this examination can unlock their own powers of innovation.

During Jobs' tenure at Apple, the company had to innovate to make complex products simple to understand and use. A design-driven approach stripped away unnecessary features to focus on the core features of a product. Apple products demonstrated amazing technical achievements and powerful capabilities that could be still be used by children.

---

[118] Tim Ferriss, "Lessons from Geniuses, Billionaires, and Tinkerers," The Tim Ferriss Show, July 7, 2016 (http://fourhourworkweek.com/2016/07/11/lessons-from-geniuses-billionaires-and-tinkerers/)

[119] Tim Ferriss, "Rolf Potts on Travel Tactics, Creative Time Wealth, and Lateral Thinking," The Tim Ferriss Show, Episode 41, November 11, 2014 (http://fourhourworkweek.com/2014/11/04/rolf-potts/)

[120] Drake Baer, Shana Lebowitz, "14 Books That Inspired Steve Jobs," Time, November 24, 2015, (http://time.com/4125709/books-inspired-steve-jobs/)

[121] Shunryu Suzuki, "Zen Mind, Beginner's Mind," page 14

[122] Ibid, page 14

[123] Steve Jobs, Commencement Address to Stanford University, June 12, 2005 (http://news.stanford.edu/2005/06/14/jobs-061505/)

While the product design focused on simplicity and elegance, Jobs was thinking big. The strategy and products were part of a grander vision and ambition. The vision and ambition inspired his employees and customers and fostered a culture that allowed innovation to thrive.

As part of the culture and as part of his life, Jobs absorbed diverse influences. He allowed himself to be open to new experiences and ways of thinking. Bringing varied experiences together in new contexts can create new possibilities, including creativity and innovation.

15 THE SPARKS OF INNOVATION

Kurt Wall

Introduction

There are actually infinite sparks to induce, prompt, provoke, exhort, trigger and stimulate innovations. Through the centuries people have either devised or discovered different ways of inciting great ideas, thoughts, designs, inventions and innovations in their minds. It is true that most of the time one does not even need an external trigger. Ideas, thoughts, theories, conceptions inspirations and notions just emerge out of nowhere, as if were magic. The truth is that we don't know how, why or where those ideas come from. One theory holds that they come from cosmic consciousness, while others call it divine inspiration (sort of an intervention).

The truth is that we don't know yet how our minds work, or what the mechanisms inside them are that create those sparks of beautiful and thrilling creativity. There are plenty of speculations, but no one has the answer yet. If we ever find the answer to stimulating creativity at will humanity will progress at an unbelievable (and some people claim scary) rate. People have devised their own mechanisms for idea generation, which we will cover some of them in this chapter.

Idea Generation In The Business World

The business world has devised numerous approaches, methodologies, tools and techniques to aid idea generation for individuals and for teams. Here are some of the most well-known ones (without explanations or definitions as they are readily available on the internet):

    a. Brainstorming (Individual or Group)
       i. Traditional Approach
- The Stepladder Technique
- Brainwriting
- Crawford's Slip Writing Approach
- Star Bursting
- Charrette Procedure
- Round-Robin Brainstorming
- Face-To-Face Brainstorming

- • Rolestorming Reverse Brainstorming
  - ii. Storyboarding
  - iii. Collaborative Technologies
    - • Computer-based
    - • Online Brainstorming (also known as Brain-Netting)
    - • Twitter-based
- b. Mind Mapping
- c. Journaling
- d. Sketching (one of the best tools for externalizing ideas)

However, all those approaches and techniques are useless unless enterprises of all sizes prime their employees with these mentalities and attitudes first:

- a. Creative Thinking
- b. Design Thinking
- c. Breaking Thought Patterns
  - a. Learn to recognize patterns and "connecting the dots"
  - b. Learn to recognize megatrends and undercurrents
  - c. Challenging the assumptions
  - d. Rewording or reframing the problem
  - e. Expressing one's ideas in different media
  - f. Think like your key competitor
  - g. Think in reverse (by making things worse instead of better)
- d. Breakthrough Thinking (Thinking Outside-The-Box)
- e. Multiculturalism
- f. Multigenerationalism
- g. Value Of Collaboration, Synergy and Teamwork
  - i. Consensus Building
  - ii. Team Building
  - iii. Handling Objections
- h. Innovation Culture
  - i. Collaborative Culture
  - ii. Networking (Building Relationships) Culture
  - iii. Learning Organization Culture
    - • Learning-Unlearning-Relearning
    - • Listening and Learning To "Hear Voices" (Listening To The Voices (VOC, VOE (Employees), VOI (independent Individuals), VOD (Directors/ Boards), VOP (Partners), Random Input, etc.)

This is just a sample list aimed at pointing the need for the right mentalities, thought patterns, and mental models that help both groups and individuals come up with fresh new ideas that will lead to exciting new inventions and innovations.

In addition to the aforementioned items, it is also important to mention that additional techniques, such as the ones below, are also aimed at creating additional sparks in the minds of those that want to go to the next step of trying things out and learning (even if it means learning-the-hard-way):

    i. Rapid Prototyping (incl. 3D-Printing)
    j. Business Experimentation
    k. Minimum Viable Product (part of Lean Startup)

Creating Sparks In The Individual Minds

Defining The Spark – It's the trigger that generates ideas in the mind. In a way, sparks "manipulate the sensors" in the mind, and enhance the mind's unique capacity or ability to envision what is possible, beneficial and valuable to many individuals, and hopefully all of humanity. In filling such a need or a set of needs and wants is what innovation and invention is all about.

Sparks are aimed at improving cognitive skills and developing a **Cognitive Regeneration** (Reinforcement) mechanism in the mind that is constantly working like an engine that never stops "spitting out" fresh new ideas. People that understand innovation, they actually live and breathe innovation every moment of their lives. However, they too need the occasional sparks that elevate the mind and consciousness to a higher level.

So, here are **twelve of the spark generators** on top of the ones that are mentioned in other chapters (e.g.: Needs-driven, Meditation, Yoga, etc.):

1. **Fantasy**

    People always like to daydream and fantasize about brave new worlds that are based on new ideals, new beliefs, new technologies, new socioeconomic and business models, and new lifestyles. Fantasy is one the key characteristics of the human race (that differentiates us from animals) and the main byproduct of hope. Hope fuels fantasy and fantasy keeps hope alive. The human race was never and will never be short of fantasies. The problem has always been and always will be of how to turn fantasies into realities.

    Sometimes we miss the needed skills, other times we miss the right technologies and other times we miss the courage and mettle to make things happen. Then on top of all that we have to deal with politics, resistance to change, silly fears, and of course lack of funding. This was true more than 3,000 years ago and it is still true today.

2. **Fear**

    Fear is always a great motivator for both change/transformation and for innovation. Right now there several fears that are rattling our world. Here are the top seven fears:

    - Resource Shortages and/or Depletion and (incl. energy, food and water)
    - Pandemics, Plagues
    - Economic Collapse
    - Terrorism
    - Destruction of Our Planet and Wildlife
    - Extreme Disconnection, Separation Or Alienation
    - Ugly Capitalism (where only profits matter)

These fears are great motivators for people around the whole world to find new solutions and in the process, reinvent our civilization and societies. Our current foundations of building societies are wrong and/or outmoded. To continue on the path that we are on today, will be not only result in major disasters, but it may also mean the end of the world as we know it.

3.   Frustration

Frustration can be a major trigger for innovation as long as the frustrated person or group of people is determined to take positive action and do something about it. Frustration about slavery, dictatorships, bad economic systems (like Communism), and outmoded business models have proven repeatedly to be major triggers for innovation --- replacing the old models and systems with new ones.

Frustration is another one of those things that will never disappear from the human race because people naturally have the tendency to get bored with the same-old-same-old. People will never be satisfied with one model, one system, or one approach. Change is indeed the only constant. Too bad that most corporate heads and enterprise founders have not understood this point yet.

4.   Passion (The Fire of Passion)

Definition of Passion: A strong, powerful and barely controllable emotion, or compelling feeling.

Passion is the fire to push forward despite of all the obstacles, barriers and efforts of others to derail one's dreams, ambitions, and strong needs and wants. Some people will do anything to stop others from reaching their goals, fulfilling their visions, and achieving success. It is in the human nature to despise others and trying to keep them down at the same level as they are. One must be driven and have the fire in the belly to overcome all that. That's what passion is all about and it is strongest form of positive energy. People with passion have a higher chance of success in life. Passion is behind most of the greatest innovations in history --- from the wheel to the iPhone.

The passion is not only great for the individual that has it, but also for entire teams. Passion is like a magnet that attracts people to it, as it gives a purpose, a meaning and importance to what people try to do in life. Since most people live empty lives and their existence has no meaning or purpose, they are eager to latch on to someone that has all that. But the passionate person needs to be careful who s/he allows to be in her/his inner circle because not all of them will carry their weight. This is one of the major reasons why some great people with vision and passion fail.

We've heard that the real passionate person is unstoppable because s/he is like the tip of an arrow having all the energy behind her/him to propel forward and hitting the target. All that sounds good, but the reality is that if the rest of the arrow is crooked or incomplete, the tip will never find the target.

5. Following One's Bliss Or Fulfilling One's Archetype

This only applies to those people that believe in destinies and archetypes. Following one's bliss (a term coined by professor **Joseph Campbell**) could be one and the same as following one's passion, but more likely than not, passion and bliss are two different things for most people. Bliss is what makes one really happy because it is the manifestation of one's purpose (or destiny) in life. Bliss is a deep satisfaction and fulfillment that cannot be achieved any other way. When one follows her/his bliss then one gets to live a blissful life. If passion and bliss coincide, then it is great, but if they do not coincide, then big problems (usually both mental and psychological ones) emerge that can derail a person's career and very life. Joseph Campbell explains all of that in great detail in his books (of which **The Power Of Myth** is the most powerful one).

Archetype is also another term that many people dispute its existence as it tends to typecast and stereotype people, which they find very annoying and detrimental to their existence. On the other hand, we see the archetypes all around us on a daily basis. The term and concept is an ancient one, but **Carl Jung**, a Swiss psychologist, has made it popular. The purpose of bringing attention to archetypes is that some people could not invent or innovate anything because it is not part of their archetype. One has to be the right archetype in order to be leader, motivator, mentor, inventor and innovator. Not all people can fulfill this role.

The archetypes that are best suited for innovation and invention are:

- The Creator
- The Explorer
- The Sage
- The Magician
- The Hero
- The Rebel

Sometimes, archetypes are confused with personalities. The difference is that archetype what one really is deep inside (the innate personality), while personality is the one that a person portrays or assumes in life. The two (innate and assumed personality) could be one and the same or could be two different things. Here are the best personality traits for innovation and invention:

- Futurist
- Imaginative
- Risk Taker
- Experiential
- Tweaker
- Inquisitive
- Instinctual
- Collaborative
- Flexible

Note: Most people are not authentic, capable of maintaining and sustaining their innate personalities because of life's demands on earning an income, supporting a family and gaining acceptance in social environments. For example, when one chooses to be a politician or a lawyer, one automatically gives up her/his real personality. No need to explain this point.

6. Right Music and Sound(s)

Certain types of music and sounds stimulate certain brains. That includes:

- Classical
- Pop
- Big Band
- Soft Rock
- Other types of music (but very rarely Hard Rock, Heavy Metal and the like)

The more uplifting and positive the music is, the higher the probability that it will lift one's spirit, mood and temperament. The whole idea behind it is to get in a happy mood. It is not a secret that happy people are more easy-going, open-minded, even-tempered, and easy-to work-with. In other words, they are in the mood for collaboration and teamwork. Grumpy and ill-tempered people do not do well in brainstorming sessions with others because their brains are cluttered with negative thoughts, energies and emotions. One must liberate her/his soul in order to achieve new heights intellectually and spiritually.

Suggestions:

- **Blue Danube** (a waltz by the Austrian composer Johann Strauss II, composed in 1866) may be one of the best pieces of music for uplifting one's spirit. The internet now has several websites that proclaim that they offer the best music and sounds for epiphanies and enlightenment.
    - o **Caution:** Different brains get turned on by different sounds and music. There are no universal tunes that turn on everyone.
- In his landmark book, **The Mozart Effect**, **Don Campbell** states that "... *by listening to music with longer, slower sounds, one can usually deepen and slow the breath, allowing the mind to calm down …. As with breathing rates, a lower heartbeat creates less physical tension and stress, calms the mind, and helps the body heal itself. Music is a natural pacemaker.*" But it is not about healing alone. It is also about "reaching in" and tapping into one's intrinsic energies and "channels".
- Most of us are surrounded by the monotonous **60 cycles per second** hum of machines and noises of urban life. They consume our energies, dull our senses, and increase our stresses and tensions. 99% of the people out there have idea what is happening to them. No wonder many people suffer from stress, fatigue, sleep disorders and other maladies. The right music and sounds can help alleviate some of that.
    - o Avoid pounding and annoying music, as it destroys your energy, mood and frequencies. Their ugly vibrations subtract and diminish your own vibrations.

7. Silence

Some people need absolute silence not only to meditate, but also think deep thoughts. It is fascinating to see that some people need background noise in order to think and do their work, while others abhor all sounds.

8. Oils and Aromas

Certain oils and aromas can aid a person's intellectual abilities by contributing frequencies that awaken or revitalize certain parts of the brain. One can write a whole book on this topic alone, but here are just three nuggets of wisdom:

- In one study conducted by Japanese researchers, it is claimed that inhaling **lemon oil** helps cut computer operators error rates by as much as 50%.
- Another recent Japanese research has shown that synthetic floral perfumes can limit brain function, while certain **pure essential oils** enhance the range and activity of brain function within 20 seconds of inhalation. A third study has found that the test scores and alertness of students increased by 28% when pure **peppermint oil** was diffused in the classroom, while students were learning and taking tests.
- **Purified frankincense** is great healing oil, but also it is used for dealing with problems of depression, PTSD, anxiety, anger, and stress. It helps induce a feeling of mental peace, relaxation, and satisfaction. It also helps some people with mind expansion, which could result in great gains towards innovation. Other oils that help with mental clarity are **amyris and sage oils**.

9. Foods And Other Nutrients (incl. Vitamins and Supplements) That Increase Mental Health and Clarity

This is another topic that could take an entire book to discuss properly, but here we are only going to offer a synapsis of what works best based on extensive research and proven results:

- Raw Eggs
- Whole Grains
- Oily Fish (like salmon and trout)
- Plant sources like linseed (flaxseed), soya beans, pumpkin seeds, walnuts and their oils
- Blueberries
- Gala Apples
- Organic Beets, Tomatoes and Red Peppers
- Organic Raw Vegetables (esp. Broccoli, Spinach and Celery)
- Blackcurrants and Oranges
- Nuts (esp. Almonds) Chia, Sunflower and Pumpkin Seeds
- Dark Chocolate
- Krill Oil
- Omega 3 (animal based fats)
- Coconut Oil
- Curcumin Spice, Turmeric and Maca Powder

- Vitamin D
- Vitamins B6 and B12
- Aloe Vera

10. Other Habits And Practices That Increase Mental Health and Clarity – That Can Help Generate Creative Ideas

- **Exercising** regularly (oxygen enriches the blood and brain activity).
- **Reading and Learning** endlessly.
- **Constantly challenging one's mind** (beyond learning) --- changing professions, careers, employers; starting one's own business; becoming an entrepreneur.
- **Sleeping properly** (deep sleep and adequate hours).
- **Optimizing one's gut flora** (because the gut is our second brain). The well-known **Dr. Mercola** correctly proclaimed: *"Quite simply, your gut health can impact your brain function, psyche, and behavior, as they are interconnected and interdependent in a number of different ways."*
- **Drinking cold water** in the morning --- 36^0 water works to enhance the awakening of the brain.
- **Starving for a few days.** Not only it helps detoxifying the body and brain, but also forces the person to focus on the problem that it is trying to solve. In a way the mind is substituting the strong passion for food or survival with the passion of solving a difficult problem.
- **Relaxing and/or Walking Away.** Sometimes it is best to walk away from a problem in order to solve the problem. By walking away, it allows the brain to re-IPL and obtain a new set of "eyes" looking at the problem that needs solving. This is why sabbaticals are a great idea.
- **"Spanking the mind".** Sometimes by closing one's eyes for a few seconds, then opening the eyes and looking up 20^0 and holding that position for a few minutes one can come up with new ideas. It feels as if the brain is searching an imaginary database inside the head to find any relevant answers or solutions. It helps to think about a nice place to be, prior start searching. The ideas will slowly come to one's mind. Some people prefer to think about a white light that becomes brighter and brighter as one focuses on it.
- **Seeing documentaries and biopics** of great topics and people that further open up one's eyes and minds to different views and perspectives. It is helpful to even see topics that one does not agree with or people that one does not like, as they too have some valid points. Also seeing great inspirational and motivational movies (like **Pirates Of Silicon Valley** (1999), **Startup.com** (2001), and **Office Space** (1999)) helps in understanding how others experience life.
- **Seeing spiritual movies,** such as **The Razor's Edge** (1946). Expanding one's consciousness is key to feeling great about one's self and reinforcing the personal Higher Purpose.

11. Tinkering

It is known that some people need some external device, trinket, gewgaw, toy, game or other stimulus to trigger thoughts/ideas, maintain concentration, and to help synergize both sides of their brains. Harmonizing both sides of the brain creates the holistic solutions that best suited for the human race. Those "toys" can be used to enhance the brain whether one's eyes are open or closed, or whether or not one is actively involved or simply holding onto something.

Some people are able to tune out the whole world while playing sports (like soccer), playing games (like chess, puzzles, computer games), or simply exercising (like roller skating). Others use pyramids, cones, strings, wood snakes, gum, straws, bottle caps, Legos, small springs (that can be squeezed between the fingers), and a variety of other toys to improve their concentration and focus. Others prefer to just tap their fingers. It all depends on what senses one engages to understand, translate and "feel" the world around her/him. The understanding and translating of the world helps many people frame the problem and the solution the right way.

Movement and stillness offer different views of the world. Seeing and hearing (as well as the other senses) also offer different views of the world. The combination of all senses offers the holistic view of the world (including the problems and solutions). Thus, it should be clear by now that one must employ as many views, senses, knowledge, info, skills, and habits as possible in order to obtain the right perspective as to what is involved with a particular problem or issue.

Here are some of the things that people do to spike their minds and energize their senses:
- Re-realizing their childhood dream
- Walking on a curb/ or walking a rope on the ground
- Roller skating
- Riding a bike
- Dancing alone / dancing with others
- Hot air balloon riding
- Jumping a rope
- Rolling down a hill
- Stepping (softly) on their own foot
- Learning to play an instrument
- Smelling different flowers
- Laying upside down a chair or sofa
- Inventing a word or creating a statement to change the world
- Riding a horse
- Walking backwards
- Sitting in a chair upside down
- Reading upside down or backwards
- Reading every other word
- Picking each finger sensor and acknowledging it in the brain
- Sifting sand through one's feet
- Laying down in the grass
- Milking a cow
- Sailing, boating or scuba diving
- Bungee cord jumping
- Sky Diving
- Getting passes to visit the back stage
- Building a wood product (e.g. a chair or boat)
- Storm-chasing with a friend
- Visiting other cultures / Cities, Countries, States, Religions
- Crashing a party: Wedding, Funeral, Bar Mitzvah

- Picking a route from city to city and driving it alone or with a friend
- Going out in the wilderness and living there for a while
- Taking a Vision Quest trip
- Seeking Enlightenment; visiting a guru and spending time together

All of these and other activities are aimed at expanding the mind, enriching the human experience and reaching higher levels of consciousness.

12. **Other "Vehicles" That Aid Mind Expansion And Intellectual Capacity**
    - **Dreaming** --- some people have the capability of addressing their problems and issues during sleep and even coming up with solutions while sleeping. Some people keep their journals or just plain blank pieces of paper on their nightstands with the purpose of capturing their thoughts while in a semi-hypnotic state during the night.
    - **Attending workshops, seminars/webinars, shows, expositions and professional meetings** with the intent to "grab" the latest ideas, understand the emerging trends, and share ideas with peers that are in the same profession and industry. Sometimes, it is smart to attend workshops and shows in other peripheral industries because cross-pollination of ideas is a must today.
    - **Giving lectures and seminars**. As with the point above, it is one of the best ways to exchange ideas, engage in meaningful and gainful dialogues and stretch one's mind. Giving a lecture is not simply creating the PowerPoint slides and memorizing one's key points. Good presenters do their homework, which involves researching the topic, adding fresh new ideas and offering new perspectives that help everyone in the audience challenge their own values and beliefs.
    - **Seeking harmony in one's life.** Harmony with everyone and everything. *"All the tragedy in the world, in the individual and in the multitude, comes from lack of harmony. And harmony is best given by producing harmony in one's own life."* -- **Hazrat Inayat Khan** (The Music of Life). People that are in harmony with others (from all nations --- ethnic and religious backgrounds), with nature, with God (by whatever definition one wants to use, and with the universe then one is literally at the door of enlightenment. Harmony brings synergy. Synergy brings peace. Harmony, synergy and peace bring togetherness, kindness, compassion, empathy, understanding, collaboration, inseparability ... and eventually Oneness. All of these words are magical words for invention and innovation.
    - **Leveraging** (in a good way) **the frequencies and energies of others.** Every person and every living thing on the planet have frequency/vibration or energy. As was mentioned previously, some of those vibrations and energies are positive, while others are negative to the point of being detrimental. Smart people learn to associate with the ones (incl. animals) that have positive energy and putting distance (and some cases barriers) with those that exude negative vibrations and energies. One does not have to be touched or "deal" directly with that negative energy to be affected. Negative energy can affect one from miles away.
      - **Advice:** Don't "screw around" with negative energy. One cannot overcome it by just increasing her/his own positive energy. It does not work that way. Negative Energy retreats, but it does not go away.
      - **Eye Opener:** The right pet can help one with coming up with innovative ideas. Scientists do not know yet, if it is the animal itself or the love that is

born out of the strong relationship with that animal that generates the positive energy that feeds the heart, soul, and mind. It may be both.

- **Feeding one's Pride and Self-Esteem.** Smart and innovative people have an extreme high need to be recognized, accepted and rewarded. Their sense of self-esteem and actualization can be wounded if recognition and appreciation are not expressed properly and frequently. Although mentally strong people don't really need that, the truth is that everyone loves some credit and respect. Smart leaders know how to show their appreciation and "love" for those that need it most. But the smart and balanced individuals do not really expect others to recognize them. They appreciate and reward themselves. That's what makes them extra-special. Being proud of one's self shows up in the passion and results that one achieves.

- **Shifting Perspectives and Paradigms.** Consciously or subconsciously, we all are fixated (and in a way stuck) on certain types of perspectives and paradigms, which yield predetermined notions of how things should be or should work. In order to open one's mind sometimes it is necessary to blow up the old perspectives and paradigms and "see" the problem from a different lens. By shifting one's perspective and using a set of new paradigms, new solutions emerge.

- **Playing the "If I were" or the "What if?" games:** When some people assume other people's identities such as pretending to be Steve Jobs, or John Rockefeller one forces herself/himself to see the problem and the solution in a different light. The same applies to the "What if" game, where all the assumptions are thrown out and one starts with no assumptions at all.

- **Employing Personal and Business Enablers.**

    Personal Enablers include:

    - **Believing in yourself**
    - Seeing yourself as a **leader, a mover and a shaker,** or **the "savior"**
    - **Changing the setting and environment.** Working in your favorite place (like a park or a Starbucks store on the beach)
    - Allowing yourself to enjoy **creative loafing time** (incl. taking a nap and playing Mario Brothers)
    - **Shutting out distractions**, especially email, texting and social media. Turn off the phone shut the computer down, close the door and put a "Do NOT Disturb" sign on it. It's OK to anger some people, especially the energy vampires that want to suck all your energy in order to feed theirs. Utilizing one's time and treating one's self as a special asset is smart. Thus, **Time Management and Personal Management** are critical in succeeding

    Business Enablers include:

    - The company's own **strategic enablers**, such as Lean 6-Sigma, Going Green, Sustainability, Conscious Capitalism, etc. There are nuggets of wisdom inside each one of them that can help in coming up with new fresh new ideas
    - In-house **mentors and sages**
    - The **company's history, legacy and artifacts**. Although the trapdoor exists of following the old paradigms, certain legacies can create sparks of pride, which in return create sparks of innovation

Conclusion

It is clear that people have a huge array of things to choose from in order to help themselves and their companies in "playing the innovation game". There is no "one way" and there is no "the best way". All ways have their value. The smart thing for a person to do is choose her/his own favorite triggers for innovation and invention. Every person likes certain things and dislikes others. A lot of it depends on one's upbringing, education, skills/competencies, culture, personal values and beliefs, and numerous other factors. The best advice that one can give in today's world is to **make innovation and invention a team sport**.

We live in a very complex world that is getting even more complex with each passing day. It is extremely difficult for one person to master all aspects of introducing a new product or service in the marketplace. This is exactly why having the right team of people is crucial to achieving results and shortening the cycle of going-to-market. Having a team with complementary skills and experiences is not only crucial, it is imperative (sort of a superordinate goal for every startup).

There are other important triggers that were not discussed in this chapter, such as Rewards, Tangible and Intangible Benefits, Social and Economic Pressures, Competition, and the like. Those triggers are the traditional triggers that have been with humanity forever and there is nothing new to add to them.

EPILOGUE

When we started writing this book some of us thought that that we could identify a specific pattern and approach to innovation; sort of a well-defined process that always leads to the great results. But in the process of exploring, researching, and comparing experiences it became very clear that there is no such thing as one approach, one process, one style, one culture, one trigger, or one anything for innovation --- and that is reflected in our chapters. Outlining different approaches and processes to innovation is only aimed to highlight the point that *"There is more than one way to skin a cat"*. People automatically improve and innovate as it is in their nature to do so. Sure, there are some ways that are better than others, but overall smart people will invent, innovate and improve under any circumstances and conditions, including the most dire and dismal settings.

Personal Anecdote: It may sound strange, but I did my sabbatical serving as a jail guard in a County and Federal Jail in Sherman, Texas. I saw inmates create and invent things out of the simplest things in life, such as gum wrappers, strings from their own blankets, and even food. People with limited resources have to invent things not only to improve their lives, but also keep their minds and bodies busy and healthy. There should be no question about people's ability to do whatever it takes to improve their lives and their environment.

BTW, the number one benefit for working in jail was discovering that I had suffered mental castration working for big corporations for over 30 years. I had become timid, coy, and risk averse. It was then and there that I realized what mental castration does to people and enterprises. Enterprises do not administer lobotomies and mental castrations willingly and knowingly. It is one of the things that happen naturally by working in such environments where the pressure is always on to conform, abide, fit, and belong. Rigid processes, strict rules and unyielding procedures hurt people's abilities to think outside-the box and do their thing. All of that represent an implied authoritarian style of management, which negate all the touchy-feely attitudes and good intentions of managers. Then, we wonder why people are afraid to make the big tough decisions and make the necessary changes.

What constraints people's imagination is not the imagination itself, but rather having the means, tools and funding to execute. For every idea that found its way to the market place and society in general, there are at least 20 other ideas that beat the dust, not because all of them were bad ideas, but because there were no sympathetic ears to listen and to help. Some ideas need time to catch on with the public; others need time to find the right trigger and right vehicle for execution, while others yet lack the technology and expertise to make them happen. Many sci-fi movies offer us a glimpse of what is possible and promising.

We also realize that it is difficult to decipher how the brain works and what makes it so different from one inventor/innovator to the next. Many people have read the story of how **Nicola Tesla** came up with the idea of the rotating magnetic field (which became the basis for the electromagnetic motor) while walking with his friend through a city park in Budapest, Hungary (in February, 1882). According to the story, Tesla was reciting verses from Goethe's Faust book, and staring at the sunset, when suddenly the idea came to him as how rotating magnets around a core could produce an electric current. That was the elusive solution that he so desperately searching for in his mind. Somehow at that moment he connected the sun and planets with rotating magnets and a core. How his mind was able to make the connection between them is a mystery, but this is a perfect example how the mind of the inventor and innovator works. They see associations and linkages that other people do not see.

That discovery is now ranked among the top ten discoveries of all time. His invention is credited of greatly accelerating the Industrial Revolution. Tesla had the gift of visualization on top of having a great IQ and an excellent memory. Tesla was able to fully develop his ideas/inventions in his mind and keep them there until he was ready to put them down on paper (usually at a much later time).

People have different ways of seeing the world, drawing conclusions, making deductions, connecting the dots, understanding the big picture and "knowing" what is needed to solve a problem, dilemma or a challenge. However, we know that some of the main characteristics of inventors and innovators are: being obsessed in getting results, being single mindedly focused and driven (sort of being "on a mission from God"), finding meaning and purpose in their lives through their creation(s), and manifesting their destiny. The stronger those characteristics and traits are the higher the probability that the individual will be successful in her/his quests in achieving greatness. And this is one of the main things that investors now pay more attention to, than the financial projections and ROI. This is exactly what differentiates the likes of Bezos, Musk, Jobs, and Gates from the masses. They acted like Moses (having the attitude of "I know how to take you to the Promised Land. Just follow me").

It is also not a secret that one's character, IQ, EQ, SQ, personality and profession make a big difference in the innovation arena. People that like to control, measure and analyze things (like accountants and auditors) cannot think outside-the-box because it is not in their makeup. The control mentality kills all innovation. Others pursue professions that are not conducive to innovation, such as Quality Control personnel, truck drivers, plasterers, road maintenance crews, and so on. 90% of people are in professions that thwart the innovation spirit. On the other hand, marketing, design engineering and consulting (among other professions) encourage and promote innovation. But the truth is that most people have the gift of innovation inside them, but don't know how to tap into it and leverage it.

Most people either by their own choices in life or by the circumstances and bad luck they find themselves lobotomized, neutered and otherwise "fixed" to the point that totally ignore their ability and gift of innovation. Even people that are in the innovation arena get tripped up inside their own heads with questions, such as these:

- Is it right?
- Is it good?
- Will I look foolish?
- What will they think of me?
- Will if it hurt my performance review, career, chances for advancement and pocketbook?
- What if my boss gets pissed off at me? (for a variety of reasons, of which getting fired is on the top of the list)

Getting back to the awarenesses in our research, our team also faced several myths and misunderstandings pertaining to innovation of which one of the most important ones is that Technological or Technical Innovation is the only one that matters. However, there is more to innovation than Technical Innovation … a lot more. There is Societal and Social Innovation, Professional Innovation, Food Innovation, and even Personal Innovation. People use different names to describe the different forms of innovation, such as rebirth, transformation, renovation, regeneration, renaissance, resurgence, reawakening, revitalization, revival, reinvention, modernization, and many more that have the same flavor and intent of inventing new ways of having, doing and enjoying something.

Innovation and Improvement are the essential ingredients of evolution, progress, advancement and civilization. Our society and civilization is being reinvented dramatically and technology is only one of many factors that enter into the picture. Other factors include the awakening of forgotten or suppressed talents and abilities, the emergence of new beliefs and dogmas, climate change, overpopulation, preposterous debt, timid governments, shocking and callous business leadership (the likes of Wells Fargo and Countrywide), savage global competition, and so many others.

That said, Technical Innovation is now one of the major economic drivers that will fuel progress, advance our civilization to higher levels of existence, and create wealth of unprecedented levels. Technology is here to stay; and the forms that technology can take is endless --- a bottomless pit for innovation. As a result **Transhumanism** (abbreviated as **H+** or **h+**) is now (per Wikipedia's definition) an international and intellectual movement that aims to transform the human condition by developing and making widely available sophisticated technologies to greatly enhance human intellectual, physical, and psychological capacities. In a way, Transhumanism (according to www.whatistranshumanism.org) is a way of thinking about the future that is based on the premise that the human species in its current form does not represent the end of our development, but rather a comparatively early phase. Transhumanism should be taken serious as it may result into a new species that will drastically transform life and the planet as we know it.

Another major misunderstanding pertains to the notion that nearly all innovation comes from industry, and that academia simply brings form and structure to it after the fact (teaching it in college). However, major universities now participate as actively in the innovation arena as any company or industry and in some cases they are ahead of industries, as is the case with sensor technology being implanted inside the body (on organs), and exploring technology-aided telekinesis and telepathy.

Another popular myth is that innovation only happens by thinking outside-the-box. There are numerous great innovations that are products of thinking and innovating inside-the-box. On the other hand, there are several people that badmouth creative and disruptive innovation on the basis that they represent unbridled innovation, which can lead to financial ruin if the products and services generated are unmanageable, occur too quickly, are phased in improperly, are unprofitable, etc.

Personal Anecdote: I was one of the first people to get involved with Knowledge Management, e-Learning and e-Consulting. Unfortunately, the public and the corporate world were not ready for those ideas and I paid a serious price in life by losing my personal wealth and health. I had to declare bankruptcy and give up my companies. The lesson learned was that there is such a thing as "getting ahead of one's self and the market place". I knew that lesson from IBM, GE, and other smart companies that I had the privilege of being associated with, but then I got caught in the excitement of the moment because I believed that those concepts (such as e-Learning) were so perfect and so logical that their acceptance by the public and business world was going to be automatic and immediate. I was wrong, very wrong. As a matter of fact e-Consulting has still not caught on (17+ years later after since its inception). E-Learning was accepted rather quickly, but not quick enough for me to save my company.

There are several other myths and misunderstandings, as well as lessons learned, but it is not worth debating them here. It is best to discuss, as a closing point, the value of the (Engineering) Design Process (EDP) (which is the mechanism of translating ideas into viable products and services) because it is a one of the best processes in achieving results. **The Design Process** is aimed at coming up with a solution or solutions to a problem or a challenge. Sometimes the solution involves designing a product that a) meets certain criteria, b) accomplishes a certain task or tasks, c) devises a new way of doing things (no criteria involved), and d) conceives a new way of doing nothing (there is an art behind all that). The main goal of the Design Process is making things right.

The process combines (or should combine) pure know-how, wisdom, engineering, science, art, music, spirituality … and "secret sauce". The methodology, tools and techniques that creative people have or utilize are part of their secret sauce. They may not even know themselves or be able to describe to others what that secret sauce is all about, but they got it. As with all previous subjects in this book, the **Design Process has many "flavors", hues and approaches.** Practically every engineering department has its own version that according to them works best (for them). All that is perfectly understandable and even preferable, as people work best when they own the process and feel that the process reflects their knowledge/know-how, skills, tools available to them, and even their habits and culture. "Canned processes" do not work for all people.

Making things right implies creating things and providing solutions that are fresh, creative, original, efficient, effective, economical, pleasant/pleasing, enjoyable, inspired and brilliant. In other words, they are focused on a lot more things other than action and results. They combine functionality, artistry, imagination and even amusement into one whole. That is exactly one of the main aspects of Holistic Innovation.

Holistic Innovation offers unlimited options. Let's look at an example. Let's look at shaving. How many innovations were already introduced to the single blade of shaving since it was first invented? And there will be more in the future. Imagine one day where people simply wear a mask and all the facial hair is gone in seconds! Or one changes the DNA for people not to grow hair at all. Or one applies a cream that gets rid of hair forever. And you thought that shaving was a simple exercise that was resolved long time ago! We have a long way to go before we run out of ideas.

As was mentioned in Chapter6, the intersection of Business Viability, Technical Feasibility and Human Desirability create the sweet spot for innovation because it is there that the best and optimal designs appeal to all stakeholders, including customers, public, investors, stockholders ... and technocrats. Technical Feasibility and Business Viability are easily understood by everyone, but Human Desirability is less understood, and in a way it is still an art to understand people's needs, wants and desires.

Human Desirability is more than aesthetics (incl. style), value (incl. price) and quality. Today, desirability also addresses knowledge content (incl. knowledge enhancement), networking ability (connectivity), and environmental friendliness, among other things. The additional aspects of human desirability are promoting **human-centered design**, which is about creating a human experience that exciting and stimulating. And the more exciting and exhilarating that experience is the more value it has. Experiences now are more important than plain products. The main aim of experiences is not to simply address needs and wants, but to improve and transform lives.

The best designs integrate human factors ergonomics, aesthetics, functionality, usability, manufacturability, serviceability, recyclability, reusability, and many other factors. Designs today are more complex than ever and require a blend of multiple skills. This is why **designs today are a team effort.** In order for a team to be creative and thrive, it needs the right people, talents/skills, structure, leadership, culture and environment. Culture is usually the most overlooked factor because most companies do not really know how to develop a meaningful one. The main tendency is to automatically accept the founder's culture as the corporate culture. However, great leaders have the audacity to form the right culture even if it does not fit the founder. As **Edgar Schein**, author of "**Organizational Culture and Leadership**", put it, "*The only thing of real importance that leaders do is to create and manage culture. If you do not manage culture, it manages you, and you may not even be aware of the extent to which this is happening*" (and slowly destroying your company by killing creativity among other things).

Developing and fostering a strong corporate culture isn't simple, and there is no one recipe to success that everyone agrees to. However, one of the most important aspects of corporate culture is encouraging employees to accept the fact that **Innovation is everyone's job and that change is constant**. People like stability, calmness, and immovability because they translate all of that as strength and permanence. Most people really believe the adage of "*If it ain't broke don't fix it*". They don't see or understand that we live in an **era of hyper-change**. By the time something is introduced, it is already becoming obsolete because **the Technology Innovation Curve of Innovation-Acceptance-Saturation is now shorter than ever before**.

The business environment is always changing as well, and leaders' job is to ensure that the organization adapts and evolves to meet those changes --- and more importantly that the people are leading the change themselves. They don't wait for the company or "the boss" to help them evolve and adapt. Employees are the champions and catalysts of innovation and change.
Design is also about comprehending that the process involves both Understanding and Making. Here is a synopsis of the two key ingredients and why they matter:

Understanding: What to make, why (for what purpose), how to make, the limitations or hurdles, the opportunities, the options, the synergies, the "connections", linkages and hooks, relationships, etc.

Making: Requires externalization of ideas, thoughts, and inspirations (translating cognition into tangible things). It also creates interactions and communications. It demands action (rather than planning to take action). The point that can be made here is that "making" is the best tool for innovation, as most people have to build things and play with them, and make the right tweaks and adjustments for a while prior to settling on the final version --- no different than making a song.

Cycles of low-investment prototyping are important to experimenting and improving one's design. It is hard for some people to say that "I made this, but it is not finished yet" and some people stop their efforts prematurely. The whole idea is to continue solving, and tweaking until the final version is out. Imagine how many unfinished songs and dreams died out in our history because people did not see them through. **Perseverance is key to execution and accomplishment.**

For more Nuggets Of Wisdom and Great Quotes Pertaining To Innovation, please visit our website:

www.holisticinnovationbook.com

ABOUT THE AUTHORS

Phillip Andrews

Mr. Andrews is the Managing Director of Biz Smarter, a business consulting firm. He previously worked for other business consulting firms as VP of Consulting Services, Practice Leader and Senior Project Director. His client list (among many) includes General Motors, Caterpillar, Case Corporation, 3M, HP and Colgate-Palmolive. Mr. Andrews' background includes senior positions with EDS, Case Corporation, and General Electric. He has also worked for IBM, Deere & Co., and Ford Motor Company. Mr. Andrews holds BSIE and MBA degrees, and has several certifications and diplomas from professional organizations.

He has served on the Board Of Directors of Digitran (a high-tech company) in Logan, UT, and the Boards of three NPOs ("Achieving Leadership Institute", "The Holistic Education Institute", and "International Innovation Centers". He is also involved as a senior advisor for the "Cleantech Open", "Texas Consilium", and SMU's Entrepreneurship Club. In the past he was involved with STARtech, DFW Innovation Center and other incubators and accelerators. He has been involved with several exciting startups. Mr. Andrews also serves as a business consultant to Small and Medium Size Enterprises.

Mr. Andrews' current areas of focus are: a) Total Sustainability Management, b) Holistic Innovation, and c) Creative Disruption as Growth Strategies. He is a frequent speaker at conferences, workshops and symposia. For more information on Mr. Andrews' background, work experiences and clients, please visit his LinkedIn page: https://www.linkedin.com/in/phillip-andrews-748574/ and website: www.phillipandrews.com.

Lynn Wilford Scarborough

Lynn Wilford Scarborough is a strategic business consultant, author and innovative coach who specializes in helping companies, individuals and non-profit organizations accomplish their immediate and long-range goals. Ms. Scarborough has worked with over 200 news organizations and conducted thousands of coaching and corporate training sessions. Ms. Scarborough uses her extensive media experience, business contacts and communication skills to help them tell their story through all media venues.

For public relations and media training, Scarborough is able to facilitate immediate improvement so that clients can maximize their effectiveness with enhance presentation skills, increased media exposure, multi-dimensional communication, and high impact messaging. Ms. Scarborough assists clients and campaigns through keen analysis, strategic planning, specific action plan and coaching to help accelerate outcomes and profitability.

Douglas M. Berman

Mr. Berman is an attorney based in Dallas, Texas whose legal practice is focused on corporate and securities transactions and general business, commercial and compliance matters. Mr. Berman also advises early stage companies in business and strategy matters, including as a co-founder, investor and advisory board member. Mr. Berman is also the Chairman of the Board of PollCart, Inc., software developer of a Social Commerce messaging platform focused on increasing online customer engagement and organic viral marketing.

Mr. Berman's legal practice has spanned such industries as technology, pharmaceuticals and health care, finance, oil and gas, mining, real estate, consumer products and manufacturing. He has represented public and private companies, entrepreneurs, investment banking firms, private equity firms, financial institutions, real estate firms and other businesses in a wide variety of matters and transactions, including mergers and acquisitions, sales and divestitures, public and private offerings of debt and equity securities, SEC reporting and stock exchange matters for public companies, management-security holder relations and takeover contests, corporate governance and advising management of firms in a wide variety of industries. Mr. Berman launched his solo practice in 2012 after almost 15 years in large law firms. Mr. Berman received his BA from Florida State University and his JD from Vanderbilt University.

Kurt Joseph Wall

Mr. Wall is the Vice President of Global Water Group, an extensive business alliance partnership focused on solving water shortage and supply issues worldwide. He serves as a board member for Water Wishes, LLC, and services several clients regarding water, and lean transformation. He previously worked on projects involving the rapid deployment of Homeland Security including a multi-stage Airport of the future project for Boeing Corporation.

Mr. Wall's background includes senior positions with the National RFID Center DWF Innovation Center, and Convergence of Technologies. He has worked with IBM, DHL, Motorola, SBC Communications, Siemens, Sun, Intermec, Cisco Systems, Best Buy, Starbuck Co. Alliance Texas, Federal Reserve, Nextel Communications, Texas Instrument, Intel, Ryder, American Airlines, and Samsung to establish meetings and worked centered on RFID projects.

He has served on the Board of Directors of National Innovation Centers, DFW Innovation Centers, as well as on the Boards of multiple for- and non-profit organizations focused on innovation in Dallas-Fort Worth Metroplex. He is also involved as an empire builder and as a venture capitalist in convergent technologies. In the past, he was involved with STARtech and other incubators and accelerators. He in an expert in Homeland Security as it relates to water and transportation, and does additional consulting in areas involving intelligent water design.

Mr. Wall's current areas of focus are: a) Innovation Measurement and Validation, b) Global Water Solutions, and c) Creative Disruption and Growth Strategies. He is a frequent speaker and organizer of conferences, workshops, and focus groups. For more information on Mr. Wall's background, work experiences and clients, please visit his LinkedIn page: https://www.linkedin.com/in/nationalrfidcenter.